GIDEON·RACHMAN

Gideon Rachman is the chief foreign affairs columnist for the *Financial Times* and author of the acclaimed *Zero Sum World*. In 2016 he won the Orwell Prize for Journalism and was named Commentator of the Year at the European Press Prize awards. Previously he worked for *The Economist* for fifteen years, and has served as a foreign correspondent in Washington, Bangkok and Brussels.

ALSO BY GIDEON RACHMAN

Zero Sum World

GIDEON RACHMAN

Easternisation

War and Peace in the Asian Century

VINTAGE

1 3 5 7 9 10 8 6 4 2

Vintage
20 Vauxhall Bridge Road,
London SW1V 2SA

Vintage is part of the Penguin Random House group of companies
whose addresses can be found at global.penguinrandomhouse.com.

Penguin
Random House
UK

Copyright © Gideon Rachman 2016
Preface © Gideon Rachman 2017

Gideon Rachman has asserted his right to be identified as the
author of this Work in accordance with the Copyright,
Designs and Patents Act 1988

First published by Vintage in 2017
First published by The Bodley Head in 2016

penguin.co.uk/vintage

A CIP catalogue record for this book
is available from the British Library

ISBN 9781784700744

Printed and bound by Clays Ltd, St Ives plc

Penguin Random House is committed to a sustainable future
for our business, our readers and our planet. This book is made
from Forest Stewardship Council® certified paper.

MIX
Paper from
responsible sources
FSC
www.fsc.org   FSC® C018179

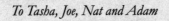

To Tasha, Joe, Nat and Adam

Contents

Preface: Trump and the Decline of the West

For more than 500 years, ever since the dawn of the European colonial age, the fate of countries and peoples in Asia, Africa and the Americas was shaped by developments and decisions made in Europe – and, later, the United States. But the West's centuries-long domination of world affairs is now coming to a close. The root cause of this change is the extraordinary economic development in Asia over the last fifty years. Western political power was founded on technological, military and economic dominance – but these advantages are fast eroding.

The shift of power and wealth to Asia is the process that this book calls 'Easternisation'. By 2014, according to the IMF, China had become the world's largest economy, ranked by purchasing power. The US is now number two, relinquishing the top spot that it had held since the late nineteenth century. China's rise is part of a broader shift in economic power to Asia (see pages 8–9). The IMF figures also showed that three of the world's four largest economies are now in Asia, with Japan at number three and India at number four. In 2009, China also became the world's largest merchandise exporter – a position that the US had held since the Second World War. The East's rising wealth is now translating into political and military power. An arms race is under way in Asia. India, along with Saudi Arabia, has become the world's largest importer of weaponry. And, by 2020, China is likely to have a larger navy than that of the United States.[1]

This erosion of America's strategic and economic dominance formed the backdrop to the election of Donald Trump as the forty-fifth president of the United States. In pledging to 'Make America Great Again', Trump implicitly promises to reverse the process of Easternisation – restoring America to its unrivalled position, both in terms of living standards and global power

Some of Trump's most important advisers have made a direct link between globalisation, the rise of Asia and the decline in American wealth and influence. Steve Bannon, who was appointed as chief strategist in the Trump White House, argues that 'The globalists gutted the American working class and created a middle class in Asia.'[2] In his view, the increasing wealth of Asia, far from being the mutually advantageous process envisaged by mainstream economics, has impoverished the United States. Bannon has also speculated openly about the possibility of a war between the US and China. In early 2016, just months before Trump's election, he told a radio show that 'We're going to war in the South China Sea in five to ten years. There is no doubt about that'.[3] During the election campaign, Trump himself was visceral in his denunciations of China, proclaiming that 'We have a $500 billion deficit with China … We can't continue to allow China to rape our country … It's the greatest theft in the history of the world.' Candidate Trump had threatened China with tariffs of up to 45% and, as president, Trump appointed Peter Navarro – a noted protectionist and author of *Death by China* – as the head of a new White House trade council.

Much of this book is concerned with the slow but steady increase in geopolitical rivalry between America and China during the Obama years. The arrival of Trump in the White House clearly threatens to accelerate this process significantly. The deliberate but careful attempt of the Obama administration to push back against Chinese ambitions in Asia and the Pacific have been replaced by a new Trump approach that is much more impulsive in style – and potentially much more confrontational. Under President Xi Jinping, who came to power in Beijing in 2012, China itself has also moved in a much more nationalistic direction. Well before Trump pledged to 'Make America Great

Again', Xi had made a similar pitch to nostalgic nationalism, promising a 'great rejuvenation' of the Chinese nation. With Trump and Xi in power in Washington and Beijing, the stage is set for a potential clash between American and Chinese nationalism in the Pacific.

The last years of the Obama administration had already seen rising alarm in Washington about China's programme of 'island-building' in the South China Sea. The Chinese government had set about re-enforcing its disputed territorial claims through land-reclamation exercises that converted reefs into islands, and then turned these islands into military bases – complete with runways and missile silos. The threat that Beijing might one day seek to control access to these seas – the busiest commercial waterways in the world – is clearly rising.

In his confirmation hearings before the US Senate, Rex Tillerson, Trump's new Secretary of State, signalled a significant hardening in the American attitude to the South China Sea. Tillerson likened the island-building to Russia's illegal annexation of Crimea, and said that the Trump administration intended to let Beijing know that 'your access to those islands is not going to be allowed'.

Taken at face value that sounded like a threat to blockade the islands. China would almost certainly attempt to break such a blockade by sea or air. The reaction to the Tillerson statement in China's state-controlled media was ferocious. The *Global Times*, a nationalist paper, warned of the possibility of a 'large-scale war' between the US and China, while the *China Daily* spoke of a 'devastating confrontation between China and the US'.

As well as intensifying existing tensions in the South China Sea, Trump also threatened to create a new US–Chinese confrontation over Taiwan. In December 2016, even before formally taking office, Trump had a ten-minute phone conversation with President Tsai Ing-wen of Taiwan – a call that reversed almost forty years of precedent. When the US and China restored diplomatic relations in 1979, Beijing successfully insisted that Washington break formal diplomatic ties with Taiwan. The US president-elect's decision to speak to the leader of an island that China deems a mere 'rebel province' came as a thunderbolt in Beijing. Behind the scenes, American and Chinese officials have openly discussed the possibility that their two countries might one day go to war over Taiwan (see pages 10–1). Much Chinese military spending – in particular investments in submarines and missiles – has been designed to prepare China for a possible invasion of Taiwan.

Yet as swiftly as Trump had ramped up his anti-China rhetoric, so he backed down. Xi Jinping dealt with Trump's apparent threat to repudiate America's 'one China policy' – that recognised Beijing's theoretical sovereignty over Taiwan – by simply refusing to speak to Trump until the policy was reaffirmed. Only when Trump had climbed down were the US and Chinese leaders able to have their first telephone conversation, in February 2017.

In the same way, the Trump White House's early bellicose talk of preventing China from gaining access to artificial islands and military bases that it was building in the South China Sea was swiftly dropped. After a few weeks of fevered speculation, following Tillerson's Senate testimony, General James Mattis, Trump's new Defense Secretary, calmed the atmosphere by stressing that the US was not planning any sudden military moves in the South China Sea.

The biggest Trump reversal of all came over trade. The protectionists, it became apparent, were not the only influential voices in the Trump White House. A rival group, labelled 'the globalists', moved swiftly to dissuade the president from starting a trade war with China. This group, centred around Gary Cohn – Trump's chief economic adviser and a former banker at Goldman Sachs – seemed to win the early bureaucratic battles. A crucial moment came with the first visit by the Chinese president to the US. Xi Jinping visited Trump at his Florida estate, Mar-a-Lago, known as the Winter White House, in April 2017. The Chinese president did a masterful job of charming his American counterpart. Months later, Trump was still waxing lyrical about their relationship, telling an interviewer 'We got along great. I like him a lot. I think he likes me a lot'.[4] The end result of the first

US–China summit of the Trump era was not the swingeing tariffs that the president had promised on the campaign trail. Instead, a joint working party was set up to look into difficulties in the US–China trading relationship. Its first results, announced a few weeks later, amounted to little more than a reheating of Chinese promises on better market-access for American agriculture and finance that had first been made under the Obama administration.

Four months into the Trump presidency, it seemed as if the US president had already been comprehensively outmanoeuvred by his Chinese counterpart. Three rounds of high-stakes diplomatic poker had been played – over Taiwan, trade and the South China Sea – and China had won all three hands. Far from 'Making America Great Again' in the Pacific, Trump appeared to be accelerating its decline. His dazzling switches in rhetoric and policy undermined America's reputation for seriousness and consistency of purpose in Asia, unnerved American allies and frustrated analysts attempting to identify coherent strands of thought in Trump's approach to the world. They should also serve as a warning against assuming that any entente between Xi and Trump will necessarily last. The US president is so volatile that he could easily switch back to a more aggressive stance against China.

One key to understanding Trump's early reversals in Asia was his preoccupation with the nuclear threat from North Korea. The rapid progress of North Korea's nuclear-weapons programme and the threat that Pyongyang is close to developing ballistic missiles that could hit the continental United States, ensured that North Korea was one of three major topics discussed by Obama and Trump in their first meeting at the White House following Trump's election. Trump's initial comments on the subject focused on the idea that increased pressure from China could force the North Koreans to abandon their nuclear programme. As a result, the new president discovered that dealing with North Korea required him to secure the co-operation of countries, such as South Korea and China, which he had once threatened with a trade war.

It is certainly true that North Korea is desperately poor and hugely dependent on its wealthy Chinese neighbour. Yet the Chinese have always denied that they have the leverage to 'deliver' North Korea. The real truth may be that they are loath to provoke a crisis in a dangerous and unstable neighbour – which also remains an ally, albeit an infuriating one. Faced with possible diplomatic frustration over North Korea, Trump made it clear that he was prepared to contemplate military action. He even boasted of sending a 'very powerful armada' towards the Korean peninsula, with the clear implication that a pre-emptive strike was in the offing. To many Americans, this kind of tough talk sounded like common sense and polls suggested that a US strike on North Korea would command majority support. However, America's Asian allies were deeply alarmed by Trump's confrontational language, since they are well aware that any American attack would probably provoke conventional or even nuclear retaliation by North Korea – a devastating prospect since many South Korean and Japanese cities are well within range of North Korean missiles.

Trump's unpredictability is a profound worry for America's closest allies in East Asia: Japan and South Korea. Both countries know that they would be in the front line if a war were ever to break out on the Korean peninsula, or in the South China Sea. But Japan, which is painfully aware of its reliance on the US security guarantee in the face of a rising China, had little option but to humour Trump. This was all the more difficult for the government in Tokyo, since it was the Japanese – not the Chinese – who were the main victims of Trump's early protectionist instincts. Trump was perfectly happy to pose for a reassuring photo op with Shinzo Abe, the Japanese prime minister, shortly after winning the US presidency, but his actual policies are considerably less comforting for Japan. Just four days after meeting Abe in November 2016, Trump announced that he intended to renounce the Trans-Pacific Partnership (TPP) on his first day in office. The TPP is a painstakingly negotiated trade deal between twelve countries, with Japan and the US as the two most important signatories. Abe had expended enormous political capital both to negotiate the TPP and to force it through Parliament in Tokyo. For him, the significance of the TPP was as much strategic as economic (see Chapter 5). Like President Obama, he saw the negotiation of a giant new trade deal that included Japan and the US – but very pointedly did not include China – as a way of heading off Chinese dominance of the Asia-Pacific region.

The Japanese government, like the Obama administration, understands that the likeliest route to a China-dominated Asia is through commerce rather than conflict. Twenty years ago, America was the most significant market for all the major Asian economies, and Japanese multinationals were the largest foreign investors across South East Asia. But those days have gone. Now China is the most important trading partner for South Korea, Japan, Australia and most of the nations of South East Asia. Chinese investment is also increasingly important and attractive to neighbouring countries in Asia. The 'One Belt, One Road' policy promoted from Beijing – essentially an effort to promote Chinese investment in infrastructure across Asia – has further increased Beijing's economic clout. As Abe and Obama both realised, the growing importance of Chinese trade and investment across the world has considerable geopolitical significance. Asian countries will be much less willing to confront China – or side with the US or Japan in a territorial dispute – if their economic futures depend on goodwill from Beijing.

For the Abe administration, the TPP represented a last effort to push back against the creation of a China-dominated co-prosperity sphere in East Asia. Donald Trump's repudiation of the deal was thus a grievous blow to Japan's survival strategy for the twenty-first century.

For Trump himself, however, ditching the TPP made perfect political sense. He had campaigned against the supposedly disastrous trade deals that America had signed in the Clinton, Bush and Obama years. The TPP was the perfect symbol of the 'globalism' that Trump rejected. And Trump was hardly alone in his hostility to the idea of a big new trade deal. Opposition to the TPP was also a central feature of Bernie Sanders's campaign for the presidency. At the Democratic Party convention in Philadelphia in July 2016, anti-TPP posters were almost as ubiquitous as pro-Clinton banners – and they were brandished with rather more fervour.

Ditching the TPP was a decision driven by American domestic considerations. But outside the United States, Trump's move was widely interpreted as a symbol of an American retreat from global leadership. A couple of days after the decision was announced, I found myself in the office of a senior EU official in Brussels, who remarked to me 'It's interesting, when the Brits were the world's dominant economy, they were also the main promoters of free trade. And then when America became the world's dominant economy, they became the main promoters of free trade. And now America is losing its faith in globalisation and China is becoming the main advocate of free trade. You can feel the wheels of history turning'.

Traditionally, the US approach to Asia had maintained a rigid division between military and economic affairs. So America's military commitment to Japan was never used as leverage in trade disputes between the two countries. Trump's instinct seems to be very different. He sees military and security commitments as part of a connected set of issues that can be used as bargaining chips in a broad-ranging negotiation.

To America's security establishment this approach is anathema. Military alliances are meant to be sacrosanct. If they are thrown into the mix as part of a negotiation, then American 'credibility' – and the doctrine of deterrence attached to it – is gravely weakened. The possible consequences for allies like Japan – and for the Taiwanese – of this new Trump approach are also disturbing, since it implies that their security could be traded away as part of a broader negotiation with China.

The volatile and unreliable nature of the Trump White House has also handed China a remarkable propaganda opportunity. During the

Obama years, the US had often suggested that China was an irresponsible international actor – whose actions over climate change, or the South China Sea, threatened the international order. The arrival of Donald Trump in the White House presents Beijing with an opportunity to turn the tables. Now it is the United States that can be presented as a dangerous player, over issues such as North Korea, trade and climate – while China plays the role of the supporter of international norms and agreements. At the World Economic Forum in Davos in January 2017, Xi gave a speech in defence of globalisation – using language that could have been employed by Bill Clinton in the 1990s. Shortly afterwards the Chinese warned the US not to walk away from the Paris climate accords. When Trump threatened military confrontation with North Korea, it was left to China to issue appeals for international calm.

The chaos that swiftly engulfed the Trump White House – exemplified by the sacking of his National Security Adviser, Michael Flynn, and of the FBI director, James Comey – also marked a striking contrast with the apparent calm and long-term thinking in Beijing. In May 2017, as Washington was convulsed with speculation about the possible impeachment of Trump following the sacking of Comey, President Xi hosted an international summit to promote China's 'Belt and Road' initiative. The largest group of foreign dignitaries to assemble in Beijing since the Olympics in 2008 heard the Chinese government pledge to spend $150 billion a year on infrastructure investment across sixty-eight countries.

Yet while China deployed its wealth to create a new network of partners, Trump threatened to alienate traditional allies. He is the first US president since 1945 to express far more admiration for the leader of Russia than for the chancellor of Germany. While Trump consistently praised Putin as a strong leader during the presidential election, he attacked Angela Merkel's willingness to admit over a million refugees into Germany as 'insane'. Trump was even widely reported to have presented Merkel with a fake 'invoice' for $376 billion, which he claimed Germany owed in dues to Nato. While the White House denied these stories, there was no disguising the tension between the American and German leaders – which made a marked contrast with the bonhomie between Trump and the Russian foreign minister Sergei Lavrov, who visited the Oval Office a few weeks later. For Trump's advisers like Steve Bannon, antagonism towards the EU has an ideological element – since Brussels and Berlin are seen as standard-bearers of the internationalist and 'globalist' philosophy that they have consistently denounced. Through his Breitbart news service, Bannon has forged ties with far-right and anti-EU parties in Europe, including the National Front in France and the Alternative for Deutschland party in Germany.

The traditional 'West' as a political concept has always had two pillars – North America and Europe. But if the US and the EU end up at loggerheads during the Trump years, the Western alliance will be in profound trouble. Trump, as an advocate of 'America First', might not worry about antagonising Europe. But the weakening of the Western alliance would actually gravely undermine Trump's plans to restore American greatness – since it would decrease the power of the United States to shape world affairs. In so doing, it would also hasten the shift of wealth and power to Asia that so troubles Trump and his supporters.

The political effects of the rise of Asia have been slowed by the continuing strength of the Western alliance. But if the West itself now falls into disarray, the process of Easternisation will accelerate still further – and with it, the decline of American power.

Introduction

In Chinese history, foreign visitors to the imperial court were often treated as 'barbarians' who were expected to pay tribute to the emperor. There are echoes of this in the way that modern China's leaders engage with the rest of the world, as I discovered in November 2013, as part of a small group of visitors received by President Xi Jinping in Beijing. There were plenty of eminent people in our party, including former prime ministers such as Gordon Brown of Britain, and Mario Monti of Italy, as well as a smattering of Western billionaires.[1] Yet the foreign grandees were treated a bit like a class of schoolchildren.

First, we were ushered into the cavernous central area of the Great Hall of the People; then we were lined up on benches in preparation for a group photo with the president. After a little while, President Xi swept into the room and shook a few hands ('I touched him', gasped Francis Fukuyama, the famous academic, in mock awe) – before posing for the photo.

A few minutes later, the president's discourse began. Seated at the centre of a banqueting room, with a giant mural of the Great Wall of China behind him, chandeliers above him, and a semicircle of former Western leaders arranged in front of him, President Xi began his remarks by reminding his visitors that 'China is an ancient civilisation with over 5,000 years of history.' It was, in some respects, a boilerplate remark. Yet China's awareness of its thousands of years of history is fundamental to the country's understanding of itself. It also inevitably means that China, in some ways, regards the United States as an upstart nation – a country that has been in existence for less than 250 years, a shorter lifespan than many Chinese dynasties.

President Xi's determination to rebuild the wealth and power of his nation was the central theme of his speech. One of his most favourite slogans, which he tried out several times on his foreign audience, was 'the great rejuvenation' of the Chinese nation.[2] But the president was also keen to reassure his audience that China's rise would not lead to conflict with the outside world: 'We all need to work together to avoid the Thucydides trap – destructive tensions between an emerging power and established powers,' he insisted.[3]

Xi's reference to 'the Thucydides trap' showed that he (or his staff) had obviously been following the American debate about the rise of China. Graham Allison, a Harvard professor, has coined the phrase to describe the dangers of a period in which an established great power is challenged by a rising power. Allison calculates that in twelve out of sixteen such cases since 1500 the rivalry ended in war. He calls this recurrent pattern 'the Thucydides trap' after the ancient Greek historian's observation that war between Athens and Sparta in the fifth century BC had been caused by Sparta's fear of a rising Athens. For Allison, 'The defining question about global order in the decades ahead will be: can China and the United States escape Thucydides' trap?'[4]

The risk of conflict between the United States and China has also worried the White House, throughout the Obama years. For much of his time in office, President Obama's energies have been consumed by a rolling series of crises in the Middle East. The many long nights he has spent in the situation room deep in the basement of the White House usually contained scant reference to Asia – beyond the occasional late-night order for takeout Chinese.

But President Obama knows this is not how it should be. He sees through eyes clouded by the smoke of Middle Eastern fires that the rise of China is an epochal event that requires a response. That response must be both forceful and sustained if the US is to preserve its privileged position in global affairs. But it must be measured and nuanced if it is to avoid plunging America into a potentially disastrous conflict in Asia.

The central theme of global politics during the Obama years has been this steadily eroding power of the West to shape international affairs. This erosion is closely linked to the growing concentration of wealth in Asia – and in particular the rise of China. One of its consequences is a dangerous rise in diplomatic and military tensions within Asia itself, as a rising China challenges American and Japanese power and pursues its controversial territorial claims with renewed aggression. The US, for its part, is pushing back against Chinese power, shifting military resources to the Pacific and strengthening its network of alliances, with nations such as India and Japan, in what has become known as the American 'pivot to Asia'. This process is described in the first part of the book.

The second section describes how Easternisation is transforming politics in the world beyond Asia. Most of the foreign-policy crises of the Obama years have taken place outside Asia – whether it is the civil war in Syria, the dramatic deterioration in Western relations with Russia, or the political and economic disarray in the European Union. But the red thread connecting these seemingly disparate events is the West's growing inability to function as a pole of stability and power, imposing order on a chaotic world. Of course, even in the heyday of American or European power, there were always wars, conflicts and revolutions that perplexed and frustrated the powerbrokers of the West. But what is new is that the political, strategic and ideological dominance of the West is now under challenge in entire regions, all over the world – in Asia, in the Middle East, in eastern Europe, in Latin America and in Africa.

This weakening of Western power is most obvious in the Middle East, where a political order set up by European powers in the aftermath of the First World War, and supported by the US after 1945, is now crumbling. The result has been war, terrorism and the collapse of several states. The United States, chastened by its inability to win clear victories in wars in Iraq and Afghanistan, has hung back from using overwhelming force to restore order in the Middle East. A European Union, wracked by economic crisis, has also been unable to respond effectively to the fires of conflict burning along its borders. Instead, Europe itself has been destabilised by refugee flows from a collapsing Middle East.

I believe that the Obama years will eventually be seen as a hinge point in history – in which the erosion of Western power became much more evident. While many of the president's critics argue that Western weakness is the fault of Obama himself, there are much deeper forces at work. The most important is the long-run shift in global economic power – which has made it harder for the US and Europe to generate the military, political and ideological resources needed to impose order on the world.

A historic shift

To understand the significance of the era we are living through, you need to go back more than 500 years. At the beginning of the 1400s, China and the Islamic world were at levels of economic and political power and sophistication that were at least equivalent to those attained in Europe.[5] The global balance of power began to tip with the great European voyages of exploration of the 1490s. In 1492, Christopher Columbus, a Genoese explorer employed by the Spanish crown, crossed the Atlantic. In 1498, Vasco da Gama, a Portuguese explorer, reached India. It was the Portuguese and Spanish who began the process of transforming the relationship between Europe and the rest of the world. Over the succeeding centuries, Europe's edge in military, seafaring and industrial technology allowed other European nations to build global empires. Russia expanded eastwards across Asia, all the way to the Pacific Ocean. The Dutch built an empire that reached as far as Indonesia. France's colonies extended from Indochina to West Africa and the Caribbean. Britain gained control of India in the eighteenth century and led the 'scramble for Africa' in the nineteenth century. By the early twentieth century, the British Empire alone covered almost a quarter of the world's land area. The global domination of the 'white races' was almost total. As the Stanford historian Ian Morris puts it, 'By 1914, Europeans and their colonists ruled 84% of the land and 100% of the sea.'[6]

Two world wars and a wave of decolonisation led to the collapse of European imperialism during the second half of the twentieth century. India gained independence from Britain, France was forced out of Indochina, the Dutch quit Indonesia. But the emergence of the United States as the world's pre-eminent power, in the aftermath of the Second World War, prolonged the hegemony of the West. Even the Soviet Union – which represented the alternative to the political 'West' during the Cold War – was a European power.

These centuries of European and American dominance were based on economic might. It was Britain's leadership of the Industrial Revolution that allowed the UK to build a global empire. The growth of Germany's industrial power in the nineteenth century allowed it to challenge Britain. After 1945, it was America's position as the world's largest economy that allowed the US to form the bedrock of the Western alliance in the Cold War and to emerge as the sole superpower following the fall of the Berlin Wall.

It is economic might that allows nations to generate the military, diplomatic and technological resources that translate into international political power. But, over the past fifty years, the West's dominance of the global economy has steadily eroded.

The economic transformation of Asia first became evident in Japan in the 1960s and then in South Korea, Taiwan and parts of South East Asia in the 1970s. The expansion and evident wealth of the Japanese economy, in particular, was so dramatic that by the late 1980s, many Americans began to fear that the US might be eclipsed by its old Second World War adversary. But the population of Japan, at just over 120 million in 1990, was too small to shift the global balance of economic power on its own. The rise of China and India – two countries each with populations of over 1 billion people – is a different matter. From 1980 onwards, the Chinese economy began to grow at the double-digit rates pioneered by Japan in the 1960s. India also grew strongly, albeit not quite as fast, after economic reforms in the early 1990s.

A symbolic moment was reached in 2014 when the IMF announced that, measured in terms of purchasing power, China was the world's largest economy. The United States had been the world's largest economy since the early 1870s; now China was 'number one'. China's rise is just part of a larger shift in economic power. According to the IMF, three of the world's four largest economies were now in Asia. China came first, America was second, India was third and Japan was fourth. I grew up in the world of the G7, a grouping of the world's leading economies, which first convened in 1975. At that point, six of the world's seven biggest economies were in Europe and North America. (Japan was the solitary exception.) But that world has gone. The magnitude of the shift in economic power that is underway was captured by an exhaustive recent report for the Australian government, which pointed out that 'Asia is set to overtake the combined economic output of Europe and North America within the decade to 2020.'[7]

The fundamental reason for the shift in economic power to Asia is simple: weight of numbers. By 2025 some two-thirds of the world's population will live in Asia. By contrast the United States will account for about 5% of the world's population and the European Union around 7%. Hans Rosling of Sweden's Karolinska Institute puts it nicely when he describes the world's pin code as 1114 – meaning that of the planet's 7 billion people, roughly 1 billion live in Europe, 1 billion live in the Americas, 1 billion in Africa and 4 billion in Asia. By 2050, the world's population is likely to be 9 billion, and the pin code will change to 1125, with both Africa and Asia adding a billion people.

For centuries, the wealth and technology gap between West and East was so enormous that Western nations dominated international affairs and business – no matter the difference in population. But rapid economic development in Asia over the past two generations means that this wealth gap has narrowed sufficiently for the weight of numbers in Asia to begin to tilt the balance of power in the world.

Many in the West are understandably anxious to believe that this is all just a temporary phase or a mirage. The IMF's estimate in 2014 that China was now the world's largest economy was widely scorned in the US, by those who insisted that the use of 'purchasing-power parity' (PPP) distorted the real picture. PPP is a means of assessing the wealth and size of economies that takes into account relative prices and purchasing power. So the fact that a haircut or a loaf of bread in China is much cheaper than it might be in the UK or the US is used to adjust estimates of relative wealth. The effect is to boost estimates of the size of an economy like China, where wages and costs are relatively lower. Some analysts argue that the use of PPP to estimate the relative sizes of the Chinese and American economies is, therefore, deeply flawed as a measure of global power – since the cost of goods within China itself is not relevant to the projection of power overseas. It is certainly true that using current exchange rates, the US was still 'number one' in 2015. But most economists regard PPP as a better measure of the size of an economy, since it avoids the absurd situation in which an economy can be said to grow or shrink by double-digits within a month – depending on fluctuations in the currency markets. Domestic purchasing power is also relevant to global power – since it translates directly into the ability to pay soldiers or to produce low-cost weaponry. In any case, the whole debate is liable to be moot by the early 2020s, when the Chinese economy is likely to overtake that of the US, in real terms as well as PPP.[8]

Even without using PPP, the evidence of growing Chinese and Asian economic weight within the world economy is stacking up. By 2014, China was already the world's leading manufacturer and its largest exporter. China was also the biggest export market for forty-three countries in the world; whereas the US was the biggest market for just thirty-two countries. (Twenty years earlier, China had been the largest market for just two countries in the world, and the US was number one for forty-four nations.[9]) China is also the world's largest market for vehicles, smartphones and oil, and the biggest single market for key Western companies and products such as Daimler-Benz, KFC and the Apple iPhone. But it is not just fried chicken and smartphones that are being consumed in Asia. In 2012 for the first time in over a century, Asian nations spent more money on armaments and troops than European countries. India was, by then, competing with Saudi Arabia for the title of the world's largest arms importer.

Western sceptics about the rise of Asia tend to highlight any signs of political or economic turmoil, particularly in China – and there is no shortage of those. In 2015 alone, China experienced a sharp slowdown in growth, a spectacular plunge in the stock market, an increasingly harsh political crackdown on domestic dissent, and the arrest or interrogation of high profile political, media and business figures as part of a crackdown on corruption. It may well be that China's economy will slow sharply in the coming years and will fall well short of the 7% growth a year that President Xi told my group was his aim, for the years running up to 2020.

But, in geopolitical terms a slowdown in Chinese or Asian growth would no longer be transformative. The economic development that allows China and India to push for great-power status has already happened. The most senior analysts in Western governments are already operating on the assumption that the shift in economic power from West to East will continue and that economic change will translate into political power. America's National Intelligence Council in Washington, which brings together all of the US's intelligence agencies including the CIA, recently predicted that 'By 2030 Asia will have surpassed North America and Europe combined in terms of global power, based upon GDP, population size, military spending and technological investment.'[10]

China's Communist system is clearly vulnerable to political and economic shocks, and India is notoriously hard to govern. But the idea that the fragility of the Chinese or Indian systems means that the Easternisation story will soon end ignores the extent to which the West's own rise was punctuated by episodes of extreme instability. The United States, after all, fought a civil war in the middle of the nineteenth century – but that did not halt its rise to global pre-eminence. The rise of Asia has already been punctuated by occasional crises. China was on the brink of revolution in 1989, just a decade after the economic reforms promoted by Deng Xiaoping had begun. South Korea, Thailand and Indonesia all suffered huge economic damage during the Asian financial crisis of 1997. Yet the rise of Asia has continued, and so has the process of Easternisation.

Measuring or predicting how this shift in economic power will change international politics, however, is an uncertain business because the relationship between economic and political power is not straightforward. When China became the world's largest economy it did not also automatically become the world's most powerful country. On the contrary, the US retained a military, diplomatic and institutional edge that continued to justify its title as the 'hyperpower'. Similarly, while the IMF may have ranked India as the world's third largest economy, even India's leaders acknowledge that their country is, as yet, still no more than a mid-ranking power in international politics.

Over the long run, though, there clearly is a strong relationship between economic might and international political power. The British Empire became unsustainable when Britain's economy was no longer strong enough to support its global commitments. The Soviet Union lost the Cold War largely because its economy was too weak to keep up with the United States. By contrast, America's 'rise to globalism' in the twentieth century would have been impossible without the might of the American economy. In time, the growing wealth of Asian nations will also translate into political power that will be felt all over the world. For the moment, however, the most obvious consequence of the erosion of Western power is a fraying of international order and a growing risk of conflict around the world.

Western weakness and international conflict

Early in the twenty-first century, the US experienced the most shocking attack on the American mainland since the War of 1812. The United States' reaction to the terrorist attacks of 9/11, led by President George W. Bush, was to try to remake the world – and, in particular, the Middle East – through a dramatic reassertion of US power, exemplified by the invasion of Iraq in 2003 and the overthrow of its leader, Saddam Hussein. By the time President Obama took office in January 2009, it was already clear these efforts to remake the Greater Middle East in the West's image had essentially failed. Even worse, the economic success and stability of the West itself was thrown into question by the financial and economic crisis that began with the collapse of Lehman Brothers in September 2008 – just four months before Obama took the oath of office. Faced with a military quagmire overseas and an economic crisis in the US, President Obama decided to concentrate on 'nation-building at home' – an effort to focus American resources on rebuilding the US economy, while drawing back from draining and unsuccessful engagements in the Middle East.

The president's deep scepticism about US involvement in further military action in the Middle East has been a central theme of US foreign policy during the Obama years – even as turmoil in the region has spread, following the Arab uprisings of 2011 and the Syrian civil war. The underlying thinking was easy to understand, given the memory of the Iraq debacle, the challenge of a rising China and economic problems at home.

But America's inability to restore order in the Middle East, combined with the European Union's paralysis, fostered a sense of declining Western power – and may well have encouraged security challenges to the US in Asia and Europe. Indeed, as the Obama years come to a close, the US-dominated global security order is under challenge all over the world.

In the Greater Middle East itself, several states – including Syria, Libya and even Iraq – have slipped into violent anarchy. In 2014, an Islamist terrorist group that styled itself 'Islamic State' took control of a swathe of territory in Syria and Iraq as large as the United Kingdom. The following year, Russia staged a military intervention in Syria. In Afghanistan, where the US and its European allies fought a twelve-year war after 9/11, the Islamists of the Taliban are once again gaining ground.

In Europe, Russia's occupation of Crimea in 2014 represented the first forcible annexation of territory on the European land mass since 1945. For two decades after the end of the Cold War, the US and the EU based policy on the hope that Russia would join the community of Western, democratic, capitalist nations. But that hope was abruptly ended by the annexation of Crimea – and the subsequent crisis in Ukraine. Instead, the threat of war between Russia and the West has returned to the European continent. Before the financial crisis of 2008, the European Union could be regarded as the second major pillar of Western power. It had peacefully incorporated most of the old Soviet Empire and its aspiration to spread wealth and democratic norms south and east – to North Africa and to Ukraine and Russia – seemed realistic. But the profound economic and political crisis that has engulfed the EU over the last decade has instead seen the forces of disorder enter the EU. The growing sense of crisis within Europe is undermining the legitimacy of the EU and leading to the rise of populist and nationalist parties in countries such as Greece, Poland, Hungary – and even France.

Meanwhile, in East Asia, China has challenged American and Japanese power in the Pacific with much greater determination. Its pressure on Japan over disputed islands in the East China Sea has come perilously close to provoking a clash between Chinese and Japanese forces. In the South China Sea, China's programme of 'island-building' to reinforce its disputed maritime claims, has led to a sharp rise in tensions between the US and Chinese militaries.

The emerging contest for supremacy in the Asia-Pacific between the US and China already looks quite finely balanced. The United States still has a much larger military than China – and Washington is the centre for a network of global alliances that Beijing cannot match. But China can concentrate its resources on asserting power within its own immediate neighbourhood, while the US has global commitments. During the Obama years, it has become increasingly evident that the US will struggle simultaneously to remain the dominant power in Asia, the Middle East, Europe and Latin America – in a world in which economic power is shifting east. As a result, America depends on its network of Asian allies as a political and strategic counterweight to the growing might of China. But those alliances also carry risks for the United States. In particular, there is a danger that the US will get sucked into regional conflicts if its allies clash with China.

In the self-absorbed world of American politics, this accumulation of challenges to US power is often blamed on President Obama – whose opponents routinely accuse him of 'weakness'. Chris Christie, one of the more moderate contenders for the Republican nomination in 2016, captured the general tenor of his party's campaign when he called the US president a 'feckless weakling'. But the 'weak Obama' thesis misses the point in two crucial respects.

First, the United States is easily the healthiest part of the Western alliance. Much of America's 'weakness' in the Obama years was, in reality, the weakness of its allies. Japan, the keystone of America's alliance system in Asia, has made valiant efforts at national renewal under its prime minister, Shinzo Abe. But the country is burdened by a crippling national debt and an ageing and shrinking population. Meanwhile, the economic crisis has turned the EU inwards and made it increasingly unable to take on burdens beyond its borders. By the middle of the Obama years, the US accounted for almost 75% of the military spending of the twenty-eight-member Nato alliance, up from 50% in the year 2000. Tellingly, when crises broke out on Europe's borders in the Middle East, it was left to the United States to lead the military and diplomatic response.

The second reason why the 'weak Obama' thesis misses the point is that it fails to understand the extent to which the process of Easternisation is rooted in deep historical and economic forces that are beyond the power of any single US president to change. It is not that President Obama is weak – it is that he has been dealt a weak hand. The same will be true of his successors. No American president is going to be able to wave a magic wand and make the rise of Asia simply go away. Even America's strategic planners acknowledge that a profound shift is underway that goes beyond the policies of any single president. The National Intelligence Council argued at the end of 2012 that 'Pax Americana – the era of American ascendancy in international politics that began in 1945 – is fast winding down.'[11]

As a result, the challenge to Western power, and the rise in international tensions associated with it, are likely to continue well beyond the Obama years. In Asia itself, tensions between China and the US will wax and wane. But over the long term they are likely to become more intense as the power gap between the two countries narrows.

As the changes in Russia under President Putin have illustrated, there is also an important ideological element in the process of Easternisation. In the aftermath of the collapse of Communism, Russia looked to Europe and the US for new economic and political models. But, as Russia's relations with the West plummeted, so the country's intellectuals have begun to embrace old 'Slavophile' ideas that emphasise the Asian aspects of Russian identity – such as the country's Mongol heritage and its vast Asian hinterland. Locked in a confrontation with the West, Russia's leadership has seized upon the idea that power is migrating east and sought ever-closer relations with China. Dmitri Trenin, one of Russia's leading strategic analysts, argued in 2012 that 'If Peter the Great were alive he would leave Moscow and not go to St Petersburg but make his capital somewhere around Vladivostok . . . The centre of gravity in the world of economic, political and military strategy is moving to the Asia-Pacific region.'[12]

A similar intellectual reorientation has taken place in Turkey during the Obama years. After the collapse of the Ottoman Empire and the foundation of the Turkish Republic in 1923, Turkey turned its back on its Islamic heritage. The new Turkey, under its founder Kemal Ataturk, even ditched the old Turkish alphabet (which looked more like Arabic than a Western script), in favour of the Roman alphabet. Turkey has been a member of Nato since 1951, but under President Recep Tayyip Erdogan, who has been the dominant political figure in Turkey since becoming prime minister in 2003, the Turkish state has become increasingly estranged from Europe and the US. Erdogan is a devout Muslim, given to elaborate conspiracy theories about the West, and has reasserted his country's Islamic and Ottoman roots – in both diplomatic and cultural terms.

In developing Africa, meanwhile, leaders from Ethiopia to South Africa have become increasingly intrigued by the 'China model' – which seems to offer the prospect of rapid economic growth without the need to pay obeisance to Western strictures on democracy or corruption. The most violent and dangerous rejection of the West has come in the form of the jihadist movements, such as Islamic State, that have attracted increasing numbers of adherents in the crumbling Middle East.

Even within Europe and the United States, recent years have seen the rise of populist politicians – such as Marine Le Pen in France and Donald Trump in the US – whose political rhetoric is based on the idea that the West is profoundly sick. These politicians look with frank admiration to the more authoritarian leadership of President Putin and even President Xi in China.

The divided East

However, politicians and intellectuals who anticipate that a weakened West will now cede global power to an ascendant East are embracing a seriously oversimplified view of the world.

There are two main impediments to Eastern power. The first is the internal political problems of the emerging Asian superpowers. Popular rage about corruption is a common theme that links democratic India and undemocratic China. Corruption is not just a potential source of internal strife. It also points to wider problems creating trustworthy institutions that are acting as a brake on both Chinese and Indian power, in a globalised economic system. These institutional problems are rooted in cultures that are hard to change. For the moment, the West's institutional advantage has led to a continuing American and European dominance of international finance and law – which, in turn, translates into a form of political power. Access to Western financial markets, educational institutions and courts still matters to the whole world.

The second and even more serious obstacle to the smooth Easternisation of global political power is the divisions and rivalries within Asia itself. Together, North America and Europe form a loose but coherent group of allies that can legitimately be called 'the West'. That is why Nato is often informally referred to as the 'Western alliance'. Asia, however, is divided politically. China's only formal treaty ally is North Korea. Many of China's neighbours – including Japan, India and Vietnam – have territorial disputes with Beijing and fear the rise of China. There are also small but genuine risks of nuclear conflict breaking out between India and Pakistan, or on the Korean peninsula. Thus, for the foreseeable future, there will be no 'Eastern alliance' to supplant the 'Western alliance'.

Many Western analysts will take comfort from these weaknesses and internal rivalries within Asia, since they hold out the prospect that Western domination of the global order can be prolonged, even as economic power migrates east. The American 'pivot' to Asia makes sense in this context – as an effort to buy time for Western power in the Pacific, while waiting for China to change.

The internal change in China that Western policymakers are willing to advocate openly is the eventual liberalisation and democratisation of the Chinese system. It is often argued that a democratic China would be less likely to challenge Western power. That argument may well underestimate the strength of Chinese nationalism – but it is an argument that US officials feel comfortable making in public, since advocating democratic reform is uncontroversial, at least in the West. A second reason for the US to play for time in China is less easy to articulate at an official level – although it is much discussed in academia. This is the belief that China is fundamentally unstable and that some combination of economic problems, political upheaval and regional tensions may eventually stop the country's rise – or even cause it to break up.

However, political instability and rivalries within Asia also pose considerable risks for the West – and the world as a whole. The big Asian economies are now so important to the global economy that political or economic turmoil in East Asia could well spark a global economic crisis. In South Asia, India and Pakistan have probably come closer to a nuclear exchange than any other two nuclear powers in the world. The machinations or internal collapse of a nuclear-armed North Korea could provoke a global security crisis. Above all, China's Communist Party has deliberately used nationalism as a means to shore up its internal legitimacy. Any signs of political turmoil in China will increase the party's paranoia about Western plots against a rising China – and increase the temptation to focus public anger on external enemies, such as Japan or the US.

The rivalries between states within Asia – particularly between China and its neighbours – also have the potential to pull the US into a conflict. The threat of such a conflict continues to concern the leaderships in both Washington and Beijing. More than a year after I had listened to President Xi muse about 'the Thucydides trap' in Beijing, the Chinese leader returned to the subject during a visit to the United States. This time he remarked 'There is no such thing as the so-called Thucydides trap' – before adding: 'But should major countries time and again make the mistakes of strategic miscalculation, they might create such traps for themselves.' Unfortunately, as the following chapters will make clear, the risks of such strategic miscalculations are rising – in Washington, Tokyo and Beijing itself.

PART 1

Easternisation in Asia

From Westernisation
to Easternisation

The idea that the era of Westernisation is coming to a close seems self-evident, when viewed from a dynamic Asian city such as Shanghai or Singapore. It is not just that the evidence of growth and change is all around you. It is also that the Chinese, in particular, have a view of the past that is naturally cyclical. With a continuous history that extends across thousands of years, the Chinese are accustomed to the idea of the rise and fall of dynasties – with periods of prosperity and progress being followed by periods of chaos and regression. By contrast, the United States, whose history as a nation goes back only to the Declaration of Independence of 1776, has a more linear view of history. The history of the American republic has only moved one way, towards greater prosperity and global power. The notion of national decline – or even of cyclical rises and falls in power – seems much stranger and more alien to Americans than to the Chinese.

America's period as the dominant global power represents the extension of a period of Western dominance of global affairs that began in the late 1400s, with the beginning of Europe's imperial age. The voyages of discovery from Portugal and Spain that began in the

1480s opened up Asia and the Americas to European exploration and, in the process, transformed the relationship between Europe and the rest of the world.[1]

European traders, colonists and soldiers were able to reach Asia relatively swiftly by this time because of the technological lead that the West had established over the East in ocean-going ships. This was an area of human endeavour in which the Chinese had once led the world. In 1405 the Chinese admiral Zheng He led a fleet of nearly 300 vessels and 27,000 sailors from Nanjing to Sri Lanka. In other voyages, Zheng He reached the Malacca Strait, East Africa and Java. The contrast between the size of the Chinese admiral's expeditions and the early voyages of Christopher Columbus is striking. When Columbus set sail from Cadiz in 1492, 'he led just ninety men in three ships'.[2]

But China's emperors seem to have seen more threats than opportunities in the expansion of global trade that voyages like those of Zheng He and Columbus facilitated. Some thirty years after Zheng He reached Sri Lanka, China's rulers banned oceanic exploration – probably on the grounds that it was a waste of resources. By contrast, Europe's warring kingdoms and empires competed to develop new and better ships and to expand their trading opportunities around the globe. Portugal's ability to explore first Africa and then Asia and the Americas was spurred by naval innovations sponsored by Prince Henry the Navigator in the 1400s, leading to Vasco da Gama laying the foundations for the European imperial conquest of Asia, when he discovered the sea route from Europe to India in 1498.

The first European colonies in Asia in the sixteenth and seventeenth centuries, established by the Portuguese and then the Dutch, British and French, were essentially trading posts. But the Industrial Revolution of the eighteenth century led to technological advances and a drive for new markets that moved European imperialism in Asia into a new and more expansionist phase. Again Europe benefited from the fact that it had established a technological lead in a field in which Asia had once led the world. It was, famously, the Chinese who invented gunpowder and the first ever guns seem to have appeared in China in the 1100s.[3] It was in war-torn Europe, however, that firearms were developed most rapidly. The result was that when European and Asian armies clashed in the eighteenth and nineteenth centuries, the Asians were invariably outgunned.

The collision between the industrial and military might of the West and the ruling classes of Asia was a mismatch. Britain's East India Company was founded in 1600 and remained a largely commercial enterprise for the first 150 years of its presence in India. In 1756, however, when a local ruler expelled the company from its trading post in Calcutta, the company reacted by sending a naval force to retake the city. In 1757, East India Company forces defeated the Nawab of Bengal and his French allies at the Battle of Plassey, establishing the basis for British domination of the Indian subcontinent. Over the following century, the company used its military might to extend British rule across the Indian subcontinent, often in conjunction with local allies. It was not until 1858 that the British Raj was formally established in India, displacing indirect rule by the East India Company.

By the mid-nineteenth century, India had also become the launch pad for an assault on the Chinese markets. Britain's desire to sell opium produced in India to Chinese consumers led to the notorious Opium War of 1839–42. When the Chinese authorities attempted to stop the opium trade in 1839 and expelled the British official delegated to supervise the commerce, there was an outcry in Britain at this violation of trade agreements. The British dispatched the Royal Navy to China. Its new all-iron steamers ensured that the clash was an unequal fight. It was no accident that the anthem 'Rule Britannia' exulted that 'Britannia rules the waves'.

After Britain's destruction of the Chinese fleet, invading forces temporarily occupied Canton and Shanghai. In 1842 the notorious 'unequal' Treaty of Nanjing was signed, forcing the Chinese to cede Hong Kong island to Britain in perpetuity (it was returned in 1997) and to open five 'treaty ports' to European trade.[4] In the 1850s, the

Europeans returned to the offensive – in pursuit of further trade privileges. In one notorious incident in 1860, British and French armies burned the Chinese emperor's Summer Palace outside Beijing.

As the Anglo-French destruction of the Summer Palace illustrated, it was not just the British who demanded trading privileges at the point of a gun. By the end of the nineteenth century, the French, the Germans, the Russians and the Americans had all been granted trading concessions in ports dotted up and down the Chinese coast.

This pattern of the forcible opening of Asian markets by Western power was replicated in Japan. In this case, it was American gunboat diplomacy that led the way. Commodore Matthew Perry of the United States and his black ships arrived in Japan in 1852, on a mission to force Japan to open its ports to international trade. The Japanese were well aware of the military humiliations suffered by China. Rather than risk a comprehensive defeat, Japan signed a treaty in 1858 – granting the main Western powers similar trading rights to those they already enjoyed in China.

In Japan's case, however, confrontation with the West and the internal political turmoil that it set off inspired a successful domestic reform movement. The reign of the emperor Meiji from 1868 to 1912 led to administrative and economic reforms, based on the Western model, that equipped the country with a formidable industrial and military capacity. In 1905, when Japan clashed with Russia over their rival claims in China and Korea, the Japanese navy was sufficiently powerful to defeat the Russians in a major battle in the seas between Japan and Korea. In the same year, the Japanese army defeated the Russians at the Battle of Mukden in Manchuria.[5]

The vision of an Asian nation defeating a European power inspired Asian intellectuals as diverse as Kemal Ataturk in Turkey and Jawaharlal Nehru of India, both of whom were to go on to lead their nations.[6] Nehru heard the news of Japan's victory when still a schoolboy studying in England and it set off daydreams of his future role in securing 'Indian freedom and Asiatic freedom from the thraldom of Europe.'[7]

But Japan's success in defeating a European nation in a major war was an isolated example in the early twentieth century. At the time of the outbreak of the First World War, European nations and their offshoots still dominated the world. In 1914, however, Europe's great powers turned on each other. The First World War marked the beginning of the end of European dominance of the world. Even Britain and France, which saw their colonial possessions expand as a result of the post-war settlement, emerged from the conflict as gravely weakened powers.

It took the Second World War, however, to end European colonialism in Asia. Japan's role in defeating British, Dutch and French armies in the first phases of the war is the basis for the claim that Japanese nationalists often make to have 'liberated' Asia. The fact that the Japanese had themselves colonised Korea and Manchuria and were responsible for notorious war crimes, such as the 'rape of Nanjing' in China in 1937, means that Japan's claim to have played a liberating role in Asia remains controversial – to put it mildly.[8] Nonetheless, it is clear that the Second World War was a decisive moment in weakening the West's political domination of Asia – and so creating the conditions for the process of Easternisation that is currently unfolding. As the historian John Darwin puts it, 'The end of British rule in India in 1947 and the withdrawal two years later of Europe's navies from China marked the end of the "Vasco da Gama epoch" in Asian history.'[9]

The fact that decolonisation in Asia had laid the basis for a shift of global political power to Asia was disguised for decades by two crucial developments. The first was that the United States had succeeded European powers as the dominant political and military power in Asia and the Pacific. The US occupied Japan until the 1950s and still keeps more than 50,000 troops there. It also fought wars in Korea and Vietnam, in the 1950s and 1960s, that demonstrated its determination to remain the dominant power in the region. The second critical development was that Asia's two giants – China and India – turned inwards in the 1940s and pursued economic policies that thwarted their economic potential. The consequences were most extreme in China, where Mao's policies caused famine during the Great Leap Forward and political chaos and isolation during the Cultural Revolution. But even India, during the 1970s, was a byword in the West for hunger and humiliating poverty.

The economic transformations that first laid bare the potential of Asia took place instead in Japan, Korea and South East Asia – countries that pursued capitalist policies under the shelter of the American military umbrella. It was not until China and India began to pursue similar policies of export-led growth, in the 1980s and the 1990s, that the true economic potential of Asia was unleashed.

These days Shanghai and Mumbai – the commercial capitals of China and India – are also two of the most important business cities in the world. Yet the symbols of these great Asian centres of commerce are both legacies of Western imperialism.

The 'Gateway to India' – the arch that stands on the waterfront in Mumbai – bears an inscription that records that it was built to celebrate the royal visit of Edward VII to India in 1910, a period that marked the height of the British Empire. The arch still serves as a landmark and a symbolic entry-point to the city.

Shanghai now gleams with modernist skyscrapers. But a postcard of the city's most famous view is still likely to feature the domes and cupolas of the Bund – the row of riverside commercial buildings built in the early twentieth century, when Shanghai was a semi-colonial city. Although China was never formally colonised, its rulers were forced to hand over large areas of Shanghai and other coastal cities, as commercial 'concessions' to the major Western imperial powers. In these areas, white Europeans lived under their own laws and the native Chinese were second-class citizens.

The psychological and political impact of these reminders of empire is enormous. Imagine how New Yorkers would feel if, every time they glanced up at the Empire State Building, they knew that it had been built by Chinese imperialists – who had lived there, less than a hundred years ago, under their own laws, while Americans worked as their servants. Or imagine how the British would feel if Buckingham Palace had been built by the Indians – and had, in living memory, been the base for an Indian viceroy, governing the United Kingdom.

Most Europeans and Americans are incapable of making this psychological leap, partly because they are remarkably ignorant of their own imperial history. Many Americans bridle at the very idea that their nation – which was founded in revolution against the British Empire – went on to play an imperial role in Asia. Even the British, who are supposedly obsessed by their lost imperial glory, are often strikingly vague about the history of the British Empire. Tony Blair records in his memoirs that in 1997, at the ceremony in which Britain handed control of Hong Kong back to China, the Chinese president, Jiang Zemin, had suggested that Britain and China could now put history behind them. Blair confesses – 'I had, at that time, only a fairly dim and sketchy understanding of what that past was. I thought it was all just politeness in any case. But actually, he meant it. They meant it.'[10]

Of course they meant it! The humiliations inflicted on China by Britain and other imperial powers may be barely remembered in the UK, but Chinese leaders and intellectuals are intensely conscious of the idea that they are now righting historic wrongs – from the Opium War of 1839–42, to the burning of the Summer Palace. Other rising Asian nations have their own memories of battles with Western power – whether it is India and the British, Indonesia and the Dutch, or Vietnam and the French, followed by the Americans.

Pankaj Mishra, an Indian intellectual, who has written a history of Asia's 'revolt against the West', argues that 'It is no exaggeration to say that millions, probably hundreds of millions of people in societies that have grown up with a history of subjection to Europe and America – the Chinese software engineer and the Turkish tycoon, as well as the unemployed Egyptian graduate – derive profound gratification from the prospect of humiliating their former masters and overlords.'[11]

That is probably true – but that still leaves hundreds of millions, perhaps billions, who have a more complicated attitude. One complication in the notion of a generalised Asian 'revolt against the West' is that one of the most brutal imperial powers in Asia was another Asian nation – Japan. There is no doubt that in South Korea and even China, the popular and intellectual animus towards Japan is currently stronger than any rivalry with the West.

While there are doubtless educated (and not-so-educated) Asians who do yearn to humiliate 'their former masters and overlords', many have a much more complicated attitude to the West. At a dinner one evening at a smart restaurant on the Bund in Shanghai in 2013, I gingerly broached the subject of the West's colonial history with a young Chinese graduate student. Did she resent the role that Europeans had once played as the city's overlords? The answer surprised me. 'Not at all,' replied my companion. The Shanghainese, she argued, knew very well that the city's glory days had been in the 1920s and the 1930s – and that Shanghai had gone into a steep decline after the Communist revolution of 1949. Her generation, she argued, associated the West with prosperity and dynamism, rather than humiliation.

Attitudes to the West are often a marker of where Chinese citizens stand on the spectrum between nationalism and liberalism. Nationalists are inclined to dismiss Western pressure on human rights in China or territorial disputes as pure hypocrisy, given the West's own imperial history in Asia. Chinese liberals, who take a much more sceptical view of their own government's talking points, are more willing to accept that the legacy of Western imperialism is, in some respects, positive. This attitude is most visible in Hong Kong, where pro-democracy demonstrators, opposed to Beijing, are struggling to preserve some of the legacies of the British colonial period – such as the independence of the courts and the freedom of the press.

There are similarly nuanced debates in other former colonies. Narendra Modi, the Indian prime minister, is often described as a 'Hindu nationalist', and he has even broached the subject of the British paying reparations for colonising India. But his party's cultural assertiveness is mainly aimed at India's Muslim heritage, rather than the long-departed British. Some Indian intellectuals argue that it is a sign of their nation's growing self-confidence that 'we can at last acknowledge, without shame or guilt, the good the British did for us'.[12] There is a similar pattern of thought in that temple of modernity, Singapore. A fierce local pride in the city state's transformation from an imperial outpost into one of the great global cities is balanced by an equally fierce determination to protect some of the legacies of British imperial rule – whether that is the architecture of the Raffles Hotel or, more importantly, a tradition of a highly professional civil service and commercial courts system.

Yet while attitudes to the West vary across Asia – between countries and individuals – there is little doubt that a widespread process of Easternisation is underway, as Asian nations reassert their own histories and heritages, and scrape away some of the accumulations of Westernisation. You can see it in something as simple as place names. Until 1995, Mumbai was called Bombay – the name of the British imperial city that was itself derived from the earlier days of Portuguese colonialism. ('Bombay' was a corruption of Bom Bahia, or 'good bay' in Portuguese.)[13] It is not just the city itself that has been renamed. The building that was once the Victoria and Albert Museum is now the Bhau Daji Lad Museum; the Victoria Terminus Station is now the Chhatrapati Shivaji Terminus. Other Indian cities have followed a similar path. Madras became Chennai in 1996; Calcutta became Kolkata in 2001. As with cities, so with countries. The country once known as Burma became Myanmar in 1989; Ceylon had become Sri Lanka in 1972.

In Shanghai, meanwhile, some of the traces of the colonial past are also being gradually erased. When I first started visiting the city in the 1990s, its most fashionable area was still routinely called the 'French concession'. More recently, I have been gently reproved for using the old name and told 'We don't really call it that anymore.'

The speed of the transformation in Asian economies and attitudes has caught many Western opinion-formers off-guard. The ascent of China, in particular, has been stunningly fast. Figures compiled by Yves Tiberghien of the University of British Columbia show that the Chinese economy was just 6% the size of the American economy in 1990. By 2000, the figure was still only 12%; by 2008 it was 30% and by 2011 it was 50%. Measured in terms of the purchasing power of the average citizen – rather than in real exchange rates – the catch-up is even more dramatic, with China's economy 58% the size of America's by 2008 and 80% by 2012.[14] According to Professor Tiberghien, China's GDP overtook that of France in 2006, the UK in 2007, Germany in 2008 and Japan in 2010.

To understand the phenomenon of Easternisation it is important to realise that the economic balance between the US and China is just part of a larger story about the relative economic weight of Asia and the West. The OECD countries, made up of 'developed' countries largely in the West but also including Japan, accounted for 62% of global output in 1990. But the lines crossed in 2011, with the OECD now accounting for less than half of the world economy. It is growth in Asia that has largely accounted for the 'rise of the rest'.[15]

Most mainstream economists, even in the West, assume that Asian growth will continue to outpace that of the West in the coming decades. The speed of change has yet to be determined – but some of the most credible projections are startling. Laza Kekic of the Economist Intelligence Unit predicts that, over the next forty years, there will be 'a stunning shift in the distribution of global power. The share of world real GDP (at PPP) accounted for by North America and western Europe will fall from 40% in 2010 to just 21% in 2050, while developing Asia's share will double to 48.1%. The share of China alone is likely to increase from 13.6% to 20%.' These predictions are not unusual or outlandish. Goldman Sachs and the World Bank have made similar projections. Danny Quah, a professor at the London School of Economics, describes the process as a shift in the 'global economy's centre of gravity'. By calculating the average location of economic activity across geographic regions, Quah has shown how world production is rapidly shifting east. As he puts it, 'In 1980 the global economy's centre of gravity was mid-Atlantic. By 2008, from the continuing rise of China and the rest of East Asia, that centre of gravity had drifted to a location east of Helsinki and Bucharest.' Extrapolating growth in almost 700 locations around the world, Quah predicts that the world's economic centre of gravity will, by 2050, be 'literally between China and India'.[16]

Of course, all extrapolations about the future can go wrong. And in the United States, scepticism about the rise of China is strongly influenced by the memory of previous erroneous predictions, fashionable in the 1980s, that Japan would soon pose a threat to America's global position. But China is a much more plausible geopolitical rival to the United States than Japan ever was, for several reasons.

The first is that the legacy of the Second World War ensures that Japan is very much embedded in the American alliance system that is one of the bedrocks of American global power. Japan is the home to major US military bases on Okinawa and elsewhere. By contrast, China is not part of the US-led alliance network in Asia. On the contrary, it is the major challenger to that system.

The idea that Japan was ever likely to be the world's largest economy was also inherently implausible simply because the country's population is under half that of the US. (In 2014, the US population was around 350 million, compared to Japan's 128 million.) As a result, the average Japanese would have had to be twice as rich as the average American for Japan's economy to overtake that of the United States. That was always highly unlikely to happen. By contrast, there are roughly four times as many Chinese as Americans. So simple mathematics tells you that China only has to achieve a quarter of the GDP per capita of the United States to become the world's largest economy. According to the statisticians and economists at the IMF that milestone was passed – at least in terms of purchasing power – in 2014.

Opinion polls suggested that the American public already believed China to be the world's largest economy well before it actually happened. By contrast, elite American opinion has tended to err in the opposite direction. In 2012 Robert Kagan, an influential neoconservative intellectual, published a book called *The World America Made*, which argued for both the necessity and the likelihood of continued American global dominance. The book was cited approvingly by President Obama in his 2012 State of the Union speech. Yet Kagan's estimates of the relative sizes of the US and Chinese economies were far too sanguine. He wrote airily that the Chinese economy might surpass the US economy in size by 2050. In fact, 2015 would have been nearer the mark.

The political implications of this shift in economic power are profound. America became the world's largest economy in 1871, and held that title until 2014. In the immediate aftermath of the Second World War, the US alone accounted for about one-third of global economic output. America has been the world's sole superpower since the demise of the Soviet Union in 1991. But the rise of alternative power centres in Asia – and, above all, China – clearly raises the question of how long the United States can continue to dominate global politics. The very prospect of an end to American hegemony is already unsettling international politics and raising fears of war in Asia.

The Risk of War

Ten days before the American presidential election of November 2012, a four-man delegation was dispatched from Washington for Asia. With the Obama–Romney campaign in full cry, few people paid attention to this low-profile trip to Beijing and Tokyo. Yet the group that left the United States was charged with a task that was of the utmost importance to the future of America – and indeed the world. Their job, put simply, was to avert a chain of events that could lead the United States into a war with China.

The American delegation was a perfect illustration of the maxim that 'politics stops at the water's edge'. Back home, Barack Obama and Mitt Romney were hitting each other with everything they had. But Democrats and Republicans were equally represented on the mission to Beijing and Tokyo. The group was the brainchild of Jim Steinberg, who had recently stepped down as Hillary Clinton's deputy at the State Department. Accompanying Steinberg were Steve Hadley, who had run the National Security Council in the Bush White House; Richard Armitage, who had been number two at the State Department during the Bush administration; and Joe Nye, a Harvard professor who had served in the Defense Department under President Clinton. The Chinese and Japanese were to be left in no doubt that the delegation they were meeting spoke for America as a whole.

The Steinberg-led mission had been put together at short notice, in response to a growing crisis in the seas around China. A long-festering dispute between China and Japan over the ownership of some un-inhabited islands in the East China Sea had flared up to new and dangerous levels. Chinese and Japanese ships and planes were jostling and buzzing each other in the waters around the islands, known as the Senkaku to the Japanese and the Diaoyu to the Chinese. Nationalist sentiments were rising on both sides. In China, there had been anti-Japanese riots across the country that had led to the trashing of Japanese-owned shops and factories. Japan itself was about to elect a government led by Shinzo Abe – a man determined to change Japan's semi-pacifist constitution, to allow the Japanese military to fight in wars even if the country had not come under direct attack. In the judgement of diplomats, Abe would be the most nationalistic prime minister to lead Japan since 1945.

The Americans in the delegation were determined to act as peace-makers. But they were also acutely aware that America risked being dragged into a Sino-Japanese conflict. The United States guarantees Japan's defence through the US–Japan Security Treaty – and the Americans intended to make clear that the Senkaku Islands were covered by America's security guarantee to Japan. The implications were both clear and alarming. If China were to attack the islands, the United States would be obliged to come to Japan's aid. That would mean that the world's three largest economic powers were at war.

As they prepared for their meetings in Asia, the four Americans discussed a disturbing historical analogy – the outbreak of the First World War almost a century earlier. Could the Senkaku Islands prove to be a modern version of Sarajevo in 1914 – an obscure place where a small incident could spiral into a global conflict? Before the First World War, many businessmen and statesmen had believed that the network of commerce tying together Germany and Britain made a war between the two nations irrational and impossible. Today, many make the same argument about the chances of conflict between China,

Japan and the US. How could three economies that are so interlinked possibly go to war? And yet in 1914, the assassination of Archduke Franz Ferdinand in Sarajevo had set off a chain of alliance commitments that had dragged all the major European powers into a conflict. Might America find itself trapped by its alliance commitment to Japan, just as Germany had been pulled into war by its security guarantee to the Austro-Hungarian Empire? As Joe Nye later recalled, 'we wanted to avoid writing a blank cheque of the sort that Germany wrote for Austria–Hungary.'[1]

The Americans had a delicate, and potentially contradictory, task. They had to convince both China and Japan that America's security guarantees were rock solid. But they also had to avoid taking steps that could bring America closer to war.

The conversations that the Americans had in Beijing and Tokyo were not entirely reassuring. In Beijing they met with China's senior leadership, including the country's prime minister designate, Li Keqiang. In Tokyo, Yoshihiko Noda, the Japanese prime minister, also listened politely. Both sides assured their American visitors that they wanted to avoid war. The Chinese prime minister told his American visitors that China needed another thirty years of peace to achieve the levels of wealth and power that it sought. But both the Japanese and the Chinese also insisted on the importance and morality of their competing territorial claims. The Chinese warned of rising Japanese nationalism, led by a government that they said denied the crimes committed by Japan after its invasion of China in the 1930s. The Japanese warned of a rising China that was determined to dominate its neighbourhood, humiliate Japan and push the United States out of the Pacific.

The American delegation flew back to Washington, still worried about the risk of conflict. The risk, they thought, was not that the leaderships in either nation would make a deliberate decision to go to war. It was rather that war could break out by accident. Chinese and Japanese forces, operating in close proximity, could clash on the high seas. Neither side would feel able to back down. The conflict would escalate. The next US president – whoever he was – would have to steer a delicate and dangerous course in Asia. In the event, it was President Obama who won re-election – and the management of tensions between China and Japan did indeed become one of the most delicate foreign-policy tasks of his administration.

This was not a problem that could be solved simply by clever diplomacy. For while the rights and wrongs of the issue are bitterly disputed on both sides, it is a shift in economic power that ultimately lies behind the rise in tensions in the Pacific. Aware that it is now the largest power in East Asia – and still bruised from Japan's treatment of China during the twentieth century – the government in Beijing is keen to assert China's status as the dominant power in Asia. The Japanese government – acutely aware of the same trends – is desperate not to appear weak. It fears that a symbolic defeat over the Senkaku Islands would set the stage for a new era, in which a vengeful and authoritarian China dominated the region.

Both China and Japan looked across the Pacific Ocean to try to gauge the strength and position of the United States. The knowledge that the US might soon cede the title of the world's largest economy, and that the Obama administration was intent on cutting military spending, had sown doubts about America's staying power in the region. The United States was well aware of these questions – and was determined to answer them forcefully. As President Obama had himself put it in a landmark speech on Asia in November 2011, 'In the Asia-Pacific in the twenty-first century, the United States of America is all in.' The president's ringing declaration reflected a bipartisan consensus in Washington. This holds that if America is to remain the world's dominant global power, it must continue to be the pre-eminent power in the Pacific. Joe Nye argued that it was unthinkable to accept that the western Pacific would become a Chinese sphere of influence because 'such a response to China's rise would destroy American credibility'.[2] A central goal of the Steinberg–Armitage–Hadley–Nye mission was to assure both China and Japan that the United States has no intention of pulling back from its role as the dominant military power in Asia.

Yet outside the policy elite in Washington, there are academic critics who fear the United States is embarked on a perilous course. One of the most articulate sceptics is Hugh White, an Australian scholar and former intelligence official, who worked closely with the Americans on Pacific security throughout the 1990s. For White, the United States is in danger of making a tragic error that 'will lead to sustained and bitter strategic rivalry with China, imposing huge economic costs and a real risk of catastrophic war'.[3] These kinds of concerns are not uncommon amongst America's close allies. The official line in London is that America's global pre-eminence will stretch long into the future. Behind the scenes, some of the more thoughtful British officials are much less certain. In 2012, one senior Brit told me that he believed that the central challenge of the next generation would be managing the transition from a world dominated by the United States to a world in which China is the pre-eminent power.

Few American scholars or officials would dare put the situation in quite such bleak terms. But many are willing to acknowledge that periods in which an established great power is being challenged by a rising power are the moments of maximum peril for the world. Joe Nye's Harvard colleague, Professor Graham Allison, had caught the attention of leaders in both Washington and Beijing with his talk of 'the Thucydides trap' and his estimate that rising powers have gone to war with established powers on twelve out of sixteen occasions since 1500. Other eminent academics who have studied the rise and fall of great powers, place the incidence of war even higher than Allison's estimate. Ian Morris of Stanford University notes cheerily that 'Geopolitical shifts on the scale of China's take-off have always been accompanied by massive violence.'[4]

Until recently, this kind of gloomy analysis was not much favoured in official Chinese circles, where the language of economic interdependence and 'peaceful rise' was much more prevalent. But a belief that a growing rivalry between the US and China is inevitable is now common among Chinese academics and policymakers. The debate in Beijing is increasingly about how to handle this burgeoning rivalry. How hard should China push? How many risks can it afford to take?

One of China's pre-eminent strategic thinkers is Yan Xuetong. In some ways, Professor Yan is the Chinese equivalent of Joe Nye. While Nye's introductory course to international relations at Harvard has been taken by many of America's elite, Yan teaches at Tsinghua University in Beijing – where most of China's senior leadership, including the last two presidents, have studied. Yet while the two professors' current lives are not dissimilar, their youths are as different as the recent histories of China and America. In his twenties, Joe Nye was a Rhodes scholar in Oxford. Professor Yan was toiling in the fields of China, sent out there as part of Mao's Cultural Revolution. He remarks, matter-of-factly, 'I saw many people killed during the Cultural Revolution, so I got used to it.'

This brutal realism arguably now influences Yan's view of the world. He believes that foreign policy is ultimately about power. And like Graham Allison, he thinks that rising powers and established powers tend to clash. But, on the bright side, Yan believes that the fact that China and the US are both nuclear powers will prevent them ever declaring war on each other. Others are not so sure. Allison, one of the foremost scholars of the connections between nuclear weapons and foreign policy, argues that it is dangerously complacent to believe that major powers will never fight a nuclear war.

The 'realist' school of foreign-policy analysis – which holds that international relations are driven by a struggle for power between nations – tends to be particularly gloomy about the likelihood of war between China and the United States. John Mearsheimer, a professor at Chicago University who is regarded as the doyen of realist theorists, has set out the argument that 'China cannot rise peacefully' in a much-discussed book, published in 2014, called *The Tragedy of Great Power Politics*.[5]

Mearsheimer, unlike the neoconservatives who so influenced George W. Bush, does not see the behaviour of nation states in moral terms. He does not argue that the rise of China will lead to war because of the nature of the Chinese regime. Instead he believes that war is likely precisely because China will behave no differently from any other nation, including the US. Mearsheimer writes that 'If China continues to grow economically, it will attempt to dominate Asia the way the United States dominates the western hemisphere. The United States however will go to enormous lengths to prevent China from achieving regional hegemony . . . The result will be an intense security competition with considerable potential for war.'[6] Those who are tempted to dismiss this prediction as simple academic theorising might find it sobering to talk to senior US security officials, who often speak the same language of pushback and rivalry. As one such official put it to me in 2015, 'I know the US navy and it's addicted to pre-eminence. If the Chinese try to control the South China Sea, our guys will fucking challenge that. They will sail through those waters.'[7]

In fact, by 2015 the US, Chinese and Japanese navies and air forces were already regularly challenging each other at sea, flying or sailing through disputed waters in the East and South China Seas. Such challenges involve a willingness to risk a limited clash, in the belief that any conflict would be brought under control well before it escalated into a major war.

The risks of miscalculation in such a scenario, however, hardly need stating. This is particularly the case because US military plans seem increasingly to be based around the idea that a war with China could swiftly necessitate American attacks on the Chinese mainland. For the discussion of the possibility of a war between America and China is not simply confined to academic theoreticians and high-flying diplomats – it is also embedded in the military planning of both nations.

The US remains the dominant military power in the western Pacific. It is pledged to defend its treaty allies such as Japan, South

Korea and the Philippines. The armies of the US and China did fight each other during the Korean War. Ever since the end of that war in 1954 – and the division of the Korean peninsula – American troops have remained in considerable numbers on South Korean soil, and their presence and activities are closely watched by China.

In recent decades, however, the tensest stand-offs between the US and China have come over Taiwan. When the Communists finally won the Chinese civil war in 1949, the defeated Nationalists, led by Chiang Kai-shek, fled to Taiwan, just over a hundred miles off the coast of China. Ever since, mainland China has regarded Taiwan as a 'rebel province' and an inalienable part of its territory. The government in Beijing has pledged to go to war rather than accept any declaration of Taiwanese independence. The US has formally accepted Beijing's 'One China' policy, but it has also promised to resist any move by China to reincorporate Taiwan through the use of force. In 1995 and 1996 China, alarmed by the growth of pro-independence sentiment in Taiwan, staged missile tests in the waters around its 'rebel province'. In response, the US dispatched aircraft-carrier battle-groups to the waters around Taiwan, in what was widely described as the biggest display of American might in the region since the Vietnam War.

China backed off and the crisis died down, but the underlying dispute has not been resolved. In private, the Americans and Chinese can have remarkably blunt discussions about the prospect of war over Taiwan. In 2008, shortly before President Obama's first election victory, I was part of a delegation of 'scholars' from the US and Europe who visited the Chinese defence ministry in Beijing. The Chinese surmised, accurately, that several of the American 'scholars' were likely soon to take up senior positions in the Obama administration.[8] As a result, our visit to the Chinese defence ministry was treated as a semi-official occasion – with both sides making formal statements. In a cavernous meeting room, a Chinese general informed our group that China regarded the question of Taiwan as a 'core national interest' and that a declaration of Taiwanese independence would meet with a military response from China. The leader of the US–European delegation, Walt Slocombe – a former Undersecretary of State at the Pentagon – replied that, he was very sorry to hear that, because a Chinese attack on Taiwan would lead to military conflict between the US and China.[9]

That, I suppose, is what 'deterrence' looks like. But, in the twenty years since the Taiwan Strait crisis, the Chinese military has become much stronger – leading some in China to believe that, in reality, America would no longer risk fighting over Taiwan, much less the uninhabited Senkaku Islands. Chinese military spending has increased by an average of 12% a year, every year for the past generation. As a result its military power has increased at a pace that has dazzled and alarmed its neighbours. In 2000, Japan's annual defence spending had been three times as large as China's. By 2015, China's defence budget was double that of Japan – and the gap was increasing each year.[10]

The nightmare for the United States would be if China eventually closed the military gap with America itself. In the aftermath of the Cold War and the collapse of the USSR, it was common to observe that America's military budget was bigger than that of the whole of the rest of the world combined. But with China's military budget increasing so rapidly and US military spending set to decline, the gap is narrowing. Indeed, the much-respected International Institute for Strategic Studies has argued that by 2023, Chinese military spending could actually surpass that of the United States itself.[11] That projection depends on the US enacting the deepest cuts mooted under its sequestration law, designed to balance the US budget – and that is unlikely. The double-digit increases in Chinese military spending of recent years could also tail off, if China's economy slows. But, even so, the general direction of travel is clear – the gap in military capabilities between China and the US is narrowing. What is more, the US is attempting to maintain a position as the dominant military power all over the world. China, by contrast, is simply attempting to be the dominant power in its region.

The focal point of Chinese–American military rivalry is the control of the western Pacific. The idea that US control of the Pacific can no longer be taken for granted still remains rather shocking in Washington, for as Bob Gates – who served as Defense Secretary for both President Bush and President Obama – explains, the Pacific had 'for all practical purposes been an American lake for our navy since the end of World War Two'.[12] But the Pacific is now contested territory. The US navy – which numbered almost 600 warships during the Reagan era – now has fewer than 300 ships.[13] After a dramatic building programme over the last twenty years, the Chinese navy now has more than 300 ships.[14] The sheer number of vessels is a crude measure. The sophistication of most Chinese ships is still no match for the US navy. For example, the US has eleven modern aircraft carriers whereas in 2015, China had only one, the *Liaoning*, which had been bought second-hand from Ukraine. Plans have been announced for the domestic production of aircraft carriers in China, but that will take time. However, there are also some important categories of ship – such as submarines – in which the Chinese navy already easily outnumbers the Americans in the western Pacific.

What is more, much of the weaponry that China is buying is specifically designed to make it harder for the US to maintain naval dominance in the South and East China Seas. New generations of Chinese cruise and ballistic missiles and submarines are aimed at targeting the aircraft carriers that are the basis of America's naval dominance in the oceans around China. These 'carrier-killer' missiles were given their first public outing in a giant military parade staged in Beijing in September 2015, to mark the seventieth anniversary of the defeat of Japan in 1945. In any future Taiwan Strait crisis, or in a showdown in the East or South China Seas, the US would have to be aware of the new vulnerability of its carriers. That might well mean that the Americans would be reluctant to sail these vulnerable behemoths to the Taiwan Strait, as happened in the 1990s.

China has also spent heavily on weapons that can target American satellites. In the information age, the US military is hugely dependent on mapping systems and communications technology that allow it to do everything from targeting missiles to co-ordinating troop movements. Yet Chinese military exercises have demonstrated the country's ability to shoot information satellites out of the sky – potentially forcing the US military to 'fight blind'.

In response to these new Chinese capabilities, US military doctrine underwent a rethink. A new concept called 'Air-Sea Battle', adopted by the Pentagon in 2010, specifically targeted China's new weaponry that is known in military jargon as having 'anti-access and area-denial' capabilities – because of its ability to deny the US navy access to areas close to the Chinese coast. The advocates of Air-Sea Battle argued that it represented a necessary updating of American military strategy to combat China's new capabilities. They believe that it is an inevitable and necessary response to China's military build-up. As one senior US official put it to me, 'If there was no rise in tension between the US and China, we wouldn't be doing our jobs properly.'[15]

A rise in Sino-US tensions may indeed be inevitable. But committing America to a military doctrine that calls for taking the offensive early in a conflict with China could be a risk too far. The difficulty with the doctrine of Air-Sea Battle is that carrying it out would probably require America to escalate any conflict quickly – by attacking missile and surveillance systems based on the Chinese mainland in extensive bombing raids.[16] The assumptions built into military plans can matter hugely in a crisis – as became apparent in 1914, when the German army's plans for rapid mobilisation, using a strict railway timetable, proved very hard to reverse in a crisis. Jim Steinberg, Hillary Clinton's deputy at the State Department, is clearly aware of the risks involved in Air-Sea Battle as a concept, pointing out that America's adoption of this military doctrine was being interpreted by some in Asia as a 'prescription for unfettered rivalry' between the US and China.[17]

Alarmed by the implications of Air-Sea Battle, even some American hawks argue that, in the event of conflict with China, the US should instead seek to strangle China economically through the imposition of a blockade. The various scenarios discussed include naval operations close to the Chinese coast or much further away – including an effort to close the Strait of Malacca that connects the Indian and Pacific oceans.[18] Yet, if such a blockade was successful in closing off China's access to oil or world markets for its goods, it might just turn out to be a slower route to the all-out conflict that critics of Air-Sea Battle fear.

Contemplation of scenarios such as these have inevitably led both sides to weigh their relative military strengths and intentions. For US officials, even talking about America's military plans involved a delicate balancing act. If America put too much emphasis on its strengths, it risked sounding bellicose and playing into the hands of China's hawks. But if America played down its military prowess, it potentially ran the opposite danger – feeding the Chinese perception of American weakness and perhaps risking a challenge. In a 2012 *Washington Post* article Jim Steinberg attempted to tread this delicate line, arguing first that: 'While US defense spending and capabilities will still appear astronomical to China . . . officials in Beijing should keep in mind that perhaps half of US defense capability is intended for other parts of the world . . . The United States is no declining superpower, but the country is nonetheless war-weary and financially strapped. US leaders are cutting military spending even as they speak of "rebalancing" towards Asia.'[19] But then Steinberg and his co-author, Michael O'Hanlon of the Brookings Institution, tacked back to send a different message, one of strength and confidence: 'The stock of modern US military equipment is worth $3 trillion: despite its spending, China is at perhaps 10 per cent of that figure. Nor does China's military have experience in modern combat operations.'[20]

The article was a carefully balanced piece of messaging towards China. But it also reflected genuine uncertainty. In Beijing, Washington and Tokyo, military and strategic planners had to make assessment of the balance of power in Asia – knowing all too well that this guess-work would only be tested in the event that a disastrous diplomatic breakdown led to war.

As well as testing capabilities, the two sides had to assess each other's intentions. Some Americans, like Steinberg (who had studied China's history), were aware of the country's historic sense of vulnerability from the ocean, derived from the experience of assault by European and Japanese imperialists in the nineteenth and twentieth centuries. Yet even sympathetic analysts like Steinberg and Henry Kissinger, whose role in restoring relations between China and the US in the 1970s make him a revered figure in Beijing, also worried that some in China might have aggressive intentions.

Like Steinberg, Nye, Hadley and Armitage on their mission to Beijing, Kissinger was drawn to the parallel between US and Chinese relations at the beginning of the twenty-first century and the rivalry between Britain and Germany at the beginning of the twentieth century. In the epilogue to his book *On China*, which was published with great fanfare in Beijing and Washington in 2011, Kissinger dealt explicitly with the vexed parallel of the outbreak of war in 1914. Specifically, he quoted the 'Crowe memorandum' – a famous analysis written by the British diplomat Eyre Crowe in 1907 that foresaw an inevitable confrontation between Britain and Germany, and which speculated that Germany's naval build-up indicated that the country was seeking 'a general political hegemony and maritime ascendancy, threatening the independence of her neighbours and ultimately the existence of England'.[21]

Kissinger noted that Crowe believed that the very fact of a German naval build-up would inevitably become a threat to the British Empire, almost regardless of German intentions. But he also rejected the idea that China and the US were doomed to slip into a similar military rivalry.

Nonetheless, the starkness of the 1914 parallel was something that American analysts of China seemed unable to shrug off.[22] Senator Max

Baucus, who was dispatched to China as US ambassador in February 2014, was so impressed by Kissinger's chapter that he took to quoting the Crowe memorandum at various senior Chinese officials, as an oblique way of asking them about the intentions underlying China's military build-up. It was a slightly odd way of raising the question. But in their different ways, Baucus, Kissinger and the others were all getting at the same crucial question: is China preparing for a war with its neighbours, or even with the United States itself? What are the intentions of the rising superpower of the twenty-first century?

3

China – An End to Hide and Bide

Xi Jinping was announced as the new General Secretary of the Chinese Communist Party on 15 November 2012 – just eight days after Barack Obama had won re-election as US president. The Chinese leader lost little time in setting out his vision for the nation. On 29 November, he made a major speech on his plans for the 'great rejuvenation of the Chinese nation' at the National History Museum on Tiananmen Square in Beijing. Any foreigner wanting to understand what the fifty-nine-year-old Xi meant by that phrase would do well to visit the museum's redesigned galleries – which tell the story of China's modern history, as seen through the eyes of the Communist Party.

Visitors are told how in the nineteenth century 'imperial powers descended on China like a swarm of bees, looting our treasures and killing our people'. Acres of space are devoted to the suffering inflicted by the Japanese invasion and occupation of China from 1937–45, when some 15 million Chinese people died.

There is, however, almost no space given over to the even larger numbers of people who lost their lives during the famines and state-sponsored killings of Mao's Great Leap Forward from 1958–62.

In China, the horrors of the war with Japan are not receding with the passage of time. On the contrary, during the Xi era it seems to be official policy to keep the conflict with Japan at the forefront of the public mind. Patriotic television dramas set during the war with Japan are regularly scheduled. In September 2015, President Xi himself took the salute at a huge military parade in Beijing, commemorating the seventieth anniversary of the end of the Second World War and the surrender of Japan. China had staged many such ceremonies of remembrance in the past, but this was the first time that the anniversary had been marked by a giant show of military force – complete with missiles and goose-stepping troops. To many of China's Asian neighbours – not just Japan – the symbolism seemed ominous.

The Tiananmen parade passed in front of the National History Museum and reinforced its message: the Communist Party's mission is to right the historic wrongs inflicted on China and to restore the nation to its rightful position in world affairs. As I had noticed when I met him in Beijing, President Xi is a suitably imposing figure to deliver this message. He is almost six feet tall and has a heavy build: in a height-obsessed country such as China, that helps him to convey a message of power and authority.

By contrast, the man who more than any others was responsible for the rise of modern China was the diminutive Deng Xiaoping, who stood at under five feet tall – but who qualifies as a giant of modern Chinese history. It was Deng whose policies of economic reform and opening to the outside world – begun in late 1978 – transformed China over the course of a generation. The economic reforms unleashed by Deng succeeded in more than doubling the size of the Chinese economy every decade, defying every Western prediction that the Chinese boom would surely soon come to a close. By the time Xi took power in 2012, China was already closing in on the title of the world's largest economy.

It was also Deng who gave his Communist Party colleagues some famous advice on how a rising China should deal with the outside world. Deng's dictum – 'Coolly observe, calmly deal with things, hold your position, hide your capacities, bide your time, accomplish things where possible' – became famous and was often abbreviated in Western foreign-policy circles as 'hide and bide'. In English that three-word phrase can sound like an injunction to be deceptive and scheming. In reality, Deng's emphasis on humility and co-operation in international affairs made good sense for both China and the West. It was a policy that gave China the room and time to transform its economy while allowing the West to share in the wealth that China was creating. In that way, a potentially alarming development – the rise of China – was presented as a 'win-win', to use a piece of Western jargon that was swiftly adopted by China.

Deng's successors followed similar policies and adopted similarly reassuring slogans. Under Hu Jintao, who headed the Communist Party from 2002 to 2012, China followed a policy that became known as 'peaceful rise' – until even the phrase 'rise' was deemed too threatening to outsiders, at which point Hu began to favour the phrase 'harmonious world'.

During the Hu years, one of the most articulate and prominent exponents of the view that China and the United States had a mutual interest in the peaceful rise of China was Professor Wang Jisi of Beijing University. For Wang, China's rise was only possible in the context of globalisation and it was the US that had designed and maintained the architecture of globalisation. The US, for its part, had a stake in a prosperous and stable China that was integrating into an American-led world order. China, as Professor Wang saw it, benefited from the 'benign careful use of US power in the global system', while America profited from 'an orderly yet changing China under a strong, reform-minded leadership'.[1]

Wang had spent time as a visiting professor at Princeton University in the US, which was a stronghold of the 'liberal internationalist' thinking that he espoused. Princeton professors, such as John Ikenberry and Anne-Marie Slaughter (who went on to become the first director of Policy Planning in Hillary Clinton's State Department), dedicated themselves to rebutting the notion that great powers were doomed to clash. On the contrary, argued Ikenberry, China and the US were 'status quo powers', with a strong interest in the maintenance of a global system that worked well for them both. Neither of them had any real interest in overturning the system, far less in risking a war with each other.

The influence of Wang's theories of interdependence between America and China could be seen in the official rhetoric of the Chinese government, in the decade before Xi Jinping took power. Wen Jiabao, China's prime minister during that period, said of America and China that 'our common interests far outweigh our differences'. Professor Wang was close to Dai Bingguo, who occupied the top job in China's foreign-policy hierarchy – state councillor – for five years, from March 2008. In that job, Dai had made it his business to develop a decent working relationship with the White House. Tom Donilon, the head of the National Security Council for much of the first Obama administration, came to trust his Chinese counterpart implicitly, telling confidants that 'Every time that Dai has promised me something, he has delivered.' Henry Kissinger was also an admirer of Dai, praising him as a 'thoughtful and responsible' leader.[2] In December 2010 in a much-read article, Dai had endorsed the theories of peaceful rise and interdependence, promoted by thinkers such as Wang Jisi. According to Dai, China's overriding goal – to 'bid farewell to poverty and enjoy a better life' – was dependent on a peaceful international environment. China, he argued, knew that it was 'a member of the big international family'.[3]

For all his stress on interdependence, Dai Bingguo was also perfectly capable of taking tough positions when China reckoned that its 'core national interests' were threatened. He was still in office in 2012 as China's territorial disputes with both Japan and the Philippines intensified. But, amidst these rising tensions, Dai was still seen as a calm and trustworthy interlocutor in Washington. So it was symbolic that in March 2013, early in Xi Jinping's tenure as leader, Dai Bingguo retired as state councillor.

The new face of China's foreign policy was Yang Jiechi, a man with a much more abrasive style. Yang is a former ambassador to the US, fluent in English and comfortable in Washington. But he had also shown a willingness to use confrontational language avoided by an earlier generation of Chinese diplomats, brought up in the tradition of 'hide and bide'.

For many of China's nervous neighbours, Yang's image is defined by a single notorious incident. In 2010, while still foreign minister (a position junior to that of state councillor), Yang issued a blunt warning to other Asian nations not to get above themselves in their various territorial disputes with China. At a summit of Asia-Pacific nations in Vietnam, he announced 'China is a big country. And you are all small countries. And that is a fact.'

To some of the diplomats assembled in Vietnam, that had felt like the moment when China's mask had finally slipped. 'Hide and bide' was giving way to something much tougher Even some Chinese observers were aghast at Yang's intervention, believing that it was likely to backfire and drive smaller Asian nations into the arms of the United States. But President Xi was evidently not one of those who felt that Yang Jiechi had overstepped the mark. Instead he promoted Yang to the most senior position in China's foreign-policy hierarchy.

Xi himself came to power with a reputation as a 'military hugger' – a man with much closer ties to the armed forces than his predecessor, Hu Jintao. And the new Chinese leader swiftly provided evidence that he was willing to take actions that appealed to assertive nationalists.

In December 2012, the month after Xi took over as General Secretary and head of the military, Chinese military aircraft entered Japanese-controlled airspace for the first time since 1958. Two months later, in February 2013, a Chinese frigate locked its missile-guidance system on a Japanese frigate in the vicinity of the disputed Senkaku–Diaoyu islands. In October of that year, the *Global Times*, a nationalist Chinese newspaper, wrote that 'The possibility that China–Japan frictions will escalate into military conflict is growing.' A month later, China startled the governments of both the US and Japan by declaring an 'Air Defence Identification Zone' (ADIZ), covering most of the East China Sea, including the disputed islands. China's ADIZ required all non-Chinese planes entering the area to identify themselves to the Chinese authorities.

The Chinese air force had pushed for the declaration of an ADIZ during the years in which Hu Jintao and Dai Bingguo controlled foreign policy, and had been pushed back, but Xi Jinping gave it the green light.[4] The US signalled its refusal to accept the new ADIZ by flying military planes through the area without first seeking clearance from the Chinese authorities. The possible dangers of this new situation were underlined in August 2014, when a Chinese fighter intercepted an American navy plane 135 miles off Hainan Island, in an encounter that the US Department of Defense described as 'very close, very dangerous'.[5]

In the months after the declaration of the ADIZ, evidence of a new and more aggressive Chinese foreign policy seemed to mount. China angered Vietnam by deploying an oil rig in disputed waters, provoking anti-Chinese riots across Vietnam. A visit by President Xi Jinping to India was overshadowed by the news that Chinese troops had crossed into disputed Indian-controlled territory, even as China's president was smiling and shaking hands in Delhi.[6]

The evidence that Beijing had embarked on a new and more aggressive course seemed to be mounting. In his first eighteen months in office, Xi paid more official visits to the People's Liberation Army than his predecessor had done in a decade. But China was also capable of blending charm with menace, combining threats with the promise of lucrative 'win-win' deals.

In November 2014, just over a year after he had taken office as General Secretary of the party, Xi used a Beijing summit of the

Asia-Pacific Economic Co-Operation Forum (APEC) to show a more conciliatory face to the world. The US and China announced a new understanding on climate change. And, after months of heavy lobbying from Tokyo, the Chinese leader agreed to shake hands with Shinzo Abe, the prime minister of Japan.

Meanwhile China's other Asian neighbours were wooed with offers of investment and economic co-operation. China trumpeted its plans for a new Beijing-based Asian Infrastructure Investment Bank, which would help to build infrastructure and promote trade across the continent. The new slogan in Beijing – relentlessly parroted, as ever, by the Chinese media – was 'one belt, one road'. The belt was a vision of a 'new Silk Road' recreating the ancient trade routes between China and its western neighbours in Central and South Asia. The 'road' (confusingly) was the development of new trade routes in the seas around China, roughly along the routes that had once been sailed by the great admiral, Zheng He, during the Ming dynasty.

To some, President Xi's new emphasis looked like a pronounced shift from the alarming militarism of his first few months in office and a return to the older policies based around economic co-operation. Perhaps, it was argued, President Xi had noticed that his more aggressive policies were driving Asian nations into the arms of the US and had thought again? Yet, in truth, the economic and military aspects of Chinese foreign policy under Xi served the same strategic goal – to build and extend China's claim to be the dominant force in Asia and the Pacific.

Even when President Xi took a conciliatory step, he did it in a way that seemed designed to emphasise China's growing sense of its own primacy in the region. So the Chinese president's meeting with the Japanese prime minister at the APEC summit, was not designed to look like a meeting of equals. Instead, Shinzo Abe was left to stand alone in front of the cameras, while waiting patiently to be allowed to shake Mr Xi's hand.[7] An Asian diplomat who witnessed the exchange assured me that President Xi would have rehearsed the look of pained distaste that crossed his face as he shook hands with the Japanese leader.

Any hopes that the assertive policies pursued during President Xi's first year in office would prove to be just a passing phase were swiftly dashed in the months after the APEC summit. Instead, China's territorial claims were advanced in a new and imaginative manner through a concerted programme of 'island-building' in the South China Sea. In an effort to bolster its disputed claims to territorial waters hundreds of miles from the Chinese mainland, Beijing began to pursue ambitious land reclamation and dredging programmes that converted sea-shoals into small islands. The government in Beijing argued that its land-reclamation work was intended to provide public goods such as lighthouses, and that other countries had made similar efforts. But China's island-building was on a far larger scale than anything ever attempted by Vietnam or the Philippines. The Obama administration was certainly convinced that the land reclamation had a military rationale – pointing to the construction of a two-mile airstrip on the evocatively named Fiery Cross Reef.

China's increasingly evident desire to assert its central role in the Pacific region came as no surprise to most long-time observers of the country. Lee Kuan Yew, the former prime minister of Singapore and close confidant of successive Chinese leaders, who died in 2015, had always believed that China ultimately would seek to re-establish its historic grandeur. He argued that 'Theirs is a culture 4,000 years old with 1.3 billion people, many of great talent . . . How could they not aspire to be number one in Asia, and in time the world?'[8]

The idea of China as the 'Middle Kingdom' around which the rest of Asia revolves has deep roots in Chinese history. Given China's history, size and economic dynamism, it was always likely that the policy of 'hide and bide' would give way to something much more assertive, as the country grew in wealth and confidence. By the time President Xi took office, there was already a body of new ideas and emerging policies that he could draw upon as the basis for a more assertive foreign policy. Three related ideas were particularly important: a sense of aggrieved nationalism; increasing confidence in China's strength relative to the United States; and a deep fear about China's own domestic political stability and the potentially subversive role of the West.

The Chinese Communist Party's embrace of nationalist rhetoric can be dated quite precisely. It was in June 1989 that Deng and his colleagues took the fateful decision to crush the student uprising that was challenging Communist Party rule in China. The Tiananmen Square massacre presented the Chinese government with a profound threat to the survival and legitimacy of the one-party state. In response, the Communist Party increasingly began to emphasise nationalism and national revival – the 'great resurgence of the Chinese nation' – as a way of restoring its legitimacy.

In the years after 1989, the idea that China had undergone a 'century of humiliation', only to be saved by the Communist Party from a predatory world, was drilled into a generation of school and university students through new history textbooks and museums. Modern Chinese history was made a required course in high schools from 1992 onwards. The teaching guidelines for the new history course stated clearly that 'Chinese modern history is a history of humiliation in which China gradually degenerated into a semi-colonial and semi-feudal society . . . It is also the history of the success of the New Democratic Revolution under the leadership of the Chinese Communist Party.'[9] Schools were encouraged to visit new or redesigned museums and memorial sites, pushing the same message of humiliation by foreign powers and regeneration by the Communist Party – such as the National History Museum in Beijing and a Memorial Hall for the Victims in Nanjing. By the time President Xi was elected General Secretary of the Communist Party a whole generation of young Chinese had been raised on this 'wolf's milk' of nationalism.

As leader, Xi Jinping swiftly began to flirt much more openly with nationalist ideas and language. The notion that he became most closely identified with was the 'China Dream' – an idea that was soon picked up and promulgated in China's slogan-obsessed political culture. The 'China Dream' was, of course, an echo of the 'American Dream'. Many foreign observers, encouraged by the Chinese, believed that President Xi's talk of a 'China Dream' was a direct response to an article by Tom Friedman, the influential *New York Times* columnist, in which he had urged China to develop its own 'dream' of material development, allied with a cleaner environment. Yet, well before either Friedman or Xi had uttered the phrase, many Chinese would have become familiar with the idea of a 'China Dream' through the best-selling work of Colonel Liu Mingfu.

Liu's book *The China Dream*, published in China in 2010, opens with the bold statement – 'It has been China's dream for a century to become the world's leading nation.'[10] Like the Japanese nationalists of the 1930s, Colonel Liu argues that his nation's rise is part of a broader Asian renaissance. He writes that 'When China becomes the world's leading nation, it will put an end to Western notions of racial superiority . . . Every global leader in recent history has risen from Europe and North America; however, Asia is the largest continent and by all rights it should have the world's leading nation.'[11]

For Liu, the 'China Dream' is part of a broader shift of power from west to east. China will stand at the centre of a new age of Asian prosperity and will also usher in a more harmonious world because its leadership will be wiser and more benevolent than that of the United States. Alongside this vision of ultimate harmony in a China-led world is a much tougher idea of inevitable confrontation with the United States. Like many Chinese nationalists, Liu believes that the US will naturally strive to block the rise of China as a rival – just as it once thwarted Japan and the USSR. The colonel, who is in his fifties, lives on a compound of residential buildings for military personnel in Beijing, near the Ministry of Defence. When my *FT* colleague Geoff Dyer visited him there, Colonel Liu informed him that 'As an ordinary military man, I argue loudly that China should try to be the number one, should race to be the champion country.'[12]

When President Xi adopted the term 'China Dream', he was surely aware of what it would signify to Liu's many readers. And indeed there were other hints that Colonel Liu's views resonated right at the top of the Chinese government. His book had a foreword written by Lieutenant General Liu Yazhou, a close adviser to President Xi.[13] For General Liu, the emerging contest between China and the US promised to be 'the largest game of global power in history'.

The question of how far China's leadership believes the nationalist rhetoric that it has pumped into the country's educational system is crucial to understanding whether the Chinese government believes that conflict with the US or Japan is likely – or even necessary. One view is that China's most important leaders have cynically used nationalism as a political tool, without ever really buying into the underlying arguments. Certainly China has consistently pursued policies that suggest a pragmatic desire to integrate the country's economy with that of the West – joining the World Trade Organization, encouraging inward investment and promoting Chinese investment overseas.

At a personal level, China's leaders have also shown a lively appreciation of what the West has to offer. President Xi's daughter studied at Harvard under an assumed name. Bo Xilai, a populist leader – once seen as a potential rival to Xi, before his downfall in a corruption and murder case – specialised in nationalist rhetoric. But that did not prevent him sending his son to Harrow School, Winston Churchill's alma mater – and then on to Oxford and Harvard.

Another view is that while China's leaders may retain a certain cynical distance from nationalist rhetoric in private, they are nonetheless in danger of being trapped by it. This theory holds that having raised a generation of young people on a story of national humiliation and regeneration, no Chinese leader could ever afford to back down in a crisis with Japan or the US. The Chinese leadership know their history and well remember that in 1919, demonstrations by nationalist students – outraged by the terms the country's leaders had accepted at the Treaty of Versailles – led indirectly to the founding of the Communist Party itself.

But there is also some evidence that many of China's leaders personally subscribe to some of the conspiratorial and anti-Western theories that are prevalent in nationalist circles. In an important study of Chinese nationalism, *Never Forget National Humiliation*, the academic Zheng Wang argues that China's senior leaders have internalised nationalist ideas – and the deep suspicion of the West's intentions that goes along with them. In his book, Dr Zheng quotes extensively from leaked private discussions held among the country's leaders in the aftermath of the Nato bombing of China's embassy in Belgrade in 1999. Even in private, none of the leaders accepted America's explanation that the bombing had been an accident. All saw it as a deliberate challenge to Chinese national honour and some saw it as a plot to provoke and undermine China.[14] Zheng's conclusion was that 'These leaders are not only educators and manipulators, but also believers in their new ideology.'[15]

The second factor underpinning China's increased assertiveness under Xi is the country's awareness of its growing wealth and power relative to the West. China's reaction to the IMF announcement in 2014 that it was now the world's largest economy in terms of purchasing power exhibited some of the old instinct of 'hide and bide'. In discussions at the IMF, Chinese officials had resisted the notion that China might soon officially be 'number one'. In many ways, it suited China to argue that it was still a developing nation. There was little point in alarming the Americans unnecessarily – and if China was classified as the world's largest economy it risked being asked to take on more burdens, for example over climate change or development aid.

Yet, in other respects, there was no doubt that China's leaders were buoyed by a growing sense of wealth and power. A procession of world leaders was now showing up in Beijing, with huge trade delegations in tow – hoping to catch the wave of Chinese growth. China had discovered that the lure of access to the giant Chinese market was an extremely effective tool for modifying the behaviour of foreign powers – even some of those who had once forced China to open its markets at the point of a gun. When Britain's prime minister, David Cameron, met with the Tibetan leader, the Dalai Lama, in May 2012, China responded by putting the British in the diplomatic deep freeze. The British government was so alarmed by the economic implications of its loss of access to China's leaders that it quietly modified its behaviour. The Chinese were given to understand that there would be no further meetings with the Dalai Lama – and Cameron was eventually rewarded with a trip to Beijing in December 2013.

When demonstrations in Hong Kong broke out a few months later, the British prime minister rather pointedly did not meet leaders of the Hong Kong democracy movement when they visited London in search of support. As far as Beijing was concerned, the British had been taught a lesson. Just how far Britain was willing to adjust its foreign policy to catch the China wave became evident in March 2015, when the British broke ranks with the US to become the first major Western power to sign up as founder member of China's new Asian Infrastructure Investment Bank. Commenting on the episode, Eswar Prasad, a former head of the IMF's China department, remarked: 'The fact that the old players like the UK and Germany are falling over each other to prostrate themselves before China is certainly a sign of the new world order.'[16]

The knowledge that China's growing economic power was enhancing the country's diplomatic power was doubtless satisfying to China's leaders. But the psychological pay-offs of decades of rapid economic growth went further than that. They helped to make many Chinese – in business or social life – feel less intimidated by the wealth and success of the West. The sentiment was captured by Jack Ma, an entrepreneur whose internet company Alibaba had made him a billionaire many times over. As a young man, Ma had taught himself English by working as a tour guide in his home city of Hangzhou. When he founded Alibaba in 1999, he did so with a rallying cry to his friends and colleagues that resonated well beyond business, telling them that

'Chinese brains are just as good as those of Americans and this is the reason we dare to compete with them.'[17] Within a decade Ma was not just competing with Americans but beating them, as Alibaba notched up global sales that were larger than those of American internet giants such as eBay or Amazon. The company's initial public offering of shares – made just as Xi Jinping ascended to the presidency – raised well over $100 billion.

Alibaba epitomised the growing sense of wealth, possibility and confidence in twenty-first-century China. And that sentiment was matched by a belief amongst many Chinese intellectuals, reflected in the media, that the US and the West as a whole was in decline. The financial crisis that began on Wall Street in 2008 – and shook the entire global economy – had also served to undermine the prestige of the United States inside China. Suddenly, a US that had seemed self-confident and secure in its global position appeared to be teetering on the edge of depression and bankruptcy. In Beijing in November 2008, a couple of months after the collapse of Lehman Brothers, I encountered a new mood that was exemplified by a comment from Pan Wei, director of Beijing University's Center for Chinese and Global Affairs: 'My belief,' said Professor Pan, 'is that in twenty years we will look the Americans straight in the eye as equals. But maybe it will come sooner than that. Their system is in chaos and they need our money to rescue them.'[18]

The fact that China – aided by a massive splurge of government spending – recovered from the shock of 2008 far faster than the West further bolstered Chinese self-confidence. The growing awareness of how much the US had borrowed from China also created the impression that the traditional power relationship between Washington and Beijing was changing.

The new cockiness in China's attitude to America was reflected at a meeting of the World Economic Forum in the Chinese city of Dalian in 2011 when Rui Chenggang, a popular and good-looking television anchor, publicly asked the US ambassador, Gary Locke, if the fact that he had flown in economy class to the conference was 'a reminder that the US owes China money'. Locke replied truthfully that flying economy class was simply US government policy. But Rui had (perhaps inadvertently) hit a nerve. Senior Obama administration officials dealing with China bemoaned the fact that they all too frequently arrived in Beijing for crucial negotiations shattered after flying fourteen hours in the back of the plane. One bitterly described to me boarding the plane in Washington and 'passing the Chinese ambassador sipping his champagne in business class, as I trudged to my seat in coach'.

In the years after the crash, Western diplomats, particularly Europeans, began to notice a new tone in their dealings with the Chinese. In 2011, one British diplomat – recently returned from a trip to China – told me with a laugh that China was the only country where he had been told, 'What you have to remember is that you come from a weak and declining nation.' Another very senior British diplomat confided that 'Dealing with the Chinese is becoming increasingly unpleasant and difficult.' When I responded that some of his counterparts in Washington still spoke highly of the top Chinese officials they dealt with, the UK official responded: 'There is a special tone of voice that the Chinese now only reserve for the Americans.' For all China's continuing insistence that it was still a developing nation, the government in Beijing was increasingly behaving like a superpower-in-the-making – and the only country that it still seemed to regard as a true equal was the United States.

But, under Xi Jinping, even the Americans began to notice a distinct shift in tone in China's dealings with the world. The influence of China's liberal internationalists was clearly on the wane. As another senior US official put it to me in 2013, 'People like Wang Jisi are not being listened to any more. They are hiding away in institutes and talking in code.'[19]

That was perhaps a slight exaggeration. When I visited Beijing eighteen months later, Professor Wang was still around and happy to meet for coffee. With a self-deprecating smile, he described himself

as a 'notorious soft-liner' and suggested, gently, that it might be easier if our substantive conversation was off the record. Yet, in his published writings, Wang himself had charted the shift in mood under Xi
Jinping. As he wrote in April 2014: 'In the past couple of years, China's
official media and documents have sent increasingly harsh warnings
to Chinese citizens that the US is not only trying to contain China
militarily and politically but, more sinisterly, waging an ideological war
aimed at generating chaos and disorder in China.'[20]

As Wang shrewdly pointed out, China's increasingly assertive
nationalism under Xi Jinping was a reflection of insecurity as much
as confidence. That pointed to the third factor underpinning the rise
of government-sponsored Chinese nationalism in the Xi years: a fear
that the continued rule of the Communist Party was threatened by
Western subversion.

When student demonstrators in Hong Kong formed the 'Occupy
Central' movement in October 2014 – to demand fully democratic
elections in Hong Kong – it looked like the fulfilment of China's worst
nightmare. Ever since the end of British colonial rule in 1997, Hong
Kong has been part of China's sovereign territory – but governed,
according to its own laws, under the formula of 'one country, two
systems'. It was a delicate balancing act that China had maintained
with some skill. For example, Hong Kong residents were allowed to
stage an annual commemoration of the Tiananmen Square massacre
of 1989 – something that was unthinkable in China itself – which
drew thousands of demonstrators to a moving candlelit vigil in Hong
Kong's Victoria Park.

But there were limits to how far China was prepared to allow freedom of expression and democracy in Hong Kong – and it was those
limits that were exposed in 2014. That year China made it clear that
it was willing to allow long-promised direct elections for the job of
chief executive of Hong Kong, only on condition that it could pre-
screen the candidates. For Hong Kong's students and democracy
activists that was unacceptable. When they took to the streets in late

2014 – bringing Hong Kong to a virtual halt for several days – some feared that China might respond as it had in Beijing in 1989, with military force.

In the event, the Chinese government was wise enough to allow the demonstrations to fizzle out, with relatively little direct or violent intervention. But in Beijing, the Hong Kong demonstrations had only served to heighten China's fear of a 'colour revolution'. The term has been coined to describe a series of pro-democracy uprisings in countries of the former Soviet Union and in the Middle East. The successful prototypes were Georgia's 'Rose Revolution' in 2003 and Ukraine's (first) 'Orange Revolution' in 2004. After that, branded revolutions seemed to break out at regular intervals around the world. Lebanon had a 'Cedar Revolution' in 2005 which helped to force the pull-out of Syrian troops from the country. Iran had an unsuccessful 'Green Revolution' in 2009. The uprisings that shook the Arab world began with the 'Jasmine Revolution' in Tunisia of 2010.

Shortly after the Tunisian uprising of 2010, Chinese internet users found that searches for the word 'Jasmine' were blocked. That act of censorship illustrated that the wave of revolutions in the Arab world, which continued throughout 2011, had stirred deep anxieties within the Chinese Communist Party. Popular risings against undemocratic regimes – and the chaos they could unleash – became a central focus of China's political thinking. The role of Western activists, institutions and technology in stoking these revolts was noted in Beijing. The fact that the Egyptian uprising of 2011 was labelled the 'Facebook Revolution' and that one of its most prominent early organisers was a Google executive helped to ensure that those two companies were effectively blocked in China.

Chinese official paranoia about the threat of a colour revolution was further stoked by a second revolution in Ukraine in 2014, a decade after the original Orange Revolution. Chinese officials seemed sincerely to embrace the Russian view of the uprising in Ukraine – namely that it was essentially organised by the Americans, using all their nefarious tools, from the internet to Western-funded NGOs. The Hong Kong protests, which broke out just a few months after the Ukrainian revolution, appeared to confirm Beijing's deepest fears. Viewed from government offices in China, they looked dangerously like the importation of the techniques of a colour revolution onto the Chinese mainland: the sit-down protests, the students, the foreign television crews, the use of social media and the emergence of a catchy brand name, the 'umbrella movement'. (It was raining a lot in Hong Kong at the time.)

Shock at events in Hong Kong led the government in Beijing to increase its vigilance against Western subversion. In early 2015, China's education minister, Yan Guiren, issued an edict to the country's universities that sounded like something from the heyday of Maoism: 'Never let textbooks promoting Western values enter our classes,' thundered the minister. 'Any views that attack or defame the leadership of the party or socialism must never be allowed.'

Any visitor to contemporary China might conclude that it is rather late in the day to crack down on foreign influence. The Chinese capital is the home to every Western brand you can think of – from Lamborghini to Starbucks. In the cafes near Beijing's university campuses, Chinese students gossip and surf the internet, much like their Western counterparts. Yet apparent familiarity can be deceptive. Anyone trying to log in from one of those ubiquitous internet cafes is liable to run straight into the Great Firewall of China that blocks access to Google, Twitter and many other Western sites.

Under Xi, the Great Firewall has been raised higher, amidst a crackdown on Western influence that has affected universities, bloggers and television schedules. University professors grumble that they can no longer access the *New York Times* for their research. People involved in liberal politics suffered much more directly. Human-rights organisations reported that hundreds of activists and dissidents were detained in the aftermath of the Hong Kong demonstrations. Foreign NGOs were also put under intensified scrutiny and pressure. The pressure was kept up the following year, with a mass round-up of civil-rights lawyers in July 2015. Most were released fairly swiftly, but the chilling effect was entirely deliberate.[21]

The Chinese government was self-aware enough, however, to know that not all domestic discontent was the fault of meddling foreigners. As soon as he came to power, President Xi made clear that the 'great rejuvenation' of China must include a crackdown on corruption. If the system was not cleansed, he argued, the survival of the Communist Party itself was at stake.

Many foreign and Chinese observers assumed, nonetheless, that the anti-corruption campaign would not go very deep or last very long. They were wrong. Three years into Xi's rule, some of the richest and highest-profile people in China had been arrested and disgraced. They included Zhou Yongkang, who had been in charge of China's internal security apparatus under President Hu Jintao, and Hu's private secretary, Ling Jihua. (His spending habits had come under scrutiny after his son, accompanied by two semi-naked women, had crashed a Ferrari and died in Beijing in 2012.)

Also caught up in the purges was Rui Chenggang, the journalist who had cheekily asked the US ambassador about flying economy. Six months before his arrest, I had bumped into Rui at the World Economic Forum in Davos. He was his usual clever, bumptious self. Rui even prefaced a question to Shinzo Abe, the Japanese prime minister, by noting that, when in Tokyo, he liked to use the same gym as the Japanese leader. Six months later in July 2014, Rui – who boasted that his TV show attracted up to 300 million viewers – was arrested shortly before going on air at the CCTV studios in Beijing. Some eighteen months later, he had still not been charged or reappeared in public.

As with many of the arrests in the anti-corruption campaign, there was speculation about the real reasons for Rui's disappearance. Was he genuinely corrupt or had he simply fallen foul of somebody powerful? Was it some combination of the two?

President Xi is almost certainly right that rampant corruption is a serious threat to the legitimacy and popularity of the Communist Party. The difficulty is that arresting over 100,000 people – a common estimate by the end of 2015 – risks creating political instability by another route. In the absence of a politically independent police and court system, few powerful Chinese people can be confident that they are not at risk of being swept up in the wave of arrests that, three years into the Xi era, had snared senior figures in the military, media, regional governments, big state-owned industries and high finance.

Xi's China presents a paradox. Its assertive foreign policy and rhetoric suggests that China is a country that is increasingly confident of its own power and international role. But a crackdown on dissent and corruption at home, against the backdrop of a slowing economy, points to a strong sense of insecurity at the top levels of government. The two themes – assertive nationalism overseas and nagging insecurity at home – come together in the government's fear of Western subversion.

The belief in some circles in Beijing that the Hong Kong demonstrations were inspired by American meddling played down the genuine indignation amongst the Hong Kong demonstrators. But the broader Chinese feeling that America was less and less comfortable with China's rise had rather more to it. For the Xi years have seen not only a rise in Chinese assertiveness around the world, they have also witnessed an increased American effort to push back against the rise of China. Taken together these emerging new attitudes in Beijing and Washington pose a profound challenge to the dominant ideas of 'win-win' interdependence between America and China long promoted by influential academics such as Wang Jisi and John Ikenberry – and then reflected in official statements in both Washington and Beijing.

In their more reflective moments, American officials recognise that an emerging confrontation between the US and China is not simply the product of a new mood of nationalism in Xi Jinping's China. It is also a result of an almost instinctive American response to the rise of a great new power. As Kurt Campbell, Assistant Secretary of State for Asia in the first Obama administration puts it, 'China understands something quite profound about the US that perhaps even American citizens struggle with. The US will not go quietly into the night. America has grown accustomed, psychologically and politically, to being the first among equals on the global stage.'[22] In fact, 'first among equals' is an overly modest description of America's conception of its global role. Under President Obama, no less than President Bush, the US was determined to remain the world's dominant power.

4

America Reacts

When I first met Tom Donilon, who served as National Security Adviser in the Obama administration from 2010 until 2013, it struck me that he bore a considerable resemblance to another Tom – Tom Hagen, the lawyer in the *Godfather* movies who served as *consigliere* to the Corleone family. The real and the fictional Toms were both tall, well groomed, slightly gaunt, with receding hairlines and an air of having seen it all. Both were lawyers by trade and served as key advisers to their bosses.

The comparison is, perhaps, a little far-fetched – but discussing the Middle East with Donilon or other US policymakers, I was often reminded of a quote from *The Godfather part III* – Michael Corleone's lament that: 'Just when I thought I was out, they pull me back in.' Just as Michael could never escape the Mafia, so the US can never seem to escape the Middle East. For it is one thing to make an intellectual judgement that US foreign policy needs to 'pivot' away from the Middle East and towards East Asia (Donilon actually preferred the term 'rebalance") – it is quite another to stick to the plan, amidst the relentless crises flowing from the Middle East.

It was a historic irony that the US announced its decision to rebalance its foreign policy towards Asia in 2011 – the very year that the

Middle East exploded into a cycle of revolution, repression, turmoil and war that was initially given the optimistic label of the 'Arab Spring'.

In an important speech to the Australian Parliament in Canberra in November 2011 – ten months after the overthrow of President Hosni Mubarak in Cairo – President Obama announced that the US was winding down its wars in the Middle East, in favour of a new commitment to Asia: 'After a decade in which we fought two wars that cost us dearly, in blood and treasure, the United States is turning our attention to the vast potential of the Asia-Pacific region.' This 'new focus' reflected the fact that 'The United States has been and always will be a Pacific nation.' As he attempted to flesh out the meaning of this new policy, Obama's emphasis was unabashedly on military and security issues: 'Reductions in US defense spending will not – I repeat will not – come at the expense of the Asia-Pacific . . . The United States is a Pacific power and we are here to stay.' It was only after ten long paragraphs devoted to America's military posture in Asia that the US president uttered the formulaic phrase, 'The United States will continue our effort to build a co-operative relationship with China.'[1]

The remaining years of the Obama administration were defined by a constant tension in foreign policymaking between the desire to maintain a strategic focus on Asia and the permanent distraction of the pounding headaches of turmoil in the Middle East and then Russia.

For Donilon, however, who was Obama's National Security Adviser at the time of the Canberra speech, the strategic rationale for America's rebalance towards Asia remained unassailable. As he explained shortly after leaving office in the summer of 2013, the Obama administration had 'looked around the world and asked where are we over-weighted, where are we under-weighted?' The conclusion was 'We were over-weighted in some areas and regions, including our military actions in the Middle East . . . We were under-weighted in other regions, such as the Asia-Pacific.'[2]

President Obama himself was easily persuaded of the logic of rebalancing American foreign policy towards Asia. Born in Hawaii and brought up partly in Indonesia, Obama could claim to be America's first 'Pacific president'. His determination to pull America back from wars in the Middle East fitted perfectly with his desire to pay more attention to Asia.

Hillary Clinton, who served as Secretary of State throughout Obama's first term, set out the rationale for what she called a 'strategic turn' towards Asia in a landmark article in *Foreign Policy* magazine entitled 'America's Pacific Century' in October 2011, that stressed the growing economic weight of Asia: 'The stretch of sea from the Indian Ocean through the Strait of Malacca to the Pacific contains the world's most vibrant energy and trade routes.' As for the South China Sea, 'half the world's merchant tonnage flows through this water'. Clinton did not need to spell out the significance of this fact. For, as all observers of the region well knew, China's infamous 'nine-dashed line' claims that almost all the South China Sea falls within China's own territorial waters. The nine-dashed line, which is printed in all Chinese passports, stretches hundreds of miles out into the sea from the Chinese mainland – hugging the coastline of the Philippines, Malaysia, Vietnam and parts of Indonesia.

The original drafter of the Clinton article, which appeared in *Foreign Policy* magazine, was Kurt Campbell, the US Assistant Secretary of State for Asia, and the policymaker with the strongest claim to be the intellectual Godfather of the pivot.[3] Campbell had a resumé that looked like the career path of a would-be presidential candidate. He had been a Marshall Scholar at Oxford, where he played tennis for the university and completed a doctorate on Russian foreign policy. After that he had served in the navy – both on active duty and as a reservist. But as the Cold War ended, Campbell shifted his attention away from Europe and towards Asia. A naval mission to Japan had led to an epiphany and a growing obsession with Asia – 'It was in 1988 and it just changed my life and, after that, I just couldn't get enough about Asia.'[4] In focusing on the military balance in the Pacific, Campbell was retracing his own family history. His father had fought in the Pacific as a naval officer during the Second World War. One of Campbell's hobbies was to go deep-sea diving to inspect the wrecks of ships sunk in the war in the Pacific.

During the Bill Clinton administration during the 1990s, Campbell had worked at the Pentagon on strengthening America's network of security alliances in the Pacific. One of his closest collaborators was an Australian intelligence official named Hugh White – which only sharpened Campbell's sense of betrayal, when White, alarmed by the implicit militarism of Obama's Canberra speech, became one of the most articulate critics of the US pivot to Asia. All that lay in the future, however, when Campbell was appointed as the State Department's top diplomat dealing with Asia in the first Obama administration. He believed passionately that a decade of war in the Middle East had left US foreign policy dangerously out of focus. As he later argued, 'At the core, the Middle East was an unbelievable sideshow that had suddenly taken centre stage.'[5] Correcting that imbalance was crucial to America's global power because 'By 2009, much of Asia had concluded that the US was on its way out as a Pacific power.' As a result, it was vital to demonstrate that America was going nowhere and that it was a 'resident power' in the Pacific. By 2011, Campbell and his allies, such as Jim Steinberg, had won the bureaucratic and intellectual argument for the 'pivot' towards Asia. The result was Obama's Canberra speech and Hillary Clinton's article on 'America's Pacific Century'.

But winning the intellectual battle was one thing. Maintaining America's focus on Asia and translating that into a series of consistent and effective policies was quite another. Even amongst the 'Asia hands' who agreed that US foreign policy should pivot towards the Pacific, there was considerable division about the correct mix of policies. Campbell argued that US policy was too focused on China, to the exclusion of other key powers in Asia. A 'China first' policy, he argued, tacitly accepted Beijing's view of its neighbours as 'tributary powers' that would inevitably have to adapt themselves to the interests of China itself.

It was a neat intellectual point. But, in practice, it was hard to avoid China dominating discussion of policy towards Asia. First, there was the sheer size of the country's economy – which, by 2015, was five times that of India, the other would-be Asian 'superpower'. Second, China – by the nature of its political system and the scope of its strategic ambitions – posed a much more direct challenge to a US-led world order than an American ally, such as Japan, or a fellow democracy, such as India. As Campbell acknowledged once he had left office, 'Most of our senior policymakers are still in the "China first" camp.'

A decision that China should be the focus of US policy on Asia did not, however, answer the question of what that policy should be. Any US government had to face the fact that America and China were simultaneously partners and rivals. As the two largest economies in the world, with deeply intertwined trading systems, they shared an interest in global economic stability. There were also global challenges – such as climate change – that both nations had an urgent interest in solving. And yet while they were economic partners, the US and China were also strategic rivals.

Any relationship between America and China was therefore always bound to contain elements of co-operation and competition. The question for American policymakers was how to strike the balance. Over the course of the Obama administration's eight years in power, America came increasingly to see China as more a rival than a partner. Quite how far the balance had tipped was brought home to me in the spring of 2014, when a senior White House official told me that he regarded the relationship as now '80% competition and 20% co-operation'. I was so surprised that I got him to repeat the formulation, in case I had misheard – '80% competition,' he said again.[6]

To understand the extent of the change in US policy that this implied, it is necessary to go back to the Bush and Clinton years. For many years both Republicans and Democrats had operated on the assumption that China's rise could be managed, by giving the nation a clear stake in the maintenance of the post-war international system – a system that had essentially been designed and maintained by the United States. Thus America supported China's application to join the World Trade Organization – an application that came to fruition in 2001 and which gave the Chinese economy a significant boost. The argument was that if China could see that its growing prosperity was clearly linked to the existing international order, it would have no interest in overturning that order – even though the world governance system was still dominated by the US. The idea was encapsulated in a phrase of Robert Zoellick, one of the last Republican internationalists and the president of the World Bank from 2007 to 2012, who suggested that China should become a 'responsible stakeholder' in the international system.

When President Obama took power at the beginning of 2009, he signalled a subtle shift in America's approach that was a response to the growing economic and political power of China. Washington was still focused on forging a largely co-operative relationship with Beijing, but it was tacitly prepared to grant China a larger role in the international system – an idea that was captured in the talk of China and America becoming a 'G2' that would together crack the world's toughest international problems. While the Obama team never formally adopted the G2 vocabulary, it did not disavow it too energetically either – an oversight that caused deep alarm in both Japan and India, whose governments feared that such an arrangement tacitly involved giving them subordinate roles in Asia.

The Obama team's initial interest in the G2 idea was rooted in its focus on transnational global problems – such as financial instability, climate change and nuclear proliferation. It was clear that on all these challenges, progress would be dependent on getting co-operation from China – which was the world's largest emitter of greenhouse gases, its second largest economy, a nuclear state and permanent member of the UN Security Council. Jeff Bader, who was director for East Asia at the NSC, later recalled that 'Throughout 2009 our foreign policy team was . . . working to gain Chinese support for our approach on critical global issues, which we saw as our *highest priority* in the relationship.'[7] (My italics.) At least initially, the main goal of Obama's China policy was therefore to gain Beijing's co-operation on a dazzling range of transnational issues, listed by Bader: 'denuclearisation of Iran and North Korea, restoring the world economy, combating climate change, fighting terrorism in Afghanistan and Pakistan, ending the civil war and genocide in Sudan and achieving energy security'.[8]

Yet President Obama's first visit to Beijing in November 2009 proved to be a sharply disillusioning experience. The president had gone out of his way to avoid offending the Chinese in the months leading up to the trip by declining to meet the Dalai Lama. Yet, on arrival in Beijing, he found that the Chinese were unyielding on all the key issues that the US had marked out as possible areas of partnership – from currency to climate to sanctions on Iran.[9] President Obama's efforts to use his charisma by staging a 'town-hall meeting' with students in Shanghai were also thwarted. The audience turned out to be largely made up of carefully selected members of the Communist Youth League. Popular Chinese bloggers that the Americans had attempted to invite were prevented from attending and the meeting was barely covered by Chinese television.

This rebuke made a deep impression on the new US president and his advisers, as an Indian government delegation discovered when they visited Washington a week after Obama's return from Beijing. 'We were meant to talk about a range of international issues,' recalled Shyam Saran, an adviser to Manmohan Singh, the Indian prime minister, 'but all Obama could talk about was China. He was clearly very upset.'[10] The fact that Obama was prepared to confide in a visiting delegation from Delhi also hinted at the role that India itself might play in the emerging balance of power in Asia. If American hopes for closer co-operation with China were doomed to disappointment, then India's role as an alternative partner in Asia would become much more important.

The downward spiral in US–Chinese relations continued in the weeks that followed President Obama's first visit to Beijing.

In December 2009, global climate-change talks broke down in spectacular fashion at a summit in Copenhagen. The US delegation – led by President Obama himself – found itself isolated by a Chinese diplomatic push focused on emerging powers, such as Brazil, India and South Africa. At a key stage in the conference, Obama literally had to barge his way into a meeting convened by the Chinese from which the Americans had been excluded. Climate change was meant to be the very epitome of the big global issues that would demand close US–Chinese co-operation – and yet it had led to another bruising experience for the Obama administration. The month after Copenhagen, China announced that it was suspending military-to-military contacts with the US in response to American arms sales to Taiwan. By the middle of 2010, the US had decided that it had to draw a line in the water. At a conference in Hanoi, Hillary Clinton announced that the US had a 'national interest' in 'respect for international law in the South China Sea'. This announcement was intended as a direct challenge to China's claim to suzerainty in those seas and marked an important shift in the tone of the Obama administration's approach to China. Even more important, as far as the Americans were concerned, was that the South East Asian nations present in Hanoi all seemed to welcome the US's firm riposte to China.

Despite the setbacks, the Obama administration continued to attempt to find areas of co-operation with China. But it was hard work. For all the intense preparation that went into US–Chinese summits, the Americans often found them frustrating experiences. One senior US diplomat who witnessed these summits up close later remarked: 'Chinese and American presidents find it hard to communicate. They are like computers with different operating systems.'[11] President Hu Jintao was notorious for sticking rigidly to his talking points. But even the more confident President Xi 'didn't engage much'. Some of the difficulties also came from the American side. For all his public charisma, President Obama can be a chilly character in private – and he struggled to build close relationships, even with other Western leaders. In Britain, some of David Cameron's advisers nicknamed the US president 'Spock', after the coldly logical Vulcan in *Star Trek*.

Behind the day-to-day setbacks and frustrations of managing US–Chinese relations, America was taking an increasingly dark view of China's ambitions in Asia. Viewed from Washington, China seemed to be taking an ever more assertive line on a series of territorial disputes, from the Senkaku Islands to the South China Sea and the China–India border. The idea that China would be a 'responsible stakeholder' in a US-led system began to seem less and less convincing. As one top Obama aide put it, 'It's true that China needs stability and the co-operation of the US to complete its rise. But it also sees the US as the biggest impediment to that rise.'[12]

US officials became convinced that if they did not react, their Asian allies would begin to doubt Washington's staying power and the US-led security system in the Pacific would begin to unravel. They also began to see Chinese ambitions as essentially unappeasable. 'China will keep pushing and pushing until they encounter resistance' was the conclusion of one of Obama's senior advisers.[13] Over at the State Department, Kurt Campbell had drawn a similar conclusion. When I suggested to him that perhaps it was unwise for America to say that the Senkaku Islands were covered by America's security guarantee, he replied that 'If we conceded on that point, I'm not sure the Chinese would back off.'[14]

For all the talk of economics, it was this strategic concern that was ultimately the driving impulse behind the Campbell-designed pivot – as well as the subsequent efforts to persist with the redeployment of American forces to the Pacific. From the outset, the pivot attracted both applause and criticism. But the critics often attacked the policy from very different angles. For the likes of Hugh White in Australia, the US pivot was over-militarised and provocative towards China – potentially putting the world's two most powerful nations on the path to a war. A few American critics shared this view. For example,

David Lampton of the Carter Center in Atlanta made an important speech in Shanghai in May 2015, in which he sounded the alarm about deteriorating US–Chinese relations and argued that 'America has to rethink its objective of primacy' in the Pacific.[15] Lampton worried that the US had not yet made the psychological and strategic adjustments that had to flow from its diminished weight in the global economy, noting that 'What seemed the natural order of the post-World War II period when the US accounted for 35% of global GDP is not sustainable when the United States is below 20%.' Yet while Lampton's speech got plenty of attention in China, he was a rare voice in the US foreign-policy world.

For some other critics – for example in Japan and in America's Pacific command – the pivot was an excellent idea, but it was under-resourced. According to this critique, President Obama had talked loudly in Canberra and elsewhere but had failed to produce much of a stick. Although the US was intent on deploying 60% of its navy to the Pacific, this was in the context of a military that was shrinking overall. 'I look at the resources provided to me,' complained one senior US naval officer, 'and I just don't see the pivot.'[16]

Other critics complained that the real shortage came not so much in military hardware, but in time and attention. Hillary Clinton, Tom Donilon and Kurt Campbell had been committed to the pivot. But a year into Obama's second term, they had all left office. Their replacements – in particular John Kerry, the new Secretary of State, and Susan Rice, the new National Security Adviser – seemed much less interested in Asia. At one of his first meetings with senior advisers at the State Department, Kerry was told that Hillary Clinton had quite deliberately made her first trip as Secretary of State to Asia – Kerry was advised to do the same thing. His response was disdainful. 'Forget it,' he said – making it clear that his top priority was to pursue an Israeli-Palestinian peace deal.[17] Some of the old hands at the State Department groaned at this choice – believing (correctly, as it turned out) that an Israeli–Palestinian deal would once again prove to be a mirage. Bill Burns, who served as Deputy Secretary of State to both Hillary Clinton and John Kerry, put it tactfully when he later said to me, of Kerry's Middle East mission, 'I admired the effort, I really did . . . The only challenge is there are opportunity costs, when you look at the Asia-Pacific rebalance.'[18]

Kerry dutifully did make long trips to Asia but it was always clear that the topics that most engaged him were Iran, Russia and the greater Middle East. As for Rice, she had started her career as an Africanist and had served as Obama's ambassador to the United Nations in his first term. Her job as head of the National Security Council frequently came down to crisis management – and, as Tom Donilon had discovered before her, all the most time-consuming crises seemed to take place in the Middle East.

The most telling critique of the pivot, however, was that it was over-preoccupied with the military challenges posed by China. As a result, America was in danger of missing the fact that the real basis of the challenge to its position in Asia was China's growing economic might. Nothing illustrated this problem better than the debacle over the Asian Infrastructure Investment Bank (AIIB) that unfolded in 2015. When China announced its intention to set up an AIIB in Beijing, the reaction in Washington was suspicious and hostile. This, after all, was not a case of China accepting a role in existing institutions such as the Washington-based World Bank or the Manila-based and Japanese-dominated Asian Development Bank. This was a new institution that China would clearly dominate, since it would be based in Beijing – and China would be the major shareholder. The AIIB also looked like a potential instrument for Chinese foreign policy, in particular the 'one belt, one road' strategy of building up new infrastructure across Asia, that would cement (sometimes literally) the ties between Asian nations and the dominant economy in the region – China.

Citing concerns about governance and transparency, America began to lobby its allies to refuse to join the AIIB. But in early 2015, the resistance of America's allies to the AIIB began to crumble – and the first nation to break ranks was Britain. An outraged White House official condemned Britain's pattern of 'constant accommodation' of China. (To which a senior British official replied smoothly, in my presence, 'Constant accommodation is clearly a bad idea, but surely *some* accommodation is necessary.') The sight of America's closest ally breaking ranks and joining the AIIB gave the green light to all the other US allies that also wanted a piece of the infrastructure action. Within weeks other key nations such as Australia, South Korea and Germany had also agreed to join the AIIB. The sole major hold-outs were America and Japan. But rather than looking like the bulwarks of a coherent anti-China front, Washington and Tokyo risked looking isolated and petulant.

Observing this spectacle, Larry Summers, Obama's first Treasury Secretary and a former president of Harvard, was convinced that he was watching history unfold – and not in ways that advantaged the United States. 'The past month', he wrote, 'may be remembered as the moment the United States lost its role as the underwriter of the global economic system.'[19] That verdict looks premature, since the future success of the AIIB is far from assured. But the very fact that Summers, a man usually noted for his supreme self-confidence, could offer such a mournful assessment testified to the growing alarm in the US establishment about America's position in the world.

After the debacle of the AIIB, it became clearer than ever that the US needed a more powerful economic component to the pivot. That component was called the Trans-Pacific Partnership (TPP) – a giant new free-trade deal for the Asia-Pacific region which was first mooted in 2005, and which became the most ambitious venture in the Obama administration's international economic policy. The TPP covered twelve nations, which were said to account for 40% of world trade and which included the US and Japan – but very pointedly did not include China. The Americans argued – as they had with the AIIB – that this was simply a question of maintaining standards of openness and good governance. But it was impossible not to also discern a strong strategic motive. Just as the US navy was attempting to stop China dominating the Pacific in strategic terms, so the TPP was intended to stop China dominating the Asia-Pacific in economic terms.

As he attempted to persuade Congress to grant him fast-track authority to negotiate a TPP, President Obama became increasingly explicit about the strategic rationale behind the new trade agreement, telling the *Wall Street Journal* 'If we don't write the rules, China will write the rules out in that region . . . We will be shut out . . . We don't want China to use its size to muscle other countries in the region around rules that disadvantage us.'[20] Yet putting all this strategic and economic weight on the TPP was a gamble by the American president. It was far from clear that Congress was prepared to make the difficult decisions necessary to make the new trade deal work. In fact, it had been Congress' reluctance to approve changes to national voting weights at the IMF, that would have better reflected China's economic clout, that had helped to convince Beijing that it would never get a fair deal in the Bretton Woods institutions based in Washington. Congressional scepticism reflected a wider backlash amongst the American public against free trade and globalisation in general. As Secretary of State, Hillary Clinton had been the original champion of the pivot and a big supporter of the TPP. But as a presidential candidate in 2016, competing for votes with the protectionist senator Bernie Sanders, Hillary decided that it was politically necessary to oppose the TPP deal. Many of Hillary's colleagues believed this to be a cynical decision – which would be cynically reversed if she ever made it to the White House. But the very fact that Hillary felt obliged to oppose an Asian trade deal that she had once championed said a lot about the political atmosphere in the US.

Like the Obama administration, the Japanese government faced formidable difficulties in persuading powerful domestic interests to accept a new trade deal. But the Japanese prime minister, Shinzo Abe, also saw the TPP as above all a crucial strategic thrust, aimed at

China. In a speech to a joint session of the US Congress, Abe pleaded that the TPP was about 'The rule of law, democracy and freedom . . . Long term its strategic value is awesome.'[21]

The fact that Abe was granted the singular honour of being the first Japanese prime minister to address a joint session of Congress is a sign of the increasing importance that the United States is investing in its 'special relationship' with Japan, as part of its attempt to push back against China's growing influence in Asia. Yet America's ever-closer embrace of Japan, while understandable, is also risky. The dynamic Japan of the 1980s is long gone. Today's Japan, while still rich and technologically advanced, is an ageing society with a shrinking population and an economy that has been stagnating for twenty years. It is also a country with a strong nationalist faction and a worryingly ambiguous relationship with its wartime past. No man better embodied that ambiguity than the leader who stood up to address Congress in April 2015 – Shinzo Abe.

5

The Japanese and Korean Dilemmas

Shinzo Abe has a lot in common with Xi Jinping. The two men came to power in Tokyo and Beijing within weeks of each other. Abe was elected as prime minister at the age of fifty-eight in December 2012 – the month after the fifty-nine–year-old Xi was appointed General Secretary of the Communist Party. Both men see their central task as 'national rejuvenation'. Both are charismatic leaders and nationalists. They are also linked by history. Their relatives were on opposite sides of the Sino-Japanese wars in the 1930s. Nobusuke Kishi, Abe's grandfather and political mentor, was one of Japan's chief administrators in occupied Manchuria in northern China. Xi Zhongxun, the Chinese president's father, was also in Manchuria – as a senior comrade of Mao, fighting with the Communist forces against Japan.

Yet the personal styles of the Japanese and Chinese leaders are very different. In January 2014, I had the chance to meet and interview Shinzo Abe at the World Economic Forum in Davos. In contrast to the imperial style of President Xi, Abe was strikingly informal. He bustled into a press conference, without much fuss and sat opposite me. When I asked if he was prepared to talk on the record, he agreed without hesitation. That might have been a mistake: his response to my opening question caused international controversy. I asked him if it was conceivable that China and Japan might ultimately go to war. Rather than ruling such an idea out – which would have been the obvious diplomatic response – Abe reminded his audience that 2014 marked the centenary of the outbreak of the First World War. Back then, he said, Britain and Germany had enjoyed a deep trading relationship – but this had not prevented the outbreak of war. China and Japan today, he remarked, were in a 'similar situation'. Abe's comments made international headlines and provoked a swift rebuke from China. As somebody who was present it was clear to me that Abe had not intended to threaten war – he was simply trying to explain the gravity of the situation – but such a comparison, coming from a world leader, was still rather startling.

Abe, of course, was by no means the first person to note the similarities between East Asia today and Europe before 1914. Professor Joe Nye and his American colleagues had discussed the same analogy on their diplomatic mission to Beijing and Tokyo, some fifteen months before. A few hours after interviewing Abe, I bumped into Nye in the corridors at Davos – and asked him if the situation between Japan and China had got better or worse since his mission to Asia. Nye winced and said that, on balance, the situation had only got more dangerous. Both countries were sending more planes and ships into the area surrounding the islands, testing each other's will. 'We've got to get this situation onto the back burner,' he said. 'If it stays on the front burner, it could boil over one day.'

The complication is that while the Americans are attempting to play the role of disinterested arbiters in this dangerous game, they are also crucial players. The fact that the US has a security treaty with Japan means that China will never accept America's claim to be an honest broker. Indeed many Chinese believe that the United States regards Japan as an 'unsinkable aircraft carrier' that is critical to its efforts to contain China. There are still over 50,000 US troops based in Japan, and the US Seventh Fleet, which patrols the Pacific, operates out of Japanese ports.

For the United States, the emergence of Shinzo Abe was a mixed blessing. On the one hand Abe promised to revive the Japanese economy and to revise its pacifist constitution, to allow Japanese forces to fight alongside the US – both of which are long standing goals of American foreign policy. But the flip side of Abe's dynamic nationalism is an ambivalent attitude to Japan's imperial history that threatens to alienate not just China, but also key US allies such as South Korea and even Singapore. That, in turn, complicates America's efforts to build a united front that could face down a more assertive China.

By the time Abe took office, there was little doubt that Japan was in need of radical reform. On the surface, the country remains prosperous. Its living standards are far above those of China, or indeed any other Asian nation bar tiny Singapore. Tokyo is one of the most exciting and welcoming cities in the world, but the numbers suggest that unless economic growth can be revived, Japan risks being caught in a downward spiral of debt and depopulation. Japan's population began to shrink in 2010. Demographers project that, at current fertility rates, the population will fall from 128 million to 87 million by 2060 – when 40% of the population will be over sixty-five. And while the US in the Obama years was panicking at the thought that its national debt might rise to 100% of GDP, Japan's debt-to-GDP ratio had already broken 200% by the time Abe took office. At that level, and even with rock-bottom interest rates, the cost of servicing the national debt was already consuming 25% of the government's budget. Any sharp rise in interest rates threatens fiscal Armageddon, since the cost of paying interest on Japan's national debt would soar – crowding out all other forms of spending.[1]

Faced with those kinds of numbers, an energetic, radical and patriotic reformer such as Shinzo Abe looked like just what Japan needed. The programme of economic reform that Abe adopted on coming to power is so closely identified with him that it swiftly became known as 'Abenomics'. The idea is that Japan must do everything to break the cycle of deflation (falling prices), which discourages spending and investment – since, in a deflationary environment, consumers and businesses hold on to their money in the expectation that prices will keep falling. Deflation also makes Japan's mountain of debt ever more intimidating. The goal of Abenomics is deliberately to encourage inflation of at least 2%, in the hope that Japanese workers will get a pay rise, consumers will spend and the national debt will be eroded by inflation. At the same time, Abenomics promises to push through structural reforms, to make it easier for Japanese firms to hire and fire – and to encourage Japanese women into the workforce. By allowing Japan's central bank to print money in previously undreamed of quantities, Abe excited (and sometimes horrified) economists all over the world.

But the prime minister's motives extend well beyond the technical goal of breaking the deflationary cycle that was depressing growth and drowning Japan in debt. For Abe, radical economic policies are ultimately needed to make Japan robust enough to stand up to China. As one analyst in Tokyo put it to me, 'Abenomics is not about deflation. It's about China.'

Abe's determination to strengthen Japan for the coming struggle with China has also entailed playing with some of the most incendiary material in Asian politics – Japan's history as an imperial power that colonised Korea, invaded China and rampaged across South East Asia. In December 2013, a year after his election, Abe outraged both the Chinese and the Koreans by visiting the Yasukuni shrine in Tokyo, where the souls of Japanese soldiers killed in war are said to be interred. Controversially, the veterans commemorated at Yasukuni include some who were convicted as war criminals at the Tokyo war-crimes trials of 1946. Even on a brief visit to the shrine in that year, it was obvious to me how much Yasukuni embraced a revisionist view of the Second World War that was bound to disturb the Asian and allied nations that had fought Japan. The shrine's museum contains a 'Zero fighter' – Japan's equivalent to the Spitfire or the Flying Fortress – along with a paean of praise to the plane's success in the war, as well as pictures of the plane drawn by visiting schoolchildren. I was also able to buy a coffee mug with a portrayal of the *Yamato*, the flagship of Japan's navy during the war, set against the background of the Japanese imperial flag. In the grounds of the shrine, there was a relatively new memorial to Radhabinod Pal, an Indian judge who dissented from the majority guilty verdict at the Tokyo war-crimes tribunal in 1946. Justice Pal had suggested that the men convicted as war criminals might one day be exonerated by history – and, as a result, is a hero to Japanese nationalists. On a trip to India in an earlier brief stint as prime minister, in 2007, Abe had taken the time to visit Justice Pal's son in Kolkata.

The question of how Japan's 'war criminals' are regarded is an intensely personal one for Abe, who reveres his grandfather and mentor, Nobusuke Kishi. Kishi not only administered occupied Manchuria for the Japanese imperial army – he also later served as vice minister for munitions in Tokyo during the Second World War. After the defeat of Japan, Kishi was arrested as a war criminal and imprisoned for three years. But in the new political atmosphere of the Cold War, the Americans decided that it was more important to allow skilled administrators such as Kishi to rebuild Japan as a bulwark against Mao's China and the Soviet Union, than to pursue all war-crimes allegations. Charges against Kishi were dropped. As a free man, Kishi swiftly rebuilt his political career and became prime minister of Japan between 1957 and 1960. Photographs taken at the time show him dandling a cute little boy on his knee – his grandson, Shinzo Abe. Rather than run away from his grandfather's legacy, Abe has embraced it. In his memoirs, he writes that 'In my eyes my grandfather was a sincere statesman who only thought about the future of his country.'

For Abe, a visit to Yasukuni was a necessary assertion of national pride – at a time when Japan was under great pressure to yield to China over the islands dispute. Many in Tokyo argue that it is now China, not modern Japan, that is in danger of re-enacting the horrors of the 1930s, by attempting to impose its will on the rest of Asia. Kunihiko

Miyake, a former diplomat who is close to Abe, expressed this concern to me over lunch in Tokyo in 2013: 'The Chinese are making exactly the same mistake that we Japanese made in the 1930s. They are challenging American power in the Pacific and they have allowed the military to escape from the control of politicians.'

Japan is haunted by the fear that an increasingly powerful China is out to revenge the affronts of the 1930s – and that, given free rein, it might seek to exact a terrible revenge on Japan. A successful assertion of Chinese sovereignty over the Senkaku Islands would be the symbolic assertion of the new hierarchy in Asia, with Japan reduced to the status of a tributary power. And the Senkaku Islands might be just the beginning. The Japanese are well aware that, in think tanks and government-backed newspapers in Beijing (if not yet in official statements), Japanese sovereignty over the islands of Okinawa is also increasingly under question. Okinawa, with a population of 1.4 million, is home to America's most important military bases in Japan – which makes it an entirely different proposition from the uninhabited Senkaku Islands. It is undeniably a vital part of modern Japan. And yet, as some of the franker Japanese intellectuals will acknowledge, Okinawa also has a different and distinct identity that sets it apart from the rest of Japan. The islands that make up Okinawa lie well to the south of mainland Japan and were only formally annexed in 1879. Many Okinawans also still lament the devastation wrought on the island by the bitter fighting in the Second World War and resent the environmental and social impact of America's military bases. There is enough in this cleavage between the Okinawan and Japanese identities for China to work with – if the moment were ever to arise.

Concern about the rising might and intentions of China bordered on an obsession in official Tokyo by the time Shinzo Abe took power. Even as it struggled against rising debts, Abe's Japan also sought to increase defence spending – although its officials were bleakly aware that China was already massively out-spending Japan. Abe also sought to change Japan's legal and administrative structure to prepare it for a potential cold war with China. In 2013, his government set up a National Security Council, centralising crucial security decisions around the prime minister's office – and mirroring the structures in the White House. (China set up its own National Security Council at around the same time.) Abe also launched a diplomatic offensive – making high-profile speeches at forums such as Davos and the Institute of International Strategic Studies' 'Shangri-La Dialogue' summit in Singapore. His speech there in 2014 appealed for peace in Asia and for the use of international law to resolve disputes. But his language – with its condemnation of those who sought to 'change the status quo through force or coercion' – provoked bitter complaints from China and even struck some neutral observers as verging on the provocative. Nigel Inkster of the IISS, a former senior officer in the British intelligence services, remarked that he had 'never heard peace espoused in such an aggressive manner'.

Remarks like that captured much of the Western ambivalence about Shinzo Abe and the broader nationalist coalition that supported him in power. The official Japanese explanation for visits to Yasukuni was that the prime minister was simply paying tribute to the millions who had suffered and died in Japan's many wars. To some Western ears that sounded reasonable enough. But there were other seemingly provocative gestures by the Abe administration that were harder to explain away.

In 2013, a few months before I toured Yasukuni, I had also visited South Korea – at a time when the front pages of the Korean papers were filled with photos of Abe sitting in a Japanese fighter jet, with a broad grin and giving a thumbs-up. That is the kind of stunt that campaigning politicians sometimes pull. But it was the numbers on the side of the plane that provoked horror and outrage in South Korea. Those figures were 731 – the number of a notorious wartime Japanese military unit which had conducted biological and chemical experiments, including vivisections, on Chinese and Korean prisoners of war. The official Japanese explanation was that this was just an unfortunate coincidence. But nobody I met in South Korea believed that, and they were not alone in their scepticism. Shortly afterwards, I met a senior member of the Singaporean political elite and asked him if he thought Abe's '731 moment' had been deliberate. 'Of course it was,' he exclaimed. 'And it was utterly disgusting.' If Abe's action was indeed deliberate, it was probably intended as a knowing wink towards the nationalist right – who make up an important part of his political coalition and who insist that Japan's wartime record is unfairly distorted by the nation's current and former enemies.

But nationalist gestures produced for a domestic audience carry an international price. Even Singapore's prime minister, Lee Hsien Loong, allowed himself a rare moment of emotion when I asked him what he thought of Japan's efforts to deny that its actions in the Second World War constituted aggression – 'Of course, it was aggression,' he exclaimed. 'They came to Singapore and they killed many tens of thousands of people . . . My uncle was taken way. Never came back.'[2]

The 731 incident was just the most startling of a series of diplomatic gaffes with a nationalist theme during the Abe administration. In 2013, Japan unveiled the largest battleship it had constructed since the Second World War: the vessel was nominally a destroyer but was, in fact, an aircraft carrier in all but name. The construction of the ship was a legitimate, arguably necessary, response to China's naval build-up. But by naming the new vessel the *Izumo* – the same name as one of the ships that had led the Japanese invasion of China in the 1930s – Japan handed a propaganda gift to the Chinese. And the gifts kept on coming. That same year, Japan's deputy prime minister Taro Aso, talking about the need to revise his country's pacifist constitution, cited the Nazis' rewriting of the German constitution as a possible model.[3] Abe's bows towards the nationalist right in Japan continued with his choice of appointees to the board of NHK, Japan's national broadcaster. One of the prime minister's picks had denied that the Japanese army once forced Korean and Chinese women into sexual slavery. This was a remark that was guaranteed to enrage the Koreans in particular, where the story of the so-called 'comfort women' is a source of continuing anguish. Since 1992, weekly demonstrations by surviving 'comfort women' and their supporters have been held outside the Japanese embassy in Seoul.

Nationalist gestures by the Abe administration caused both concern and debate among Japan-watchers in the West. One long-time resident of Tokyo, much consulted by Western governments, told me caustically that for some senior members of the Abe administration, 'The only thing wrong with the Second World War was that Japan lost.' Kurt Campbell, the designer of America's pivot to Asia, appeared to suggest that Japanese nationalism was as much of a problem as the Chinese variety, when he wrote that 'Both Tokyo and Beijing are determined to play to nationalist sentiments.'[4]

In private, some American officials even worried that Japan might be the major source of instability in Asia. Shortly after John Kerry became Secretary of State he startled a group of Washington-based Asia-watchers by asking them 'How can I stop Japan starting a war with China?'[5] For many of Kerry's colleagues in the White House and the Pentagon, however, this is precisely the wrong question. They believe that a rising, authoritarian China is incomparably the biggest threat to peace in Asia and to American interests in the Pacific. Even if Abe is happy to play to the nationalist gallery in Japan, it is a fundamental error to put Japan in the same box as China. Japan, after all, is a democracy with a free press, and a semi-pacifist constitution, which has not waged war on anyone since 1945. The pro-Japan lobby in Washington argued that rather than complaining about Japanese nationalism, the US should energetically support Abe's efforts to change the lopsided nature of the US–Japan security treaty – under which the US was committed to defend Japan, while Japan had no reciprocal obligation to defend America.

Under Article Nine of Japan's 1947 constitution, the country had renounced forever the right to wage war. Abe, who had long argued that Japan should be a 'normal country', would ideally have liked to scrap that provision – but he knew that he lacked the public support to do so. Instead, he settled for a controversial reinterpretation of the constitution which would allow Japanese forces not only to defend their homeland if it was directly attacked, but also to take part in 'collective self-defence'. So, for example, if the US navy was attacked in the East China Sea, the Japanese could come to their aid – perhaps through logistics, or even by fighting alongside them.

Even this modest-sounding change provoked fervent domestic opposition. When, in July 2015, Abe's government presented legislation easing the restrictions on the Japanese military, the opposition walked out of Parliament, while demonstrators chanted outside. For any foreigners worried about a resurgence of Japanese nationalism, these public misgivings were, in some ways, reassuring. The mood of the Japanese public still looked strongly pacifist – which made a striking contrast with the nationalism that often flared amongst China's netizens.

The whole episode underlines the ambivalence – in both the US and Japan – about the two countries' security ties. The Japanese security establishment is keen to make America's commitment to defend Japan as solid as possible and saw the revision of the constitution as a key part of this effort. But many in the Japanese public and the political opposition seem to have the opposite fear – that an over-assertive America might drag Japan into a conflict. Just as in post-war Germany, where the left has long been suspicious of American militarism, so liberal and left-wing opinion in Japan still harbours deep reservations about America's reliance on military strength as the basis of its foreign policy in the Pacific. The continuing strength of that sentiment raises the possibility that the assertive nationalism of the Abe government might just be a phase. The first Japanese government that Obama had dealt with, led by the Democratic Party of Japan, had spoken of weakening ties to America and sought a rapprochement with Beijing. That strand of thinking has not disappeared from Japanese debate – so it is conceivable that some future government in Tokyo might definitively shrink away from the risk of confrontation with China and tacitly accept Beijing's dominance.

There is a similar ambiguity hovering over America's approach to Japan. US policymakers sometimes seem to switch between a concern that an aggressive Japan might drag them into a confrontation with China, and a worry that a weak Japan might lose its will to resist Chinese hegemony over the western Pacific.

By 2014, however, China's actions in the region had tipped the balance towards those in the Obama administration who argued that a stronger show of support for Japan was now imperative. A range of Chinese actions – the declaration of the Air Defence Identification Zone, the expansion of naval and air patrols, increasing pressure on the Philippines as well as Japan – had convinced the US that it had to take a firm stand in support of its treaty allies in Asia. Obama came decisively down on the Japanese side on his visit to Tokyo in May 2014. On that trip, he became the first US president explicitly to confirm that the US–Japan Security Treaty covered the Senkaku Islands. It was a commitment that one of the president's close aides described colourfully to me as 'giving the middle-finger to China'. It was also exactly the kind of reassurance that the Abe government was looking for.

But even if Washington had decided to embrace Abe – warts and all – the provocative nature of right-wing Japanese nationalism was still a headache for the Americans. That was because key US allies in the region were much less prepared to forgive Abe's nationalist gestures. South Korean resentment of Japan threatened only to grow with the passage of time. The fact that the surviving 'comfort women' were dwindling in number only served to heighten Korean anger over any Japanese statements that appeared to whitewash their treatment. South Korea had its own 'islands dispute' with Japan – over the Dokdo Islands (known as the Takeshima Islands to the Japanese) – that excited almost as much nationalist fervour in Korea as the Senkaku–Diaoyu Islands did in China. When I visited the South Korean foreign ministry in 2015, I found that the lobby featured a live video-feed of the sea lapping over the (uninhabited) Dokdo–Takeshima Islands. The fact that the rocks are under the control of South Korea apparently does not lessen the emotions they arouse.

The tensions between Japan and South Korea make it much harder for these two democratic countries to work together to deal with the real security threats they both face. In the long term, the biggest threat is China. In the short run, it is the actions of the eccentric, tyrannical and nuclear-armed regime in North Korea that are even more likely to cause nervous palpitations in Seoul, and even Tokyo.

To visit the demilitarised zone (DMZ) that still divides the Korean peninsula is to step back into the Cold War. On the southern side, tourists use telescopes to stare into the North. A giant flag from the Democratic People's Republic of Korea (DPRK) – as the North styles itself – flutters in the breeze. The fact that more than half a century has passed since the end of the Korean War in 1953 makes it easy to forget the continuing dangers posed by a divided Korea. But any complacency about the situation should have definitively ended when North Korea staged its first successful test of nuclear weapons in 2003. Since then, the North is believed to have developed a significant nuclear arsenal – and it has also tested ballistic missiles that could reach as far as Alaska. America's nightmare is that the North Koreans will succeed in attaching a nuclear war head to a ballistic missile that could strike the West Coast of America.

All of the major Pacific powers are threatened in different ways by North Korea. Seoul, the South Korean capital, is just thirty-five miles from the DMZ. The US has 28,500 troops stationed in South Korea, just south of the frontier. To the north, China shares a border with the DPRK and would be seriously endangered if there were ever a nuclear exchange on the Korean peninsula. Japan is also uncomfortably close to the action. North Korean weapons tests have even seen missiles fly directly over Japan, before landing in the sea.

All of these countries have reason to fear the disorderly break-up of a nuclear North Korea. China is often seen in the West as holding the key to pressurising the regime in Pyongyang. But the Chinese insist that economic pressure on a nuclear North Korea could prove dangerously counterproductive. Geopolitical tensions also make it much harder for the North's neighbours to work together. China is wary of a reunified Korea – since that might bring US military bases right up to the Chinese border. Japan has its own concerns, since a reunified Korea of over 70 million people would create a third major power in North East Asia – and one with historical grievances against the Japanese.

Japan and South Korea also know that North Korea is not the only common problem they face. In the long run, the autonomy of both countries is threatened by the rise of an increasingly assertive China. Both countries are democracies and allies of the United States. Even so, the emotional scars left behind by history make Japanese–Korean co-operation very difficult – while creating shared grievances between the Chinese and Koreans. In 2012, Park Geun-hye, the new president of South Korea, broke with precedent and chose to visit Beijing before she visited Tokyo. It was a symbolic moment that was matched by an equally symbolic gesture by Xi Jinping, who reciprocated by visiting Seoul before Pyongyang, the capital of China's old but exasperating ally, North Korea. In September 2015, President Park also became the only close ally of the Americans to attend the massive military parade in Beijing, with which the Chinese marked the end of the Second World War and the defeat of Japan.

The growing closeness of the Chinese and the South Koreans was a serious concern in both Washington and Tokyo. It suggested that any plans to unite all the Asian democracies into an American-led alliance could easily come to grief. Behind the scenes, the Obama administration piled pressure on its two closest Asian allies to mend their differences. In December 2015, these efforts appeared to bear fruit when it was announced that the Japanese and South Korean governments had reached an agreement aimed at finally resolving the bitter dispute over the 'comfort women'. The Japanese government agreed to pay $8.3 million into a fund for the surviving victims. In return, the South Koreans promised not to press any further claims.

Nationalists in both Japan and South Korea were upset by the agreement. But in Washington, there was quiet satisfaction. One US policymaker suggested that this was Abe's 'Nixon to China' moment. Just as in 1972, the staunchly anti-Communist Richard Nixon had overcome his personal history to travel to Mao's China, so the nationalist, Shinzo Abe, had reached out to an angry South Korea. The 'Nixon to China' analogy probably overrated the significance of Abe's gesture in erasing the bitterness between Japan and South Korea. But the comparison was still telling in one important respect. Nixon had decided to try to mend fences with China in the 1970s as part of a broader geopolitical strategy. His real concern was to outflank the Soviet Union in the Cold War, by splitting off Moscow from Beijing. In the same way, Tokyo's efforts to reach a rapprochement with Seoul were part of a broader strategic game.

For both Japan and the US, the overriding strategic concern in the Asia-Pacific is now clearly the assertive behaviour of a rising China. That concern is growing in North East Asia, where Japan, China and the two Koreas bump up against each other. It is also an increasing worry in the other great arena of Asian strategic rivalry – South East Asia and the South China Sea.

The Battle for South East Asia

Standing on the roof of the Marina Bay Sands hotel in Singapore, I had a perfect view over the most important trade route in the world. It was the spring of 2014 and scores of cargo ships and oil tankers were visible through the morning haze, as they waited to pass through the narrow stretch of water that links the Pacific and Indian oceans. Every year, one-third of the world's traded goods pass through the straits of Malacca and Singapore – the main sea route connecting East Asia to Europe and the Middle East.

The basement of the same hotel provided another glimpse of globalisation in action. It featured a giant casino, whose most lucrative clients were high rollers from mainland China. The money that these Chinese tourists lost at the tables swelled the profits of the casino's owner Sheldon Adelson, a Las Vegas-based billionaire with pronounced right-wing political views. Adelson, in turn, used his fortune to fund hawkish Republicans running for the US presidency, and right-wing newspapers supporting Benjamin Netanyahu in Israel. So a spinning roulette wheel in South East Asia served as a connection between China, the US and the Middle East.

Singapore is now a global crossroads. But its rise to that status is recent and owes a lot to its position astride the main trade route between Asia and Europe. The shifting power balance between East and West is, in turn, epitomised by the history of that trade route – the Malacca Strait. In the fifteenth century, the town of Malacca on the southern shore of modern Malaysia was the home to a powerful Muslim kingdom, but the sultanate was overthrown by a Portuguese invasion in 1511. The Portuguese ships that arrived in Malacca were the advance guard of the European imperialists who were to colonise and settle most of the world over the following centuries. Portugal itself rose to be one of the world's great empires, stretching from Brazil to southern Africa to the Indian subcontinent and on to East Asia. Portuguese colonialism lasted centuries and its last Asian possessions were only recently relinquished. Macau was returned to China in 1999 and East Timor was decolonised in 1975.

By the time I was gazing down on the Strait of Malacca, however, it was already hard to believe that Portugal had once been a great global power. On a recent visit to Lisbon, I had stopped by the statue of Vasco da Gama, the explorer who had laid the foundations for the Portuguese Empire when he discovered the sea route from Europe to India in 1498. But the billboards in Mandarin at Lisbon international airport, advertising properties for sale to Chinese investors, better represented the state of modern Portugal. Beset by a debt crisis and bailed out by the IMF and the EU, Portugal was attempting to revive its economic fortunes by peddling residence visas to foreigners, who were willing to spend $500,000 on a property.

By 2014, Lisbon's days as one of the world's major power centres were well and truly over. Singapore, by contrast, had emerged as one of the great global cities of the twenty-first century. Its skyline was studded with skyscrapers bearing the names of the giants of international finance: Citi, HSBC, UBS, ANZ. Its harbour and airport were among the busiest in the world.

The reversal of fortunes between Singapore and Portugal is emblematic of the migration of wealth and power from west to east. Singapore was first established as a trading post by the British in the early nineteenth century. But as Lee Kuan Yew, the city state's found-ing father, put it at the turn of the twenty-first century, 'Singapore has existed for 180 years, but for the 146 years before 1963, it was just an outpost of the British Raj.'[1] In the 1960s, the prospects for an inde-pendent Singapore – without natural resources or even its own water supply – had looked bleak. But under Lee's determined leadership, the country made use of every advantage it had – above all its strategic position. Along with Taiwan, Hong Kong and South Korea, it became known as one of the 'Asian tigers' whose economies grew at startling rates as they moved, in Lee's phrase, 'from Third World to First'.

The goods that flow through the Strait of Malacca have become a foundation of Singapore's prosperity and a symbol of a peaceful era of booming global trade. But, under different circumstances, the Strait of Malacca could become an international flash point. At its narrowest point – between Singapore and Indonesia – the strait is just two and a half miles wide. And yet most of the oil that China imports from the outside world must pass through this thin windpipe. Three times as much oil passes through the Malacca Strait every year – en route to East Asia – as goes through the Suez Canal.[2]

The strategic importance of the Strait of Malacca is well known to both the Americans and the Chinese. Just as the Panama Canal links the east coast of America to the Pacific, so the Malacca Strait links the Pacific and Indian oceans and is China's gateway to the energy supplies of the Middle East and Africa.[3] As a US military planner once put it to me, with bracing directness – 'If there was a war, that's where we'd get 'em.'[4] In other words, China's great vulnerability is its depen-dence on seaborne imports – oil, above all, but also other crucial com-modities, such as grain and iron ore. If a conflict were ever to break out, the US navy could attempt to strangle the Chinese economy at the Strait of Malacca and the three other less-used straits (Sunda, Lombok and Makassar) that connect the South China Sea to the Indian Ocean.

China, however, is well aware of this vulnerability. The 'Malacca dilemma' has been a feature of Chinese strategic discussion for much of the past decade and has helped spur a surge in funding for oil and gas pipelines that could bring energy to China overland, from Russia, Kazakhstan, Pakistan and through the remote Chinese province of Xinjiang. The Chinese navy has also benefited disproportionately from the increase in the country's military budget, as the country seeks to lessen its potential vulnerability to a naval blockade by the United States.

The role that the Strait of Malacca plays in the strategic thinking of both the Americans and the Chinese reflects the wider position of South East Asia in the struggle for dominance of the Asia-Pacific. Since the end of the Vietnam War, in 1975, South East Asia has gone through a golden era. Foreign trade and investment have boomed, and countries as different as the city state of Singapore and the vast archipelago of Indonesia have enjoyed many years of rapid economic growth. Even nations that were once isolated by Communism or military dictatorship – such as Vietnam and Myanmar (Burma) – are now emerging as serious trading nations and as important destinations for foreign investors and tourists.

Within living memory, however, South East Asia has also been a battleground between great powers. Japan's capture of Singapore on 15 February 1942 'shattered the myth of white invulnerability' and dealt a catastrophic blow to Britain's international image – setting the stage for the end of empire, after the war.[5] Some of the bloodiest battles between Japan and the Allies during the Second World War were fought in the Philippines, Burma and Malaya. The end of the war did not lead to the end of conflict in South East Asia. As the colonial era came to a close, the British fought an insurgency in Malaya, and the French waged a losing fight against the Viet Minh in Indochina. The wars of decolonisation gave way to the bloody struggles of the Cold War. The Vietnam War cost the lives of some 55,000 Americans and well over a million Vietnamese. Neighbouring Cambodia, destabilised by the conflict in Vietnam, suffered the near-genocidal rule of Pol Pot and the Khmer Rouge, which led to the deaths of over a million

Cambodians. Hundreds of thousands more were killed as 'suspected Communists', in the bloodletting after the military coup in Indonesia in 1965, which brought Suharto, a pro-Western military dictator, to power. East Timor, no more than half an island, suffered a similar death toll after the collapse of Portuguese rule in 1975 encouraged Indonesia to invade.

Yet, from the 1980s on, South East Asia began to put its blood-soaked past behind it. As the Cold War wound down and peace returned, the countries of the region made the most of the opportunities offered by burgeoning global trade, improved communications and transport links – as well as foreign direct investment from Western and Japanese multinationals. Nations like Singapore, Malaysia, Thailand and Indonesia pioneered a formula for rapid economic growth, based on exports, manufacturing and foreign investment, that was then adopted – on a much larger scale – by China. As the historians Christopher Bayly and Tim Harper put it, 'It was not really until the 1980s with the economic renaissance of Japan, the rise of Singapore and Malaysia and the transformation of Asian Communist regimes towards free-market capitalism that Asia began to claim its place in the sun as the dominant continent of the twenty-first century.'[6]

By the time I was working as *The Economist*'s South East Asia correspondent, based in Bangkok between 1992 and 1995, the region had become central to the globalised economy. The big Japanese multinationals, such as Toyota and Sony, were using Thailand and Indonesia as a production base. And firms from South East Asia itself were among the early foreign investors in China. My first trip to Shanghai was to report on the investments made by Charoen Pokphand, a Thai conglomerate whose interests spanned everything from processed chicken to motorbikes. In 1993, the Chinese were so pleased by this investment that a brand new CP motorbike had pride of place in the centre of the luggage carousel at Shanghai airport. At that stage, the rising middle class in Shanghai were still more likely to be able to afford a new motorbike than a car. The Pudong area on the banks of the rivers – where CP had their factory – was still a run-down zone full of warehouses. Fifteeen years later, Shanghai's streets were choked with cars and Pudong was a forest of modernist skyscrapers.

For a brief period in the 1980s and 1990s the nations of South East Asia were at the hub of the development of Asia – and were even showing the way forward for China and India. But, after two further decades of rapid growth, the sheer size of the Chinese and Indian economies now means that South East Asia is once again overshadowed by giants. In the meantime, the commercial connections between South East Asia and China have become much thicker and more intense. In the early 1990s, there were just two flights a day between Bangkok and Shanghai – now there are fourteen. Countries like Thailand, which used to rely on Western tourists, increasingly look to the Chinese market, as the Chinese middle class get the travel bug.

The continued 'peaceful rise' of the Chinese economy holds out the prospect that the nations of South East Asia can continue to surf the wave of rising Asian prosperity. But the growth of Chinese nationalism also raises more alarming prospects – above all, the threat that war could return to South East Asia. The region's most thoughtful politicians are acutely aware of the potential vulnerability of the region.

For all its prosperity and glitz, Singapore nurtures an almost Israeli sense of its own vulnerability. As Lee Hsien Loong, the country's third prime minister (and Lee Kuan Yew's son) put it to me over lunch in London in 2014, 'If you take the historical perspective, not very many small countries have great longevity.'[7]

To safeguard its future, Singapore has sought successfully to cultivate warm relations with the regional giants. Indeed, it is perhaps the only country in the world that could claim to have a special relationship with both China and the United States. 'PM Lee' (as the Singaporeans invariably refer to him) epitomises his country's ability to look both east and west. He grew up speaking both English and Mandarin Chinese. Like his father, he studied at Cambridge

University, graduating with the top first in mathematics awarded that year. With some regret, Lee Hsien Loong turned down the offer to pursue an academic career at Trinity College, Cambridge and returned to the task of nation-building in Singapore – serving for some time in the army, before following his father into politics.

Both Lees were determined to position their nation to take advantage of the rise of China. Since the 1970s, it has been Singaporean government policy to ensure that the 75% of the country's population that are ethnically Chinese are educated in both Mandarin and English. The insistence that the Singaporean population should speak the language of China's governing elite – rather than regional dialects such as Hokkien, which are more likely to be spoken at home in Singapore – represented a far-sighted bet on the rise of China. The Singaporeans were early investors in China and many of Beijing's high-flying civil servants have come to the country to be trained. As China has become richer, so Singapore has also become a favourite destination for mainland money which flows into the country's property market and banks. Meanwhile the Singaporean government is positioning the nation to be the major overseas hub for trade in the renminbi, when the Chinese currency finally internationalises. As Lee Hsien Loong pointed out to me, China is capable of turning on the charm in its relations with South East Asian nations: 'The Chinese are very engaged . . . They come, they have a pitch, they have specific proposals and they back it up with resources. So they'll co-operate with you on maritime research or they'll help with education. They'll have a list of seven or eight items and they'll make sure they've covered the ground and they want that relationship to be a good one.'[8] There are political as well as economic links between China and Singapore. Like the Chinese, the Singaporeans have promoted Confucianism – with its emphasis on hierarchy and obligation – as an alternative philosophy to Western liberalism and individualism.

Yet even as the Singaporeans have cultivated China, they have hung on to the United States. Ships from the US navy regularly rotate in and out of Singapore and use it as a base for policing the South China Sea and for guarding the Strait of Malacca. The American navy is Singapore's insurance policy against its larger neighbours – such as Indonesia or China itself.

Singapore's careful balancing act between East and West reflects the current uneasy balance of power in Asia. Inevitably, it also risks antagonising both sides. When I asked Lee Hsien Loong what the Chinese thought of Singapore's vocal support for a continuing American military presence in the Pacific, he replied evenly 'They don't like it. But they understand it.'[9] As Lee explained: 'In Asia-Pacific, we depend on the Americans to be present, to play a benign but effective role – as they have been doing since the war.' Singapore's naval harbour at Changi is the regional hub for two US combat ships. In 2015, as tensions mounted over China's maritime claims, the US navy announced that a further two vessels would rotate regularly through Singapore – noting pointedly that these littoral ships were perfect for operating in the shallow waters of the South China Sea. But Lee's officials flinch at the use of the word 'base' to describe America's military presence in Singapore, and very few US personnel are stationed there.[10] As far as the Singaporeans are concerned, the US navy is not based in their city state – it is simply using the facilities.

These Singaporean sensitivities reflect the careful, sometimes tortured balancing act carried out by the country as it tries to keep on the right side of both Washington and Beijing. Certainly, when the maritime dispute between Vietnam and China flared in 2014, the press coverage in Singapore's government-controlled media was strikingly neutral. Anyone looking for a bit of South East Asian solidarity was liable to be disappointed. It was not just the Vietnamese who felt let down. One White House official complained to me that Singapore was doing nothing to promote a firm regional response to provocations from Beijing and was failing to speak out about Chinese aggression in the South China Sea. The American fear was that Singaporean policy reflected not just a natural desire to keep out of trouble in the present, but also a subtle bet on the future. As the same US official complained to me in 2014, 'They often talk as if they think Chinese domination of the Pacific is inevitable.'[11] And indeed Kishore Mahbubani, a former head of the Singaporean foreign ministry, was fond of remarking, 'We know that China will still be our neighbour in 1,000 years. We don't know if the Americans will still be here in 100 years' time.'

Since Singapore's population is less than 6 million, the country's attitude might not seem to matter much. In fact, Singapore's uniquely strong ties to both China and the West – allied to its wealth and strategic position – give it a geopolitical status that far outweighs its size. If Singapore is seen as accepting that South East Asia is gradually turning into China's backyard, the rest of the region would draw conclusions – and so would the rest of the world.

The ten members of the Association of South East Asian Nations (ASEAN), of which Singapore is a part, have also reacted uncertainly to the emergence of a more assertive and nationalistic China. Some nations, such as Cambodia and Laos, already seem to be making their accommodation to Chinese power. Others such as Thailand, Singapore, Malaysia, Myanmar and Indonesia have played a careful and sometimes ambiguous role – seeking to maintain close ties with both the US and China. But two of the largest countries in South East Asia – Vietnam and the Philippines, both of which have populations of over 100 million – are now in an openly antagonistic relationship with the People's Republic.

The source of the tension is China's notorious nine-dashed line, which sets out its claims to some 90% of the South China Sea – and which since 2012 has been printed in every new Chinese passport. The line that China has drawn is founded not on proximity to the Chinese coast, but on bitterly disputed historic claims, linked to patterns of Chinese settlement and maritime exploration that date back to the Han dynasty in the second century BC. China and its neighbours are also in dispute about the ownership of groups of small islands and shoals in the South China Sea and the waters that surround them. The Spratly Islands are claimed in full by China and Vietnam, and in part by Malaysia, Brunei and the Philippines. In recent years, China has sought to bolster its territorial and maritime claims by building concrete structures, helipads and entire airstrips on several of the reefs and shoals in the islands.[12] In 2014 and 2015, these land-reclamation efforts were stepped up as small reefs were effectively converted into islands capable of hosting military facilities – such as the new airstrips built on Fiery Cross and Mischief Reefs.

In both Washington and South East Asia, China's island-building stoked the fear that Beijing was moving into a more aggressive phase in the assertion of its claims over the South China Sea. Potentially, those claims put China in conflict with almost all the maritime nations of South East Asia, including Brunei, Malaysia and Indonesia.

However, it is the Philippines and Vietnam that are under most pressure. They point out indignantly that some of the waters claimed by Beijing are several hundred miles from the coast of the Chinese mainland, but less than a hundred miles from the coasts of Vietnam or the Philippines. If China enforced its claims it would control vital sea-lanes and gobble up prized fishing grounds – and potentially much more valuable deposits of oil and gas. Official Chinese projections estimate (somewhat hopefully) that the South China Sea may contain 130 billion barrels of oil – the largest reserves outside Saudi Arabia. For a country with a voracious appetite for energy, but just 1% of the world's oil reserves, that would be quite a prize.[13]

Depending on how it chooses to enforce its nine-dashed line, China might also attempt to shut the US navy out of the South China Sea. The Chinese argue, controversially, that states are entitled to stop foreign navies from sailing through an 'Exclusive Economic Zone' that stretches 200 miles out from their coasts. If China were able to control all the islands and reefs in the South China Sea, it could create a legal claim for shutting the US military out of those waters.[14] Given that, according to Hillary Clinton, some 50% of the world's merchandise trade passes through these seas, America has a huge interest in preventing that happening.

By 2015, this argument had moved from a legal abstraction into active shadow-boxing between the two countries' militaries. In response to China's island-building, in May 2015 the US air force flew a plane over one of the new territories. A television crew on board recorded eight verbal warnings from the Chinese military. Speaking in impeccable English, a disembodied voice warned 'This is the Chinese navy, please go away to avoid misunderstandings.'[15] The Chinese foreign ministry followed up with a formal protest. In Washington, however, Anthony Blinken, America's Deputy Secretary of State, called China's actions in the South China sea 'a threat to peace and stability' and compared it to Russia's land-grab in eastern Ukraine.[16]

Yet for all the apparent firmness of American rhetoric, many in South East Asia doubt America's long-term ability to deter China's island-building. For the Philippines, the 'teachable moment' had come at Scarborough Shoal, a rocky outpost that is more than 500 miles from the coast of the Chinese mainland – but just 120 miles west of Luzon, the island that houses Manila, the capital of the Philippines. In 2012, Philippine and Chinese vessels had confronted each other in the waters around the shoal. The US had negotiated a mutual withdrawal of the two navies, but when the Filipinos withdrew, the Chinese stayed put – effectively annexing Scarborough Shoal. The outraged Filipino president, Benigno Aquino, compared China's actions to Hitler's annexation of Czechoslovakia. But Washington failed to react to the violation of an agreement that the Americans themselves had negotiated – prompting one senior Asian diplomat to suggest to me that the Obama administration was suffering from 'attention deficit disorder'. The Obama-administration response is that the Scarborough Shoal incident is invested with far more retrospective significance than it had at the time. But even that justification is a tacit acknowledgement that the Americans lost face at Scarborough Shoal. It also points to a wider problem. Outside the small realm of Asia-Pacific security-watchers, it is hard to get anyone in the US worked up about the possession of an uninhabited shoal on the other side of the world. But in the region itself, these incidents are noted and matter a great deal. So if China plays its hand intelligently, it has a good chance of advancing its territorial claims in a rapid but incremental fashion, without provoking a decisive push-back from the US.

After Scarborough Shoal, the next rock of contention between Manila and Beijing is the Second Thomas Shoal, a rocky outcrop on which the Filipinos deliberately grounded a ship in 1999. Ever since, they have maintained a small garrison (usually less than a dozen people) whose lonely duty is to serve as formal evidence that this is Filipino 'territory'. By 2014, this obscure wreck was the focus of attention not just in Manila and Beijing, but also the White House. The Americans were watching carefully, worried that China might take action to dislodge the Filipinos, perhaps by dismantling the ship. The fear was that once again China would make a move against the Philippines that was large enough to send a message across the Asia-Pacific region – but too small to trigger a reaction from Washington. As one close adviser to President Obama put it to me: 'How am I meant to tell the president that US credibility relies on risking a war over a sunken wreck, most of which isn't even above the water half the time?'[17]

Another big maritime conflict in South East Asia also looked to be carefully chosen. When the Chinese moved a large oil rig into disputed waters 120 miles from the Vietnamese coast in May 2014 (the Chinese said the rig was in the South China Sea, the Vietnamese call the same waters the East Sea), the reaction in Vietnam was fierce. Anti-Chinese riots broke out across the country, with factories destroyed and at least four deaths.[18] Vietnam, however, had no Western protector to look to. Unlike Japan, South Korea, Singapore or the Philippines, it is not a treaty ally of the United States. China could flex its muscles in waters near Vietnam without fear of triggering a direct American reaction.

The Vietnamese received some support from Japan: in the wake of the oil-rig affair, Tokyo announced that it was giving Vietnam six naval patrol boats.[19] But the Vietnamese looked most longingly for support towards their old enemy – the United States. Even before the oil-rig incident, the government in Hanoi had sent out unofficial feelers to Washington, to see if the Americans might be interested in setting up a naval base at Cam Ranh Bay.[20] The Americans declined the offer, but the irony of inviting the US to return to the very base that its navy had used in the Vietnam War was lost on no one in Hanoi or Washington. For the Vietnamese, however, the offer made perfect sense. In its thousands of years of history, Vietnam has fought just one war against the US – but seventeen against the Chinese. It was swallowed up as part of China's Han Empire in 111 BC and it took over a thousand years for Vietnam to regain its independence in AD 939. The struggle to ward off the giant to the north has defined Vietnamese history. The Vietnamese joke that their country's coastline looks like a bent spine that reflects the crushing weight of China bearing down on them. A resurgent and nationalistic China feels like an existential threat.

As China grew more assertive in South East Asia, America attempted sporadically to push back. Hillary Clinton's statement in 2010 that the US had national interests in the region that it intended to defend was denounced in Beijing as an affront – and greeted with relief by America's allies in the region. In 2014, on the same Asian trip during which President Obama announced that the US–Japan security treaty covers the Senkaku–Diaoyu Islands, he also strengthened America's security relationship with the Philippines. In the 1980s, after the Filipino revolution had thrown out Ferdinand Marcos, the US had lost the use of air and naval bases in the country. Now it was announced that the US navy would resume regular visits to the port at Subic Bay.

The US was signalling that its alliances and security commitments in South East Asia remained rock solid – and indeed were being strengthened. Yet while America's alliance system looked strong enough to deter a conventional act of war by China, it was struggling to come up with an appropriate response to China's salami-slicing tactic of making small advances and gestures across East Asia – around the Senkaku–Diaoyu Islands, at Scarborough Shoal and in Vietnam's East Sea. As *The Economist* observed in the summer of 2014: 'China's bullying is, for now, cost-free. Diplomatic resistance has no effect. And China is probably right in thinking there is little appetite in America, and even less in ASEAN, for anything more vigorous.'[21]

In Asia – as in the Middle East and Europe – America was faced with the dilemma that its regional allies demanded military protection from Uncle Sam, while apparently being prepared to do remarkably little in their own defence. If ASEAN – whose members have a combined population of 500 million – were able to act as a determined and coherent bloc in world affairs, it would be a powerful counterweight to Chinese influence in Asia. Yet, in reality, China found it relatively easy to find and exploit divisions within the bloc. Tiny, impoverished and dictatorial Cambodia was easily influenced by Chinese money – and became a pro-Chinese voice within ASEAN, helping to prevent it form a united position on the disputes in the South China Sea. The historic antagonism between the Khmer people of Cambodia and the neighbouring Vietnamese played a part in this.

Within the ASEAN group, allegiances waxed and waned. As Myanmar moved towards democracy, it also sought to lessen its economic dependence on China – cancelling a pipeline project that China had hoped would provide an alternative route to the sea. On the other hand, Thailand – which has historically been regarded as in the Western camp – began to tilt towards China. The US–Thai relationship soured after a military coup in Bangkok in May 2014 led America to downgrade its relationship with the Thai military, and to call for a swift return to democracy. In response, the new Thai authorities moved closer to Beijing – announcing the purchase of submarines from China in 2015. Such weapons sales have a broader strategic significance, since they usually compel closer military co-operation between the two countries doing the deal.

Within this confusing firmament, the position of Indonesia is critical because it is the largest country in the region and the fourth most populous in the world. Indonesia often displays the insularity typical of many large countries. Its presidential election in 2014, which was regarded as a landmark in the country's democratic development, was fought almost entirely on domestic issues. The country's status as the largest Muslim country in the world, and its proud heritage as one of the founders of the Non-Aligned Movement of neutral states, make Indonesia disinclined to tilt decisively towards the US. Its territorial disputes with Beijing in the South China Sea were also relatively dormant for many years. By 2015, however, even the Indonesians were beginning to express open alarm about China's island-building in the South China Sea. A tightening Chinese grip on South East Asia would certainly alarm Jakarta – and might also play into Indonesia's complex racial politics. As in much of South East Asia, many of the most successful businesspeople in Indonesia are of Chinese origin. But the ethnic Chinese have also periodically suffered from discrimination – and made up a disproportionate number of the victims in the 'anti-Communist' massacres of the 1960s, when the Indonesian military seized power in a coup. If a more powerful China were ever to take on the mantle of the protector of the ethnic Chinese throughout South East Asia – as some Chinese nationalists have demanded – the regional implications would be profound.

By 2015, there were indeed some signs that mainland China was beginning to see itself as a guardian for the millions of 'overseas Chinese' living in South East Asia. In 2015, a political crisis and corruption scandal in Malaysia prompted supporters of the embattled prime minister, Najib Razak, to play the 'Malay card' – rallying ethnic Malays against the prime minister's critics in the ethnic-Chinese community. Communal tensions are always just beneath the surface in Malaysia and have increased in recent years as Islamic fundamentalism has become more common amongst the majority Malays. As tensions between Malays and ethnic Chinese grew, China's ambassador to Malaysia, Huang Huikang, spoke out – condemning extremism and racism. His remarks were carefully phrased and, arguably, justifiable, given the long history of anti-Chinese discrimination in Malaysia. But this was also one of the first times that Beijing had shown an interest in defending ethnic Chinese living outside China itself. The precedent was noted across Asia, and as far south as Australasia.

For Australia, in particular, the prospect of the countries to its north slipping into a Chinese sphere of influence is profoundly unsettling. In recent decades Australia has lived up to its nickname of the 'lucky country'. The country's 23 million people inhabit an entire continent that is richly endowed with resources – allowing Australia to prosper mightily from the boom in commodity-hungry China. Uniquely amongst the developed economies, Australia has avoided a recession for over thirty years. The global economic crisis that began in 2008 and caused deep slumps in Europe and the US barely seemed to touch Australia. The optimistic side of the Australian character has greeted the rise of Asia with exuberant enthusiasm – treating it as an unparalleled opportunity to secure Australian prosperity, long into the future.

But as the political and strategic implications of the rise of China have become clearer, so Australia's policy elite have become much more concerned. Their nation is culturally and politically anchored in the West. Australia fought with the Allies in the first and second World Wars, and with the Americans in Vietnam. It is part of the exclusive 'five eyes' intelligence-sharing arrangement that is the inner core of the Western alliance and of the anglophone world (the other members are the US, the UK, Canada and New Zealand). So if the nations to Australia and New Zealand's north become part of a Chinese sphere of influence, Australasia risks becoming an isolated Western outpost, cut off from its political and cultural hinterland.

As a result, the vision of China asserting its influence across the South China Sea and in South East Asia set off alarm bells in the Australian elite. One senior Australian diplomat put it bluntly: 'We face in Australia the greatest single threat since the end of the Vietnam War. If China can achieve its goals through coercion and the weakness of its neighbours, our independence and autonomy will be irreparably restricted . . . The states of South East Asia will very quickly bend if China can enforce its nine-dashed line and will become dysfunctional like all the other states that surround China.' He added for good measure, 'And if you see the map of Chinese naval activity, it is simply terrifying.'[22]

The acuteness of Australia's strategic dilemma means that the country has become the home of both the most enthusiastic supporters – and the most astute critics – of America's pivot to Asia. It was in a speech in Canberra that President Obama formally unveiled the pivot with his resounding statement that 'In the Asia-Pacific of the twenty-first century, America is all in.' The most eye-catching concrete action connected to the pivot was the announcement that America would be setting up a new base to train US marines in Darwin, northern Australia. That step demonstrated the strong support and encouragement that successive Australian governments have given to the pivot, as they sought to secure their nation's security.

Yet the most articulate critic of the pivot is also an Australian. Professor Hugh White, a former intelligence official, had listened to President Obama's Canberra speech with alarm. For White – as for many observers – increasing Chinese power during the twenty-first century is regarded as a given. And yet here was the president of the United States apparently pledging himself to block China's rise. White believes that since China will not compromise on its regional ambitions, the US is embarking on a path that will culminate in either a war, or in a humiliating climbdown by the United States. His argument is that rather than confronting China, the US 'should seek an agreement with China about a new order in Asia, an order that would allow China a bigger role'.[23] White did not spell out the full details of what this 'bigger role' might mean. But the clear implication is that the US should give up any thought of taking military action to thwart China in the East or South China Seas, or over Taiwan.

There are some members of the Australian establishment who are prepared to listen attentively to what White has to say – and, in 2015, one of them became prime minister. Malcolm Turnbull managed to oust his very pro-American, conservative colleague, Tony Abbott, as leader of Australia in September of that year. A lawyer, a banker and an intellectual, Turnbull had written a sympathetic review of Hugh White's book, *The China Choice*. In an allusion to the Thucydides trap, Turnbull had written that 'We should seek to ensure that the Americans, unlike the Spartans, do not allow their anxiety about a rising power to lead them into a reflexive antagonism that could end in conflict.'[24]

Turnbull's more distant approach to the Americans was reflected in late 2015, when the Australian government nodded through a deal in which a Chinese company, the Landbridge Group – rumoured to be linked to the People's Liberation Army – was allowed to buy a ninety-nine-year lease on the port of Darwin. The announcement startled the Americans because Darwin is where the US had placed its new facility to train marines.[25] Above all, the Turnbull government had not given the Obama administration prior warning before announcing the lease. Turnbull's Darwin deal was significant because it indicated that – as with Singapore and Japan – Australia's attitude to the rise of China and the America pivot was more equivocal and uncertain than it might appear on the surface.

Even amongst the majority of Australian strategic analysts who cheered Obama's decision to deploy more military muscle in the Pacific, there was a nagging fear that the pivot was largely rhetorical. Michael Fullilove, the head of the Lowy Institute, Australia's leading foreign-policy think tank, worried that 'I don't think America's heart is in the pivot. The military element is pretty underwhelming.'[26]

If the pivot was not enough to reassure Asia's middle powers – such as Australia, Vietnam and the Philippines – what else could be brought into play to balance the power of a rising China? For many Western strategists, the answer was obvious: India. As the only other country in the world with a population of over 1 billion, India is the alternative Asian superpower to China. To emphasise that strategic thinking about Asia should always include India, Rory Medcalf, an Australian strategist, has popularised the idea of an 'Indo-Pacific' region – rather than talking about East Asia or the Asia-Pacific region. The notion of the Indo-Pacific emphasises India's importance, and so challenges the idea of a region that inevitably revolves around China. It also stresses the central importance of the Indian Ocean, as well as the South China Sea. And it makes the Australians feel less lonely. Rather than being stuck out on the edges of the Asia-Pacific region, Australia could style itself as being at the centre of a vast Indo-Pacific region framed by the two democracies of the US and India.

As a concept, the Indo-Pacific region is attractive. But how does India itself view its future as a great power?

7

India, the Second
Asian Superpower

The office of the chief economic adviser to the government of India is situated in the imposing government buildings in New Delhi left behind by the British Empire. These days, however, it feels more like a reminder of the emerging special relationship between India and the United States.

The chief adviser's wall is decorated with a wooden board recording the names of all the previous holders of his office. In the spring of 2015, the two most recent names were Raghuram Rajan and Arvind Subramanian. Both men were distinguished Indian economists who had spent most of their careers in the US and were at least as comfortable in Washington as in Delhi. Despite their years working at leading American institutions such as the University of Chicago (Rajan) and the Institute of International Economics in Washington (Subramanian), both men had also maintained a certain intellectual distance from the optimistic, consensus view in the US about America's enduring global power. In 2005, Rajan had delivered a prescient warning of instabilities building up in the US financial system – which was treated sceptically at the time, but gained him a reputation as a seer after the financial crisis of 2008.

Subramanian is even more of a sceptic. In 2011, he published a book arguing that China would displace the US as the world's leading economic power. *Eclipse: Living in the Shadow of China's Economic Dominance* begins with a provocative vision of a US president in 2021 applying for an emergency loan from a Chinese director of the IMF. Subramanian argued that 'The economic dominance of China relative to the United States is more imminent . . . will be more broad-based, and could be as large in magnitude, in the next 20 years, as that of the United Kingdom in the halcyon days of empire.'[1]

Eclipse had received a hostile reception in much of the United States, where its frank 'declinism' was distinctly unfashionable. By 2015, with the US economy recovering and China slowing markedly, some argued that predictions of America's eclipse by China were now off the mark. But when I met Subramanian in his office in Delhi in May of that year, I found him unrepentant: 'The broad premise and prediction of the book have been borne out in spades,' he argued.[2]

For many Indians, the problem with the argument of *Eclipse* was not what it said about the US or China, but how little it said about India. For the election of the government of Narendra Modi had led to a resurgence of bullish optimism about the future of Asia's second would-be superpower. Modi himself had spoken of the twenty-first century as 'India's century'. And many in the country's elite dared to hope that India might 'own' the next thirty years of international economic development – just as China had dominated the three decades that had followed its opening to the outside world in 1979.

Indian optimism is, in large part, based on demographics. The Chinese population is ageing and its supply of young workers is shrinking. In 2015, China formally abandoned its famous 'one-child policy', after thirty-five years, partly because of the ageing of the country's population. But the consequences of ageing are already filtering through to the economy, as Chinese wages rise and the country begins to lose manufacturing jobs. By contrast, 65% of the Indian population was under the age of thirty in 2015, creating a healthy 'dependency ratio' of productive workers to old people. Demographers think that India is likely to surpass China as the world's most populous country, with 1.4 billion people, around 2022. And some economists reckon it might be the world's largest economy by 2050.[3] As Shekhar Gupta, one of India's most influential journalists put it to me, 'Indians now tend to believe that India is on the rise and China is going down. We are the only growing power in the world.'[4]

The Modi government was happy to stoke this optimism. Talking to Arun Jaitley, the country's finance minister and Subramanian's boss, I found him in optimistic mood – predicting that India would soon grow at 8–9% a year, making it the fastest-growing economy in the world, easily outpacing China.[5] But there was an important qualification to those figures. In 1980, when China's growth spurt began, the Indian and Chinese economies were of roughly equivalent size. By 2015, China's economy was five times the size of that in India.[6] That means that even if China is growing at 6–7% and India is growing at 8–9%, the gap between the two economies is actually widening rather than shrinking. Arvind Subramanian was well aware of the real state of play, predicting to me in Delhi that 'The underlying economic power of India will not be close to China for another twenty-five to thirty years.'[7] Subramanian's caution is wise. While India may one day be a genuine political and economic peer to China, that day is probably at least a generation away.

The development gap between India and China is clear not just in the figures, but in the streets. China is now criss-crossed by modern motorways and a network of high-speed railways. In India, by contrast, the road network is still primitive and, in 2015, some 50% of Indians even lacked access to basic toilet facilities – a national disgrace that Modi, to his credit, has made a policy priority. Levels of basic education and literacy, which were crucial to the economic miracles in East Asia, are much lower in India than in China.

For all the swagger of the Modi era, the more cautious members of the Indian elite are well aware of their country's weaknesses and know that, as a consequence, India's global power is likely to lag well behind that of China for decades to come. The difference is subtly reflected in the vocabularies used by the governments in Beijing and Delhi. While President Xi Jinping talks of his desire for a 'new type of great power relationship' between China and the US, Modi speaks of India as a 'leading power'. In other words, China is already making a claim to be America's peer; India's ambitions are more modest – to be seen as one of a number of major international players.

The question the Modi government faces in foreign policy is how to position India as a 'leading power' in a fast-changing world. Should India continue to define itself, as it did during much of the Cold War, as a leader of the 'Global South' – the poorer countries of the world that believed themselves to be disadvantaged and exploited by the industrialised nations of the North? Or should India see itself as part of the rising East – an Asian nation that is poised to correct the historic injustices and power imbalances that were imposed during the centuries of Western imperialism. The second approach would mean that India stresses its similarities to China, as two great and historic Asian cultures, oppressed by the West during the imperial era, but now seeing their power on the rebound.

A third approach sees China not as a potential Indian ally in changing the world order, but as the country's biggest emerging rival. Like many other Asian nations, India has reason to fear the rise of an assertive China. The border between China and India is the longest disputed frontier in the world.[8] The two countries fought a brief border war in 1962, in which India came off worst – and they still have an outstanding territorial dispute, with China laying claim to large parts of the Indian province of Arunachal Pradesh. If the growing power of China is likely to be India's dominant foreign-policy problem, then an entirely different foreign policy is implied. In that case, India has a strong national interest in forming alliances with Western and Asian democracies – in particular the United States and Japan.

And then, finally, there is a fourth approach. This argues that all this talk of India's global role overlooks the fact that the country still faces an existential threat right on its border, in the form of a nuclear-armed Pakistan. India and Pakistan have fought three wars since partition in 1947 – and a fourth remains a distinct possibility. For some in the Indian security establishment it is this reality – rather than dreams of a new world order or fears of an emerging rivalry with China – that should continue to dominate India's strategic thinking.

Inevitably, all four of these strands in India's strategic thinking will influence the approach of any government in Delhi of whatever complexion. Which of them comes to the fore will, to some extent, be a product of whatever unforeseen crises emerge in the coming years. But it is clear that the arrival of Narendra Modi in power has seen India draw closer to the US and Japan – and take a more wary attitude to China.

The legacy of India's anti-colonial history, however, is not easily shaken off – and continues to shape the country's instincts. For older Indians, in particular, the country's moral authority continues to derive from its status as a spokesman for the world's poorer nations and the victims of colonialism. During the Cold War, India formed a close relationship with the Soviet Union, and Indians of a certain age are still wont to say 'I was taught in school that Russia is India's closest friend.' That pro-Russian reflex still remains in Delhi, to some extent – and means that the US cannot rely on Indian support in international crises that pit Moscow against Washington.

The suspicion of Western capitalism is always likely to remain a powerful strand in Indian thinking. This, after all, was a country that was once colonised by a Western multinational – the East India Company. Traces of anti-Western and anti-capitalist thinking continue to make India a prickly partner in global trade and climate negotiations. While liberal economists might insist that India can reap enormous gains from globalisation, Indian policy is still often conditioned by a fear that a powerful West might impose disadvantageous deals on the 'Global South'.

As a result, even though India, with its huge population, scarce water resources and polluted atmosphere, is one of the countries most at risk from climate change, its governments long resisted Western pressure to reduce carbon emissions. They argued that all such deals threatened to institutionalise an unjust order that permits Westerners to consume more energy per head than Indians. India's insistence that it has a right to use fossil fuels to develop its economy – combined with the fact that by 2015, the country was already the world's third-largest emitter of greenhouse gases – made the Modi government's stance critical to the global climate-change talks that culminated in Paris in December 2015. Going into the Paris talks, some Western diplomats feared that Indian intransigence might actually prevent any deal emerging at all. In the event, the Indians found a middle way that preserved the principle that rich, Western nations must do considerably more to reduce greenhouse gases than poorer countries, while also committing India to move gradually towards cleaner forms of energy.

Indians have long argued that it is not just the global economic and environmental orders that discriminate against them. Viewed from Delhi, the global political order has also long seemed intrinsically unfair. Crucial post-war institutions such as the UN and the IMF were shaped before India had even achieved its independence in 1947 – and have proved extremely hard to reform ever since. As a result, India has often found itself as a 'geopolitical outsider'. While China is a permanent member of the UN Security Council, India remains excluded from the top table of international affairs. The five permanent members (the US, UK, France, Russia and China), as established in the 1940s, continue to play a crucial role in defining the international order. For example, they have veto rights over UN resolutions and so can decide whether a war is legal or illegal.

India's suspicion of the Western-dominated global order is reflected in its voting record at the UN. While Britain and America often praise

India as 'the world's largest democracy' and assume that this should mean they share a common world view, in practice this is often not the case. An internal exercise by Britain's Foreign Office in 2014 found that India had voted against the British position at the UN more often than any other large nation.[9]

Permanent membership of the UNSC is also closely associated with the possession of nuclear weapons. The Treaty on Non-Proliferation of Nuclear Weapons (NPT), signed in 1970 and renewed in 1995, recognised just the five permanent members of the Security Council as legitimate nuclear-weapons states. In protest at this 'nuclear apartheid', India became one of four UN members to refuse to sign the NPT. The denial of legitimacy to an Indian nuclear-weapons programme, through the NPT, threatened to formalise India's status as a second-class power

India had first tested nuclear weapons as early as 1974. It tested them again in 1998 – by which time Pakistan, India's most dangerous adversary, had also developed a nuclear-weapons programme. The initial reaction of the five 'legitimate' nuclear powers was to impose sanctions on India for its violation of the nuclear non-proliferation regime. During the presidency of George W. Bush, however, the US decided to change tack – in the interests of cultivating a warmer relationship with a rising India. The US–India nuclear deal, signed during the Bush presidency, effectively recognised India as a legitimate member of the nuclear-weapons club. The breakthrough on nuclear weapons was rightly regarded in Delhi as a mark of India's growing international status. Sanjaya Baru, head of the India office of the International Institute for Strategic Studies, argues that 'Breaking the nuclear regime is the most important geopolitical development for India in the last twenty-five years.'[10]

The nuclear breakthrough had come at a time of growing Indian self-confidence connected to the country's rapid economic emergence. The free-market reforms of the early 1990s had, at last, seen India notch up the kind of rapid economic growth previously achieved in East Asia. The emergence of globally successful hi-tech companies, such as Infosys and Wipro, gave India a new glamour and self-confidence – reflected in high-profile campaigns, such as the 'India Everywhere' campaign launched at the World Economic Forum in Davos in 2006. Indian companies blanketed the Swiss ski resort with advertisements and sponsored a gaudy and exuberant closing-night party, complete with Bollywood dancing, to entertain the assembled plutocrats. That same year, *Foreign Affairs* magazine in the US put India on its cover and proclaimed it a 'roaring, capitalist success story'.

All of this was heady stuff. A country that had been part of the British Empire within living memory was emerging as a leading world economic and political power. The renewed sense of confidence in India created an opportunity to rethink India's global role – casting the nation as part of the rising and assertive East, rather than a weak and exploited South. India's membership of the BRICS group – made up of Brazil, Russia, India, China and South Africa – gave the country membership of a group of non-Western economies that had been singled out for their size and dynamism, rather than their weakness.[11]

The assertive and dynamic image of Narendra Modi, elected prime minister in 2014, energised Indian nationalism – both within the country and amongst non-resident Indians living overseas. Modi was given an ecstatic reception when he gave a speech to US-based Indians at Madison Square Garden in New York. The 'Hindu nationalism' associated with Modi excited many of his supporters, who saw it as a promise to increase global respect for India's unique culture – as well as a mark of the country's growing power. A successful Indian space probe to Mars, in the early Modi years, was hailed as sign of national prowess.

For some of the prime minister's critics, however, 'Hindu nationalism' was either absurd or sinister – or both. They pointed to claims by Modi's more fervent supporters that ancient Indians had invented everything from aeroplanes to nuclear weapons. His left-wing critics accused the new prime minister of promoting 'xenophobic national-ism'[12] and of turning a blind eye to the mass murder of Muslims in riots that took place when he was chief minister of Gujarat in 2002. Modi's role in the Gujarat killings was sufficiently controversial for him to be refused visas to travel to the United States in the years before his election as prime minister.

The election of a 'Hindu nationalist' as prime minister also imme-diately raised questions about the future of India's relations with Pakistan – the issue that had bedevilled Indian foreign policy since partition and independence. In 2008, India had been the victim of ter-rorist attacks in Mumbai that killed 164 people. Despite strong evi-dence of links between the terrorists and the Pakistani intelligence services, India had refrained from retaliating against Pakistani targets. This restraint drew widespread international praise, given the obvious risk of a clash between two nuclear neighbours.

Nonetheless, by the time Modi won election, it was conventional wisdom in Delhi that if Pakistan ever sponsored another terror attack on the scale of Mumbai, Indian retaliation was all but inevitable. Modi's own reputation as a Hindu hardliner only increased nervous-ness about the threat of war. But one of Modi's first acts as prime min-ister was a gesture of reconciliation – an invitation to Nawaz Sharif, the Pakistani prime minister, to his swearing-in ceremony in Delhi. Those who hoped that this initial act would be swiftly followed by further efforts at bridge-building between India and Pakistan were swiftly disappointed. As one senior Indian diplomat told me, 'Our policy now is essentially to ignore Pakistan, as far as possible.'[13]

The 'ignore Pakistan' policy was not simply a reflection of Modi's own preferences. Rather it reflected a broader strategic consensus in Delhi that India's aspirations to be a 'leading power' on the world stage are dependent on breaking its 'hyphenation' with Pakistan. As long as the rest of the world sees India's place in the world through the prism of the India–Pakistan dispute, then India is condemned to be little more than a regional power, boxed into South Asia. If India aspires to be a truly global player, then it cannot allow its foreign policy to be defined by rivalry with Pakistan.

This determination to prevent Pakistan defining India's global strategy is only strengthened by the belief in Delhi that China is bolstering Pakistan, with the precise intention of keeping India preoccupied and contained. The Pakistani nuclear programme received crucial technical assistance from China. And under Xi Jinping, the Chinese moved decisively to strengthen the economic and strategic ties between China and Pakistan.

In April 2015, President Xi paid a state visit to Pakistan – the first Chinese leader to visit the country in nine years. This was more than just a courtesy call. Xi signed infrastructure contracts worth $46 billion – dwarfing the $7.5 billion in development aid that the US had directed towards Pakistan during the Obama years, despite that country's significance in the 'war on terror'. The projects that China was promising to finance in Pakistan had a direct strategic pay-off for Beijing – and posed an indirect strategic threat to India and the US. In particular, Xi promised to direct $1.6 billion towards the development of the Pakistani port of Gwadar on the Arabian Sea and, in return, signed a forty-year contract giving China the right to manage the port.

The potential strategic significance of this deal was enormous. The port at Gwadar had the potential to be the answer to China's Malacca Strait dilemma. Gwadar is not far from the Strait of Hormuz, which guards the entrance to the Persian Gulf, through which 20% of the world's oil passes. Traditionally, for that oil to reach China it then had to sail around India and through the Strait of Malacca, before entering the South China Sea. However, the development of Gwadar port offered the possibility that Middle Eastern and Iranian oil could take a much shorter sea journey to Pakistan. From Gwadar, the oil could then be transported overland, across a 3,000-kilometre land route into western China. Much of the rest of the billions that China proposed to invest in Pakistani infrastructure would be directed to creating the road, rail and pipeline links to make those shipments possible.[14]

Gwadar is also potentially useful for the expanding Chinese navy. As one Pakistani newspaper noted, the port deal would give China 'the possibility of building a naval base on the Arabian Sea'.[15] That possibility did not escape the attention of strategists in Washington and Delhi – particularly given the fact that on the same trip, President Xi agreed to sell Pakistan eight advanced Chinese-made submarines. Viewed from Delhi, it looked as if Pakistan, their old adversary, was now locked in the embrace of China. The worst-case scenario for India is that the country might one day face a two-front war against two nuclear-armed nations.

For the Indians, China's inroads into Pakistan looked like part of an alarming pattern through which China seemed to be deliberately encircling India by forming ever-closer ties to the country's neighbours. China had also invested heavily in building ports in Sri Lanka – just off the southern coast of India. In 2014, alarm bells were set off in Delhi when two Chinese submarines docked at Colombo, Sri Lanka's main port and a major trans-shipment port for exports arriving in India. China had also invested heavily in economic, political and military ties with Myanmar – a large country lying between India and China that was only just emerging from decades of political isolation. Bangladesh, another of India's neighbours, also received Chinese investment into port development at Chittagong.

China's infrastructure investment in India's neighbours seemed to fit a geopolitical theory known as the 'string of pearls'. The phrase referred to China's alleged ambition to develop a string of port facilities stretching from the Chinese port of Hainan across the Indian Ocean to the Middle East and Africa. From Beijing's point of view, such a strategy made sense as a way of securing the sea lanes that were crucial to China's ability to export manufactured goods and import energy resources. In the long term, the string of pearls might offer an insurance policy against a potential US naval blockade of China. But viewed from Delhi, the string of pearls looked unpleasantly like an effort to contain India. As Shyam Saran, the former Indian foreign secretary, put it to me: 'From Pakistan to the Maldives to Sri Lanka to Burma, we can already see the space around us constricting . . . If we don't narrow the gap between us and China, we'll be boxed into the subcontinent as China dominates our periphery.'[16]

India's efforts to break out of this Chinese box were a feature of Narendra Modi's first year in office. The new prime minister hurled himself into regional diplomacy as part of an effort to build up long-neglected relations with India's closest neighbours. An agreement to end a long-standing border dispute between India and Bangladesh was seen as an important breakthrough. The defeat of a pro-Chinese government in elections in Sri Lanka in January 2015 was greeted with delight in Delhi – and two months later Modi became the first Indian prime minister to pay a bilateral visit to Sri Lanka since 1987.

Meanwhile, India, like China, is investing in naval power – both to protect itself from being throttled by China's string of pearls and to develop leverage over Beijing, by creating a potential threat to Chinese trade routes. A second Indian aircraft carrier is due to come into service in 2017–18 and a third will be launched around a decade later.[17] India's determination to build up its own naval power is also a hedge against the possibility that – despite the Obama administration's 'pivot' to Asia – American power in Asia may decline. Shivshankar Menon, who served as India's National Security Adviser between 2010 and 2014, sees the chaos in the Middle East as a harbinger of the decline of the 'traditional Western-dominated world order'. His conclusion is that 'We can no longer assume that others will guarantee the safety of the sea lanes that carry our foreign trade.'[18]

Yet Menon, a tall courtly man who has also served as India's ambassador to Beijing, is not resigned to the idea that China and India will be antagonists. He knows that all this jockeying for regional advantage with China does not – and cannot – mean that the Indian government is resigned to a straightforwardly adversarial relationship with the government of China. China is, after all, India's largest trading partner – although the huge trade surplus in favour of China is a source of discontent in Delhi. The two countries also need to co-operate on regional issues and international issues – from Afghanistan to climate change to the management of water resources. Any Chinese move to dam the rivers of Tibet would potentially pose a mortal threat to India's water supplies. Like many of China's neighbours, the Indians are also interested in the possibility of Chinese investment in local infrastructure – as part of China's 'one belt, one road' strategy.

When Xi Jinping visited India in September 2014 – the first such visit by a Chinese leader in nine years – the Indians did their best to make him welcome. Rather than starting the visit in Delhi, the Chinese leader was invited to Gujarat, Modi's home state. The two leaders visited Gandhi's ashram and exchanged warm words about mutual economic co-operation, with Xi arguing that there was a natural fit between the world's factory (China) and its back office (India). Yet, even as the Chinese leader shook hands in Ahmedabad and Delhi, Chinese troops were crossing into the disputed territory of Arunachal Pradesh.[19] The incident left the Indians confused and concerned. Could this troop incursion by China have been the initiative of a local commander, pursued without Xi's knowledge? Or had the order been a deliberate message from the Chinese president himself? Reflecting on the incident some months later, one of India's most senior diplomats concluded: 'The Chinese troops stayed for three weeks. This was not an accident.'[20] The message from Beijing could only be interpreted one way – as a threat.

The troop incursion during Xi's visit helped to tilt Indian foreign policy towards the West. Those in Delhi who argued that India must now seek to pursue closer ties with the United States soon had their opportunity. Just two weeks after Xi's visit to India, Modi paid his first visit as prime minister to Washington. For a man who had been banned from the US for some years, he received a strikingly warm welcome – with Obama taking the time to give the Indian prime minister a personal tour of the Martin Luther King Memorial. Four months later, the seal was put on the emerging special relationship between

Delhi and Washington when Obama visited India – becoming the first US president ever to be guest of honour at India's Republic Day celebrations. Modi seemed intoxicated by his new closeness to the US president – hugging him on the tarmac and referring repeatedly to him as 'Barack' in a joint press conference.

Beyond the ceremony, there was real substance. The two nations issued a joint statement that was designed to get the attention of Beijing. It began grandly: 'As leaders of the world's two largest democracies . . . we have agreed on a Joint Strategic Vision for the region.' But the most eye-catching sentence came further down: 'We affirm the importance of safeguarding maritime security and ensuring freedom of navigation . . . especially in the South China Sea.'[21] With that statement, the US and India had essentially joined forces to resist China's burgeoning maritime ambitions.

The strategic understanding between India and the US was underpinned by an economic and cultural convergence. As the cheering crowds that had gathered to see Modi at Madison Square Garden underlined, there is now a substantial Indian diaspora population living in the US. By 2015, there were estimated to be 3.3 million people of Indian origin living in the US, over half of whom had arrived since 2000.[22] Indian expatriates are particularly visible and successful in Silicon Valley and on Wall Street. Sundar Pichai, who was named as the new CEO of Google in 2015, was born in Chennai in southern India and only moved to the US as a graduate student. Vikram Pandit, another Indian-born businessman, served as CEO of Citigroup from 2007–12. Deloitte, the largest accounting firm in the world, which is based in New York, appointed Punit Renjen, another expatriate Indian, as the firm's global CEO in 2015. The network of personal and business ties between India and the US is growing steadily thicker. Business-minded Indians based in the US are amongst Modi's strongest supporters. They are also a natural constituency from which to build a 'special relationship' between India and the US.

Obama's commitment to that special relationship built upon the efforts of his predecessor, George W. Bush. In the early Obama years, as the new president had courted China, Delhi had felt rebuffed and anxious. But as the relationship between China and America had soured, so Obama had returned to the courtship of India – as the only country large enough to balance a rising China within Asia. As the Obama administration committed itself to its pivot towards Asia, it became obvious that India had a central role to play in that strategy. Leon Panetta, Obama's Defense Secretary in his first administration, argued that India was indeed the 'lynchpin of the rebalance'.[23] India's strategic and defence relationship has got steadily closer throughout the Obama years. By 2013, the US had also displaced Russia as the largest arms supplier to India. By 2014, India was doing more joint military exercises with the US than with any other nation.

An emerging India was indeed being courted on all sides. Xi had become the first Chinese leader to visit India in almost a decade. Obama had become the first US president to pay two state visits to India. Perhaps the most ardent suitor of them all was Shinzo Abe, the prime minister of Japan – who let it be known that he followed only three people on Twitter, one of whom was Narendra Modi. Abe had also wisely invested early in his personal relationship with the new Indian prime minister, visiting him twice when Modi was chief minister of Gujarat. Returning the favour, Modi paid his first foreign visit outside mainland Asia to Japan, praying with the Japanese leader in a Buddhist temple in Kyoto. In a speech in Tokyo, Modi seemed to endorse Japan's fears of a rising China, saying: 'Everywhere around us, we see an eighteenth-century expansionist mindset, encroaching in other countries, intruding in others' waters, invading other countries and capturing territory'.[24] He did not name China, but there was no mistaking whom he was referring to.

The emerging strategic logic was clear. As China rose, so India, Japan and the United States were drawing perceptibly closer together. It was not quite the policy of 'containment' that China feared, but it was clearly a conscious effort to balance the power of a more assertive China on the global stage.

By 2015, however, India also increasingly mattered in its own right, not simply as part of a strategic balancing act with China. *Eclipse* author Arvind Subramanian is certainly right to dismiss the idea that India will catch up with China in the next twenty years; but look ahead a little further, to 2050, and it is possible to envisage a world in which India could be both the world's most populous country and its largest economy. While the last years of the twentieth century and the beginning of the twenty-first century had been shaped by the emergence of the Pacific Rim as the new core of the global economy, by the mid-twenty-first century, the rise of the Indian Ocean Rim – linking India with a fast-growing African continent – could well be the next centre of global economic dynamism.[25] It is with this thought in mind that the futurologist Hans Rosling likes to recommend that investors buy beachfront properties in Somalia.

The idea that India might one day be at the fulcrum of global economic development underlines the point that the story of Easternisation is about much more than China – and indeed about much more than Asia. The shift in economic and political power from west to east is reshaping the whole world.

PART 2

Easternisation Beyond Asia

Rasterisation Beyond Asia

The Question of American Power

Perhaps the most famous image from Barack Obama's period in office was the photo taken of the president and his team watching the raid on Osama Bin Laden's compound in Pakistan. The president is seated off to one side, hunched slightly and watching the screen intently. Hillary Clinton has her hand over her mouth, gasping in shock at some unseen development. Tom Donilon, the National Security Adviser, stands at the back with his arms folded, looking impassive.

If you visit the room itself, it is even smaller than it appears in the official photo. (The image was taken with a fish-eye lens that exaggerated the size of the space that the president and his aides had crowded into.) On the day of the raid, the president's national security team had assembled in the famous situation room in the basement of the West Wing of the White House, just down the corridor from the annex where military staff where monitoring the video-feed of the raid. As the day unfolded, the key players had moved down the corridor to the annex, to watch the raid as it happened.

The killing of Osama Bin Laden was a stark demonstration of the continuing reach, power and ruthlessness of the United States. It stood President Obama in good stead when he ran for re-election in 2012. But if the president had hoped that the successful pursuit of the world's most famous terrorist would come to define the Obama years, he was to be disappointed. Instead, as Obama's eight years in office drew to a close, it was clear that his presidency was being defined, both at home and abroad, as a period when American power was challenged all over the world – but especially in East Asia, Russia and the Middle East.

The Chinese challenge to the Western-led world order – which was examined in the first part of this book – is part of a global phenomenon. In Europe, an angry and resurgent Russia slid into open confrontation with the West over the fate of Ukraine and Russia's annexation of Crimea. As a result, the stability and peace of Europe and the power of the Western alliance was faced with its most severe challenge since the end of the Cold War.

In the Middle East, meanwhile, the state system that had been created by France and Britain in the aftermath of the First World War was crumbling under the impact of the revolutions and civil wars that were convulsing the Arab world. After the Second World War, the United States had emerged as the underwriter of the security order in the Middle East. As that order crumbled, many in the region and around the world pointed accusing fingers at the Obama White House. In June 2015, *The Economist* gave expression to a widespread complaint, when it lamented that 'The Middle Eastern order sustained by the United States has collapsed . . . The Middle East desperately needs a new, invigorated engagement from America.'[1]

All of these regional crises came to be seen as connected by a general thread of American retreat from the world. In its crude form, this idea was a serious oversimplification. Throughout his term in office, Obama consistently displayed a willingness to use military force – witness his administration's plentiful and controversial use of drone strikes on suspected terrorists in Pakistan, Yemen and elsewhere. When the jihadists of ISIL seized a large chunk of Iraq and

Syria in 2014, Obama was prepared to use American air power to strike back – although he remained characteristically reluctant to commit ground troops. The US also remained deeply involved in international diplomacy from Iran to Ukraine. It was America that led the international effort to forge a deal over Iran's nuclear programme, which came to fruition in a controversial deal in 2015. The imposition of tough American sanctions on Russia after the annexation of Crimea in 2014 also helped to push the EU to take similar measures. Indeed, in comparison to a Europe that was consumed by financial and refugee crises, the US remained the most confident and outward-looking part of the Western alliance.

Nonetheless, in international affairs, image can swiftly shape reality. By the closing years of the Obama administration, the notion that a timid America was losing its grip on world affairs was in danger of becoming conventional wisdom – from Beijing to Berlin to Brasilia.

The killing of Bin Laden in 2011 had failed to create an enduring aura of strength. Instead America's image was being defined by events in Crimea, the South China Sea and Syria. In particular, the president's failure to enforce his own 'red line' over the use of chemical weapons – by taking military action against the Assad regime in Syria in 2013 – came to be seen as emblematic of a US government that was unwilling to back up harsh words with appropriately tough actions.

The origins of the red-line controversy lay in a remark by President Obama in August 2012, a year into the Syrian civil war, when – justifying America's policy of non-intervention – he had said that if the Assad regime used chemical weapons it would cross a red line and change his calculations. When, almost a year later, clear evidence emerged that the Syrian government had indeed used poison gas on its own people, US military intervention looked inevitable. Plans for air strikes were drawn up, and support from allies such as France and the UK was canvassed. But when Britain's House of Commons rejected military action in Syria in August 2013, a clearly torn President Obama decided to seek approval for military action from the US Congress. This decision was announced just hours before bombing raids on Syria were due to begin. Over the following week, congressional support crumbled. Eventually President Obama shelved the whole idea of military action in favour of a Russian-led diplomatic initiative to force Syria to give up its chemical weapons voluntarily.

The administration attempted to spin this episode as a diplomatic success and Obama later insisted that he was 'very proud' of his decision not to take military action in Syria.[2] But the impact on Obama's international image was very damaging – erasing the decisive picture established by the Bin Laden raid, and replacing it with a less flattering image of a vacillating president who was unwilling to use force, and who had lost control of events. The French, whose pilots had been in their briefing rooms preparing for the attacks on Syria when the news came that the raids had been called off, were particularly scathing. Francois Heisbourg, a French strategist, summed up the emerging general view when he commented acidly, 'The Americans are very good at drawing red lines, but they are not very good at enforcing them.'[3]

While the episode of the Syrian red line was the most famous example of dithering by the Obama administration, there were others. People noticed that Susan Rice, the president's National Security Adviser, had warned that Russian military intervention in Ukraine in 2014 would be a 'grave mistake' – language that many interpreted as a threat of a military response.[4] In practice, the US contented itself with economic sanctions against Russia, and then refused to supply arms to the Ukrainian government. In Asia, many felt that the US had turned a blind eye to Chinese aggression around Scarborough Shoal, emboldening the Chinese to take a more aggressive stance in the East and South China Seas. Every time the US hesitated to enforce a red line in one part of the world, it raised questions over American security commitments elsewhere. As Clyde Prestowitz, one of Washington's veteran Asia hands put it, 'It makes no more sense for Americans to die over the Senkakus than it does for them to die over Ukraine.'[5] So if Russia could get away with the annexation of Crimea without triggering a military response, and President Assad could survive his use of chemical weapons, what conclusions might Beijing draw?

For Obama all of these accusations of weakness – both at home and abroad – were a source of frustration and irritation. The president, after all, had run as an anti-war candidate and had been rewarded with electoral victory at home and with a Nobel Peace Prize overseas. He believed, with some justice, that the lesson of the Iraq and Afghan wars was that military force was often counterproductive and he appeared bewildered by the speed with which that lesson had been forgotten – lamenting in 2014, 'Why is it that everybody is so eager to use military force after we have just gone through a decade of war at enormous cost?'[6]

The notion that he was presiding over a period of American decline clearly infuriated Obama. In his State of the Union speech to Congress in 2012, the president proclaimed that 'America remains the one indispensable nation in world affairs . . . Anyone who tells you otherwise, anyone who tells you that America is in decline or that our influence has waned, doesn't know what they're talking about.'[7]

It was a ringing declaration – but also one that was tellingly defensive in tone. Obama knew that no US president or senior official could ever admit publicly that American power was in decline. The projection of strength was a political necessity at home and a foreign-policy necessity abroad. Hillary Clinton embodied this tone when she proclaimed in her 2011 *Foreign Policy* article 'America's Pacific Century', 'Our military is by far the strongest and our economy is by far the largest.'

Yet, in reality, the Obama administration took a much more nuanced and cautious view of American strength. Indeed a key theme of the Obama years was the president's cautious adaptation to a new world of rival power centres – a shift that was made all the more cautious by the fact that the president could not openly acknowledge his thinking, lest this be interpreted as further evidence of American weakness.

Clues, however, could be found in statements made by key members of the president's team. In a little-noticed interview, given about a year before he became Defense Secretary in the second Obama administration, Senator Chuck Hagel had openly acknowledged the changing world order, arguing that:

> Almost every American alive today has lived over the last 65 years in a world where America has dominated, unrivalled in any way. We call the shots, no matter who, no matter what. It isn't that way anymore and it isn't going to be that way. Now that doesn't mean we're not the senior power in the world. Not at all, but there's a new reality of accommodation now, that's going to have to be factored in.[8]

President Obama would, of course, have been well aware that these were Hagel's views before sending him to the Pentagon. Indeed, the fact that Hagel was aware of the shifting balance in global power was part of the reason that he was given the job.

Even Hillary Clinton, as a presidential candidate in 2008, had said that economics constrained America's ability to confront China. Clinton's argument was that since the US budget deficit was, to a significant extent, funded by Chinese purchases of US Treasury bills, China was effectively America's banker, and 'How do you get tough on your banker?'[9] Clinton's analysis of the leverage China's ownership of US Treasuries gave to Beijing was disputed by many economists, who argued that a mass sale of US Treasury bills by the Chinese would damage their own interests by driving down the value of China's savings. But the broader point about the political consequences of shifting economic power was hard to dispute. A wealthier China has more leverage over the West – witness the queue of European leaders seeking contracts in Beijing.

The notion that the basis of American global power is ultimately economic is rooted in American history. William Seward, Abraham Lincoln's Secretary of State, asserted that 'The nation that draws most from the earth and fabricates most, and sells the most to foreign nations, must be and will be the great power on earth.'[10] Seward was also clear that the key to global economic power lay in the area that later came to be known as the Pacific Rim: 'You want the dominance of the world. This must be looked for on the Pacific.'[11] This statement may have sounded a little outlandish when it was made, little more than a decade after California was admitted to the Union – and at a time when the major industrial powers of the world, with the exception of the US itself, were all still in Europe. But from the standpoint of the twenty-first century, Seward's words seem prophetic.

By the early twenty-first century, when China had emerged as the dominant economic power in the Pacific and was rapidly closing the economic gap with the United States at a global level, American foreign-policy thinkers – particularly in the 'realist' school – began to take a more cautious view of America's global reach. Stephen Walt of Harvard University noted that 'It is highly unusual for a country with only 5% of the world's population to be able to organise favorable political, economic and security orders in almost every corner of the globe and to sustain them for decades.'[12]

Walt advocated a foreign-policy strategy known as 'offshore balancing' which argued that America should adapt to the relative decline in its power by avoiding large military deployments around the world, and instead using regional allies as proxies to balance potentially hostile powers.[13] To some nervous allies, the Obama administration's policies in East Asia, the Middle East and Europe began to look suspiciously like the beginnings of offshore balancing.

Although the Obama administration would never publicly embrace a policy as controversial as offshore balancing, advocates of similar-sounding policies were appointed to influential posts in the administration. One example was Charles Kupchan, who was appointed Europe director at the National Security Council during Obama's second term. When still a professor at Georgetown University in 2012, Kupchan had published *No One's World*, in which he argued bluntly that 'The United States still aspires to a level of global dominion for which it has insufficient resources and political will.'[14] Kupchan's book appeared in the very year that Obama told Congress that 'America is back'. The fact that Kupchan's views did not prevent him being appointed to the NSC the following year suggests that the president's team was more tolerant of private 'declinism' than his public rhetoric might suggest.

Those who continued to proclaim that American dominance could continue into the foreseeable future were not quite sure how to deal with the idea that the US was on the brink of losing its position as the world's largest economy. For some, the solution was simply to assert that it wasn't happening. In 'The Myth of American Decline' (an article that inspired Obama's rallying cry of 2012), Robert Kagan wrote that 'Optimists about China's development predict that it will overtake the United States as the largest economy in the world sometime in the next two decades.'[15] Yet, within two years of the appearance of Kagan's article, the IMF announced that China was already 'number one'.[16]

For America's 'anti-declinists', this was a tricky moment. They responded, in part, by arguing that the unit of measurement was faulty. Joe Nye in *Is the American Century Over?* pointed out that the estimates were based on purchasing-power parity (PPP) rather than real exchange rates. Nye argued that while PPP was useful for measuring levels of welfare within societies – because it adjusts for the cost of living within individual countries – 'current exchange rates, although they may fluctuate depending on currency values, are often more accurate in estimating power resources'.[17] That is because while a haircut is best measured at PPP, 'imported oil or parts for an advanced aircraft engine' have to be bought at the prevailing exchange rates.

Nye had a point – but perhaps not a decisive one, for the lower cost of living and wage rates in China do have an impact on 'hard' military power. So while Nye was right to point out that 'China's 11 percent of global military expenditure is far less than America's 39 percent', he did not acknowledge that America gets less bang for its buck, partly because of the enormous costs of US military equipment.[18]

The expense of American military programmes is illustrated by the story of the US Air Force's F-22 Raptor fighter which proved so expensive to produce – at a 'through-life cost' of $670 million a plane – that the Americans were only able to buy 182 of them, as opposed to the original plan to purchase some 650. The result was to significantly reduce America's military capacities. As Mark Urban, the BBC's defence correspondent, notes: 'If America held back some squadrons for home defence, it is unlikely that it could deploy more than a few dozen Raptors in any confrontation with China, with its hundreds of fighter jets.'[19] The F-22 was not an isolated example. The new stealth B-2 bomber – the most modern bomber plane the US possesses – is 'so colossally expensive to procure that at the time it was calculated that an aircraft made of the same weight made of solid gold would have been cheaper'.[20] As a result, America has been able to build only nineteen B-2s, of which just six are likely to be deployable on any given day.

The decline in American naval power is also striking. In the 1980s, the US was aiming for a '600-ship navy'. But the navy was half that size by 2009. That still made the US fleet the world's most powerful by a long way – with eleven aircraft carriers, nine more than any other country. But while America's carriers were a symbol of the country's power and global reach, they were also increasingly vulnerable to advanced missiles and submarines – of the sort that China was developing.

Overall, American defence spending was decreasing as a share of the economy. Under George W. Bush, the US had spent over 4% of GDP, a year on defence. By 2014 that had declined to 3.9% and it is scheduled to fall to 2.9% by 2017.[21] The result will be a decline in America's ability to intervene militarily around the world. As Robert Gates, who served as Defense Secretary under both President George W. Bush and President Obama, put it: 'We need to be honest . . . a smaller military, no matter how superb, will be able to go to fewer places and be able to do fewer things.'[22]

As America's defence spending has declined as a proportion of GDP, and non-Western powers – such as China, Russia, Saudi Arabia and India – have increased their military budgets, so America's once unquestioned lead in military power has begun to shrink. During the Clinton years, the US spent more on defence than the rest of the world combined. By the end of Obama's period in office, the US accounted for less than 40% of global military spending.

Under these circumstances, it became increasingly important that America's allies should share the burden of upholding the Western alliance. But, in fact, the opposite was happening. The countries of the European Union, beset by an economic crisis, were spending less and less on defence. As a result, the twenty-eight-member Nato alliance – essentially the armed wing of the West – became increasingly dependent on American military spending. In the year 2000, the Americans accounted for roughly 50% of Nato spending, with the Europeans and Canadians accounting for the other half. By 2012, however, the US accounted for over 70% of Nato's military spending.

In theory, Nato members were all committed to spending at least 2% of GDP on defence. In reality, only the US, the UK and Greece (which was worried about Turkey) were meeting that commitment by 2014. In that year, it became apparent that even the British were thinking about slipping below the 2% target – despite public commitments made by David Cameron. The reaction in the United States was something close to despair. Both President Obama and Ashton Carter, who had succeeded Chuck Hagel as Defense Secretary, publicly urged the British to stick to the 2%. In private, Obama told David Cameron that if the UK failed to meet its 2% commitment, the 'special relationship' between the UK and US would be over – an extraordinarily stark warning.[23] In an article entitled, 'Britain Resigns as a World Power', Fareed Zakaria, one of America's most influential foreign-affairs commentators, noted that Britain's army was scheduled to shrink to just 80,000 men – its smallest size since just after the Napoleonic Wars. There was even speculation in the British think-tank world that the army could shrink to just 50,000 troops.[24] In the event, domestic and American pressure persuaded the British to stick to the 2% target. But, even so, the UK's military capacity has already been seriously eroded. The Royal Air Force was only able to participate on American-led strikes on Islamic State in 2015 by delaying the retirement of part of its ageing fleet of strike aircraft. When the British army has been shrunk to 80,000 soldiers in 2018, the entire force will be able to fit into Wembley Stadium, Britain's biggest football ground – and there would still be 10,000 empty seats left over.

Even after the announcement of these cuts, Britain and France remained the only two EU powers that aspire to the ability to project military force around the world. Nato's bloody and unsatisfactory involvement in the Afghan war has made European countries still more suspicious of taking on military roles outside their continent. Even within Europe, the Europeans looked to the United States to provide the military muscle to deter Russia. General Sir Richard Shirreff, who until 2014 was the senior non-American officer at Nato, complains that 'European countries have effectively disarmed themselves.'[25]

Behind these military statistics there lies a fundamental economic reality. While the headlines focused on whether China or America was the world's largest economy, there was a broader shift going on between West and East. As Nye acknowledged, 'From 2001 to 2010, the West's share of the world economy shrank by 10.33 percentage points, more than the combined loss of the previous forty years.'[26] More of the world's wealth is being generated in Asia and that, almost inevitably, will translate into more of the world's military power also being generated in Asia. Indeed, while Western military spending is going down, an arms race of historic proportions is underway in Asia. Shivshankar Menon, India's National Security Adviser between 2010 and 2014, comments that 'Asia-Pacific has seen the greatest arms build-up ever in the last few decades.'[27]

Even within Asia, America's allies are spending less than its potential adversaries, such as China. Australia, although it was one of the leading cheerleaders for increased US military involvement in the Pacific, has consistently fallen below the 2% of GDP benchmark for military spending – a situation that, in 2014, the Abbott government promised to rectify over the course of the next decade.[28] A frightened Japan announced its largest ever defence budget in 2015 – but Japanese spending was still dwarfed by that of China. And there were clear limits to how far Japan could bolster its military, given the country's colossal national debt of over 200% of GDP.

The failure of America's friends and allies to share the burden of maintaining Western military dominance threatens to turn one of the US's greatest strength – its network of allies – into a potential liability. In making the case for continued American dominance of the global system, Nye had noted that 'Washington has some 60 treaty allies; China has few . . . Of the 150 largest countries in the world, nearly 100 lean towards the United States, while 21 lean against.'[29] However, allies that are too weak to defend themselves – but which enjoy a security guarantee from the United States – risk dragging America into conflicts that it might otherwise avoid.

Under the circumstances, the temptation for the US to pull back from its global commitments is likely to increase. That option came to seem more viable with the energy revolution, brought about by America's successful exploitation of shale oil and gas. Shale had hardly featured on the world energy scene when Obama took power in 2009, but in little more than five years the explosive growth of the industry transformed the global energy picture. By 2014, Daniel Yergin, one of the world's leading energy analysts, could predict that 'The US is going to give Saudi Arabia and Russia a run for their money in terms of being the world's number-one oil producer.'[30]

The shale revolution dramatically reduced America's dependence on imported oil, making it much more feasible for the US to pull back from its global commitments. If America is no longer dependent on imported oil from the Gulf, why exactly does it need to continue to maintain massive naval and air bases in Bahrain and Qatar? Why, for that matter, does America need to insist on naval dominance in the Pacific, when the oil that sails through the Strait of Malacca is bound for China, not California?

In the ranks of the US foreign-policy establishment, it is rare for these questions to be debated openly. Ever since the Cold War, the US has remained determined to retain its global dominance – almost as an end in itself. As the Pentagon's Defense Planning Guidance had proclaimed in March 1992, just three months after the dissolution of the Soviet Union, 'Our first objective is to prevent the reemergence of a new rival . . . This requires that we endeavor to prevent any hostile power from dominating a region whose resources would, under consolidated control, be sufficient to generate global power. These regions include Western Europe, East Asia, the territory of the former Soviet Union and southwest Asia.'[31] One senior member of the Obama administration put it to me rather more succinctly when he commented that 'the United States is addicted to primacy'.[32]

Sometimes when discussing the roots of America's 'addiction' to primacy with senior US policymakers, I found that the conversation became almost circular. Using the US navy to push back against China's ambitions in Asia was, for example, justified on the grounds that not to do so would corrode American power. It was not felt necessary to examine why the erosion of US power was obviously a bad thing. That was simply assumed. If this kind of reflexive defence of American power was so ingrained even in the 'weak' Obama administration, it was even more pronounced in the chest-thumping wing of the nationalist right in America.

Around the world, however, the Obama years still saw a growing number of countries question whether the US will ultimately be willing to pay the price for its 'addiction' to primacy. Nothing has raised that question more pointedly than America's unwillingness to deploy its full military might in the Middle East, even as the region has descended into violent anarchy.

The Middle East – the Crumbling of the Western Order

During the Obama years, revolution and then war has engulfed the Middle East. The unwillingness of the United States to intervene and reimpose order has become exhibit one for those who argue that America is in decline as a global power.

America's dominant role in the Middle East has not, however, been ceded to a rival hegemon. One of the reasons that the region is so torn by conflict is that none of the local powers – Saudi Arabia, Iran, Egypt, Israel, the jihadists of Islamic State – is in a position to exert control over the entire region. Nor is there another outside power to take on the role of imperial overseer. Russia's military intervention in Syria in 2015 changed the course of the war there – bolstering the Assad regime, weakening the 'moderate' opposition backed by the West, creating new waves of refugees and making the US look like an impotent bystander. But President Putin's tactical triumph was a risky and draining venture for Russia. And nobody yet imagines that Russia has the power or the regional support to become the dominant power in the Middle East as a whole. The emerging super-powers of Asia – China and India – are also not yet militarily or psychologically ready to intervene in the Middle East. The result has been violent anarchy – the collapse of states, the deaths of hundreds of thousands and the creation of millions of refugees.

Viewed more broadly, the decline of US influence in the Middle East during the Obama years is part of a bigger, historical process of declining Western influence. Throughout the twentieth century, Western nations were – for better or worse – the dominant outside influence in the Middle East. The decline and eventual collapse of the Ottoman Empire, from the mid-nineteenth century onwards, ended the period of Turkish domination of the region. Britain and France, the biggest imperial powers in Europe, carved up the former territories of the Ottoman Empire between them. The borders of the modern states of Syria, Lebanon and Iraq were delineated by the Sykes–Picot agreement of 1916, negotiated by the British and French diplomats Sir Mark Sykes and Francois Georges-Picot. Between the first and second World Wars, the Middle East was essentially divided into French and British zones of influence. After the Second World War, it was the United States that emerged as the dominant power in the Middle East – something that became all too apparent after the Franco-British intervention in the Suez crisis of 1956 was thwarted by a disapproving White House.

Throughout the Cold War, the US jostled with the Soviet Union for influence in the Middle East. In general, it was America that was more successful, securing the most important regional powers – Saudi Arabia, Turkey, Israel and, after 1973, Egypt – as its allies. There were setbacks for US power in the region – most notably the overthrow of the shah of Iran in 1979. But the collapse of the Soviet Union in 1991 removed the major external challenger to American power in the Middle East. That same year, the US assembled a giant inter-national coalition to defeat Saddam Hussein of Iraq, after he had invaded Kuwait. The decisive victory of the 'Desert Storm' campaign underlined America's strategic dominance of the Middle East.

The terrorist attacks on New York and Washington that swiftly became known as 9/11 opened a new phase in America's relations with the Greater Middle East. The administration of George W. Bush launched wars in Afghanistan in 2001 and Iraq in 2003, justified as part of a 'war on terror'. In reality, Bush's aims were far more ambitious than simply inflicting a military defeat on terrorism. His goal, and those of the neoconservatives who influenced him, was to remake the political culture of the Middle East by building democratic states in Iraq and Afghanistan and, ultimately, across the region.

By the time Barack Obama was campaigning for the presidency in 2008, Bush's dream of creating a democratic Iraq as a showcase state had turned into a nightmare of continual warfare and sectarian violence. Some 4,000 US troops had lost their lives in the Iraq War and the total figure for casualties, including civilians and Iraqi troops (while highly contested), was probably over 200,000.[1]

Obama campaigned as a peace candidate, making much of his opposition to the invasion of Iraq. Once in power, he set about extricating the US from its wars in the Greater Middle East and rebuilding US relations with the region – emphasising diplomacy, rather than force. In June 2009, less than six months after being sworn into office, he gave an important speech in Cairo, appealing for a fresh start between Islam and the West. While many of George W. Bush's supporters had been pushing for an attack on Iran's nuclear programme, Obama was determined to avoid yet another US military engagement in the region. The effort to negotiate a nuclear deal with Iran, and then a broader rapprochement, absorbed an enormous amount of American energy (or 'bandwidth' to use the modish Washington phrase) in the early Obama years – and only came to fruition late in his second term in 2015. The president's determination to define a new American approach to the Greater Middle East helped to win him a Nobel Peace Prize shortly after setting foot in the Oval Office – an award that even the Americans found embarrassingly premature.

For his first two years in office, Obama struggled to maintain the uneasy balance between extricating the US from wars in the Middle East while continuing with violent counter-terrorism operations (in particular, the controversial drone strikes in Pakistan and Yemen) and forging a new relationship with the Islamic world.

Then, all these delicate calculations were overturned by the wave of revolutions across the Middle East that soon came to be known as the 'Arab Spring'. The first uprising to shake the Arab world took place in Tunisia in December 2010, after a vegetable seller named Mohamed Bouazizi set himself on fire in protest at local corruption and injustice. Within days, Tunisia was being rocked by nationwide protests against President Zine El Abidine Ben Ali – a dictator of twenty-three years standing with close ties to the French and Saudis.

Within a month, Ben Ali had been toppled and the demonstrations had spread to Egypt. I was in the United States when President Hosni Mubarak was forced from power in Egypt in what became the signature event of the Arab Spring. It was January 2011 and – despite the fact that Mubarak was an old American ally – the reaction in the US media was overwhelmingly positive. Americans appeared to recognise something of their own country's revolutionary past in the pictures from Tahrir Square in Cairo. Commentators rushed to point out that new internet technologies and websites – texting, Twitter, Facebook – had been used to organise the uprising. This too felt rather flattering for the United States. The revolutionaries in Cairo were portrayed as young, pro-Western liberals outwitting fusty old generals by using the latest technology from Silicon Valley.

The overthrow of old established autocracies in the Middle East – first in Tunisia, then in Egypt and in Libya – was initially greeted with a degree of euphoria in the wider West as well as in the US. Many informed Americans had long felt uneasy about the moral compromises involved in embracing Arab dictatorships for reasons of realpolitik. The Arab Spring looked like a chance to resolve those unpleasant ethical dilemmas. By embracing the revolutionaries, the

US could 'put itself on the right side of history' and finally align its interests and its values. What is more, the Arab world finally appeared to be embracing Western values and democracy. Perhaps the Bush administration's hopes for a democratic Middle East would finally be realised – but this time through internal change, rather than outside intervention.

The fact that one of the early organisers of the revolts was an Egyptian executive working for Google appealed to American techno-evangelism. Within days Wael Ghonim was unofficially appointed by the US media as the face of the Egyptian revolution. While some of the veteran Middle East hands in Washington counseled caution about the revolutionary forces that had been unleashed, younger White House aides were caught up in the revolutionary excitement of the moment. As the author James Mann noted, the young idealists in the White House viewed the upheavals in the Arab world as 'an epochal change in line with their own views of themselves as a new generation'.[2] President Obama himself was sensibly more cautious than most, telling his aides 'What I want is for the Google guy to become president. What I think is that this will be a long drawn-out process.'[3]

Obama's instincts were amply vindicated. Visiting Egypt a couple of months after the overthrow of Mubarak, it swiftly became apparent to me that the Western-educated liberals formed a very thin layer at the top of Egyptian society. This, after all, was a country where one in three of the population was illiterate and the most powerful cultural influence was not Facebook – as the West fondly imagined – but fundamentalist Islamist preachers, beamed in by satellite television from the Gulf. Later that year, Wael Ghonim came top of *Time* magazine's list of the hundred most influential people in the world. A year after that, he was living in exile in the United States – forced out by the increasingly radical and illiberal turn in Egyptian politics.

Political Islam in the shape of the long-repressed Muslim Brotherhood – and the even more fundamentalist Salafist forces – was the rising force in the new Egypt. In April 2011, I met the liberals' presidential hopeful, Mohamed ElBaradei, at a country club on the outskirts of Cairo. A charming and gentle man, ElBaradei was a former senior official at the United Nations, who told me that he was now more comfortable speaking in English than Arabic. He was the kind of new leader that the West yearned to see emerge from the Egyptian morass. Yet, as ElBaradei admitted to me, even he was baffled and alarmed by some of the emerging Islamist forces in Egypt: 'Some of them, well, there is no common ground with them,' he confided. 'They want a completely theocratic state.'[4]

ElBaradei never stood a hope of winning the Egyptian presidency. The elections in 2012 saw the Muslim Brotherhood's candidate, Mohamed Morsi, become president. The Egyptian revolution had not made the country more 'Western'. Instead, in Egypt and much of the Arab world, it had unleashed Islamist political forces that were deeply antagonistic to Western ideas. But faced with the electoral success of the Muslim Brotherhood, the Obama administration and the European Union felt compelled to stick with their own Western democratic principles and to give the Brotherhood a chance of governing.

That chance was ended by a bloody Egyptian counter-revolution in June 2013, which overthrew the Brotherhood and restored a military government to power. Once again, the US and the EU were faced with a dilemma. Idealism suggested that they should stand by democratic principles and condemn the coup. Realpolitik suggested embracing the coup and re-forging a strategic partnership with Egypt. In the event, both the Americans and the Europeans adopted an ambiguous middle ground that ended up antagonising everybody. The Islamists of the Muslim Brotherhood believed that all their suspicions about Western double-dealing had been vindicated and accused the CIA of being behind the Egyptian coup. But the new Egyptian government and its Saudi allies would not forgive the Americans for their role in pushing Mubarak from power and allegedly embracing the Muslim Brotherhood. The new Egyptian government under Field Marshal el-Sisi attempted to rally support at home by embracing a virulent nationalism, combined with strong anti-American rhetoric. In February 2015, President Putin became the first leader of a major power to visit Sisi in Cairo – thoughtfully presenting his host with a Kalashnikov rifle as a mark of esteem.

The regional turmoil unleashed by the Arab Spring forced the Obama administration, against its better judgement, to spend more and more of its time on the Middle East – just at the time that it was trying to 'rebalance' American foreign policy towards East Asia. As Philip Gordon, director of the Middle East department of the National Security Council during Obama's second term, explained to me: 'The White House is often about crisis management. And, in foreign policy, 90% of the crises are in the Middle East.' For those who work in the West Wing of the White House, the pressure of these crises is relentless – which is partly why it is almost unheard of for any senior official, except the president and vice president, to last the entire course of a two-term presidency.

By the latter stages of the Obama administration, the US was experiencing the worst of both worlds in the Middle East. It was far more deeply involved in the affairs of the region than Obama had ever wanted or intended. And yet, simultaneously, American power was being challenged in the Middle East as never before. Both developments had significant implications for America's ability to refocus its foreign policy on Asia. The time and energy spent on Middle Eastern affairs inevitably made it much harder to 'rebalance' towards Asia. And the fact that US power in the Middle East was clearly ebbing had implications for the perception of American power in Asia. If the US was perceived as weak in the Middle East, it was more likely that China would also see it as potentially weak in Asia.

The Obama administration's Middle Eastern dilemmas were a perfect illustration of the way in which world events are always likely to overturn preconceived notions about foreign-policy strategy. As a candidate, Obama had campaigned to get America out of wars in the Greater Middle East, in particular in Iraq and Afghanistan.

As president, his major foreign-policy insight was the pivot to Asia. And yet events kept dragging him back to the Middle East.

By 2013, when the coup against the Muslim Brotherhood took place in Cairo, the whole of the Middle East was in ferment. As well as the turmoil in Egypt, in 2011 there had been uprisings in Libya, Syria and parts of the Gulf, including Bahrain. Improvising wildly, the West had given military support to the Libyan uprising, stayed out of the Syrian civil war and tacitly encouraged the repression of the uprising in Bahrain, which threatened the Gulf monarchies that were close Western allies. Amidst all this, the White House team struggled to retain the original focus on Asia – and the president's determination not to get sucked into fresh conflicts in the Middle East.

When Colonel Gaddafi's troops threatened to overrun Benghazi in Libya in 2011 and massacre the inhabitants, Tom Donilon, the head of the NSC, and Robert Gates, the Defense Secretary, were amongst those who counselled against intervention. Other close advisers to the president, including Hillary Clinton and Samantha Power who later became US ambassador to the UN, argued that America had to intervene to prevent a humanitarian catastrophe – arguments that were supported by the French and British governments. In the event, President Obama settled for a compromise. The US would lead the first wave of missile strikes; but European air forces, led by the French and the British, would carry out the subsequent air raids – with American logistical support. Above all, there would be no question of US troops on the ground. This was the policy that was named – in an anonymous briefing by a White House official – 'leading from behind'.

This cautious policy on Libya allowed the Obama team to argue that, amidst the maelstrom of events, they were maintaining their determination to 'rebalance' US foreign policy away from the Middle East. But, in 2013 and 2014, that policy was temporarily abandoned. Four key events sucked America back into the Middle East: the arrival of John Kerry at the State Department, the civil war in Syria, the prospect of a diplomatic breakthrough with Iran and – above all – the rise of the militant jihadists, who styled themselves as 'Islamic State'.

By the time John Kerry made it to the office of Secretary of State, in early 2013, he was already sixty-nine-years old. Eight years previously, he had missed becoming president of the United States by the narrowest of margins – fewer than 120,000 votes in Ohio had swung the 2004 presidential election for George W. Bush. The State Department offered Kerry his last opportunity to make his mark on history – and he was determined to do it in the most traditional of arenas for American diplomacy: the Middle East. Within weeks, the new man had embarked on a rush of shuttle diplomacy aimed at restarting the moribund peace process between the Israelis and the Palestinians. To some observers it looked like Kerry was stuck in a time warp – imagining himself to be a Henry Kissinger or a Bill Clinton – striving to create peace between Israelis and Arabs.

Even within the Middle East, the Israeli–Palestinian stand-off hardly looked like the top priority – with Egypt in turmoil and Syria in flames. As for the pivot to Asia, it seemed to have been forgotten, as Kerry shuttled to and from Jerusalem. The Chinese noted the new Secretary of State's preoccupation with the Middle East with a mixture of bemusement and delight. In Beijing, that summer of 2013, I discovered that Chinese policymakers had interpreted Hillary Clinton's and Tom Donilon's rebalancing as an effort to block the rise of China. If Kerry was determined to go back to the old policy of pouring money, treasure and attention into the Middle East – so much the better from Beijing's point of view.

Kerry's obsession with Middle Eastern diplomacy might have ended up as little more than a personal idiosyncrasy had it not been for developments in Syria. Amidst the unfolding horror of the Syrian civil war, Obama had initially stuck grimly to his determination not to get involved militarily in the region. In 2013, he had come perilously close to launching air strikes on the Assad regime, to enforce America's 'red line' over the use of chemical weapons. The president and his team were initially relieved when a diplomatic initiative offered an alternative to military action. But the US still paid a heavy price for its undignified vacillation over the Syrian red line.

The episode swiftly came to be seen as emblematic of American 'weakness' around the world. It had strengthened the global impression that the US was increasingly unwilling to use its mighty military – and that American politics was so bitter and inward-looking that Washington politicians would willingly damage the nation's international standing, by rejecting the president's call for air strikes in return for a small political gain at home. Even before the Syrian crisis, some critics of the Obama administration had charged the president with presiding over a catastrophic decline in American global influence. Vali Nasr, a prominent American academic who had served in the first Obama administration, lamented that 'We have gone from leading everywhere, to leading nowhere.'[5]

The irony was that Obama's refusal to punish the Assad regime for crossing his red line did not even achieve its aim of keeping the US out of war in the Middle East. In 2014, the conflict in Syria – which by then had probably cost 200,000 lives, around 40% of them civilians – finally pulled the US back in. Almost off the radar, ISIL had been making significant territorial gains in both Syria and Iraq. In June of 2014, ISIL shocked the world by seizing Mosul, Iraq's second city. More than a decade after the US had led an invasion of Iraq as part of the 'war on terror', a group that was even more extreme than al-Qaeda had gained control of a significant part of Iraqi territory.

Even more shocking for television audiences in the US was the beheading of Western hostages captured by the group. In response, President Obama – beset by charges of weakness at home and fearing that ISIL might even take Baghdad – took the step that he had long resisted. He pledged once again to commit American military might to change the course of the wars in Iraq and Syria. Speaking about US involvement, the president also made it clear that 'this is going to be a long-term project'. Even so, the US and its allies insisted that they would not repeat the mistake of the invasion of Iraq in 2003. This time there would be no boots on the ground.

The Obama administration's belated commitment to a new air war in Syria and Iraq in 2014 did little to silence the chorus of voices claiming that American influence in the Middle East was on the wane. That was partly because the American commitment still stopped a long way short of 'whatever it takes'. Indeed a year of US-led bombing raids was unable to inflict a decisive defeat on Islamic State, which by the middle of 2015 still controlled an area spanning parts of Iraq and Syria that was the size of Britain. The sense that the US had lost control in the region was further heightened when Russia startled the West by beginning its own bombing raids in Syria in late 2015 in support of President Assad.

Western policy as a whole was an incoherent mess. In Syria, the US was simultaneously committed to the removal of the Assad regime and to the defeat of the jihadist rebels fighting the Assads. Together with their European allies, the US made an unconvincing effort to inject some coherence into this policy, by training and supporting Syrian 'moderates' who opposed both the jihadists and the Assads. But even in the White House few believed that the Syrian 'moderates' stood much chance of prevailing in the conflict – particularly once the Russians began bombing them in earnest.

The confusion surrounding US policy in the Middle East sowed continuing doubt amongst America's traditional allies in the region about US staying power. For amidst all the military turmoil in the region, the big picture now is that a once settled regional order – which had the US at its very heart – is now in turmoil.

Traditionally, American power in the region has rested on 'special relationships' with four very different countries: Turkey, Egypt, Saudi Arabia and Israel. But all of those relationships have become much shakier during the Obama years. The erratic and emotional rule of President Erdogan in Turkey – and his Islamist and regional pretensions (see pages 202–207)– has gravely damaged Washington's special relationship with Ankara. The Egyptian generals who retook power in Cairo in 2013 were also very slow to forgive the Obama administration for what they regarded as the 'betrayal' of Mubarak.

The deeply conservative Sunni monarchy in Saudi Arabia bitterly resented the Obama administration's flirtation with revolution in Egypt – as well as its slowness to intervene against the Shia regime led by the Assads in Syria. Above all, the Saudis feared America's efforts to strike a deal with their enemies in Iran over Tehran's nuclear programme. The announcement of just such a deal in the summer of 2015 was hailed by the Obama administration as marking a decisive breakthrough in the fight against nuclear proliferation. But the Saudis share Israel's fear that the Iran deal is a naive sell-out that will not only fail to put a permanent stop to Iran's nuclear ambitions, but that might also empower Tehran to pursue a more expansionist policy across the region.

In the background, there is also a Saudi fear that the shale revolution in the US is gradually removing the underlying rationale for an American commitment to the security of Saudi Arabia. It is indeed true that the origins of the US–Saudi special relationship lie in the oil beneath the Saudi desert. But by 2015, as the US itself was moving to become the world's largest oil producer, Saudi Arabia began to hedge against its reliance on the American security guarantee. One alarming development is the burgeoning of close nuclear co-operation between Saudi Arabia and Pakistan. In Western intelligence circles, it is widely feared that the Pakistani bomb is a surrogate Saudi bomb – which could be moved to Saudi Arabia at a moment's notice, should the security situation in the Middle East require it. The Saudis have also begun to do much more to cultivate the largest customer for their oil – which is now China, not the United States. By 2014, more than two-thirds of Saudi oil was being sold to Asian markets, with China the largest single customer, and just 8% was going to the United States. The US ships that guard the Strait of Hormuz in the Gulf – ensuring that Saudi oil can continue to reach its markets – are essentially safeguarding China's energy needs. The first foreign trip made by King Abdullah of Saudi Arabia, after coming to power in 2005, was to China and India. As Bruce Reidel, an aide in the Obama White House put it, 'Long before the American pivot, Saudi Arabia had reoriented its economic and policy priorities to South and East Asia.'[6]

Perhaps the most surprising change in the American position in the Middle East has come in the fourth pillar of its alliance system in the region – the US relationship with Israel. Benjamin Netanyahu, the Israeli prime minister throughout the Obama years, is practised in presenting a forbidding visage to the world. Western television viewers are used to seeing him issuing grim-faced warnings about the threat of a nuclear Iran or uncompromising justifications for Israeli army actions in Gaza. But the Netanyahu I met in his office in Jerusalem towards the end of 2013 was a rather different character. Leaning back in his chair, puffing expansively on a cigar with a large map of the Middle East behind him, Netanyahu seemed relaxed, even optimistic as he surveyed Israel's position in the world.

As we spoke, it became apparent that Netanyahu's good mood stemmed partly from the openings that he saw for his country in Asia. The previous May, he had visited China and had received the kind of lavish, ego-boosting welcome that the Chinese are especially adept at delivering. In many hours of meetings with political and business leaders, Netanyahu had discovered a deep Chinese fascination with Israel's prowess in high technology. China was in the midst of a foreign investment boom – the 'going out' policy that was intended to diversify the country's economy and to provide a safe and productive home for the billions that China had amassed during the years of growth. In 2013 China had invested $107 billion overseas of which $7 billion had gone into Israel alone – not a bad return for a country of just 8 million people. For the Israelis, this surge in Chinese investment made a welcome contrast with the burgeoning 'BDS' (boycott, divestment and sanctions) movement in Europe and the US. The ambition of most Israeli tech start-ups was still to list on the stock exchange in New York. But, for a growing number, particularly those with an expertise in agriculture, water or cyber security, China also looked like an increasingly promising market and source of investment.

The Israelis and the Chinese saw something in each other. As part of their flattery campaign, the Chinese emphasised that the two nations were both ancient cultures, with a strong emphasis on education. They also seemed to appreciate each other's willingness to focus on business and to put politics (and human rights) to one side. As one Netanyahu aide put it to me, 'We spent seven hours with the Chinese leadership. You know how long they spent on the Palestinians? Roughly twenty seconds.' The Chinese, for their part, also saw Israel as likely to welcome investment in high technology, without raising awkward objections about politics or national security. As Yasheng Huang of MIT put it at a conference in Tel Aviv in 2014, 'The Chinese feel more comfortable investing in Israel than in the US because there is not so much political hostility or suspicion.'[7] America has watched the burgeoning Israeli–Chinese relationship with a degree of discomfort – intervening behind the scenes on a couple of occasions, to warn their Israeli allies not to sell sensitive military technology to China.

China was not the only potential opening that the Israelis spotted in Asia. The advent of the Modi government in India in the middle of 2014 brought about a distinct change in Indian foreign policy. As one of the leaders of the Non-Aligned Movement, India had traditionally championed the cause of the Palestinians. But the Modi government's preoccupation with the threat of Islamist terrorism and its own Hindu nationalism meant that it was much more in tune with Israeli concerns. Rajnath Singh, Home Secretary in the Modi government in 2014, made his first official trip overseas to Israel to discuss defence and security issues. Under Modi, India also chose to spend over $500 million on Israel's Spike anti-tank missile, in preference to the American Javelin missile. Within months, the Modi administration was being called 'the most pro-Israel government in India's history'[8].

Previous Indian administrations had kept their close security co-operation with Israel under wraps. As one Indian analyst joked to me, 'The Israelis complained that we treated them like a mistress and would only meet them in secret.'⁹ But under the new government in Delhi, the intimacy of the relationship was increasingly out in the open. When Netanyahu won re-election in 2015, his victory was greeted with ill-disguised gloom in Washington. By contrast, Narendra Modi tweeted his congratulations to the Israeli prime minister – in Hebrew. That same year it was announced that Modi would become the first Indian prime minister ever to visit Israel.

Israel's tilt to Asia had a wider significance. To both its friends and its foes, Israel was often portrayed as a lonely outpost of the West in the Middle East. Israel's friends saw the nation as an isolated democracy. Its foes argued that the Jewish state was essentially an outpost of colonialism. But both sides agreed that Israel was part of the wider West. During the Obama years, however, even Israel began to look east – and to seek to develop new relations with a rising Asia. Political changes in both Asia and the US underpinned this change. Relations between Israel and the US became increasingly fractious, as the Netanyahu government repeatedly defied the Obama administration's calls to halt the expansion of Israeli settlements on occupied Palestinian land.

As relations between the US and Israeli governments deteriorated, so many in Israel, particularly on the right, looked to Asia as an alternative outlet. Avigdor Lieberman, who served as Israel's foreign minister under Netanyahu, put it bluntly when he said 'Ties between Israel and the US are weakening. The Americans today are dealing with too many challenges . . . and they also have economic and immigration problems.'¹⁰ For Naftali Bennett, the rising star of the Israeli far right, America was feckless and Europe was intrinsically anti-Semitic. Instead, Israel should look to the rising economies of Asia.

It helped Israel that China under Xi, India under Modi and Russia under Putin were all increasingly preoccupied by the threat of Islamist terrorism at home. All three governments had no qualms about using harsh methods and military repression in the struggle against Islamist-inspired separatism in Xinjiang, Kashmir and Chechnya. As a result, none were liable to have a deep-rooted objection to the many civilian deaths caused by Israeli tactics in Gaza – in marked contrast to the outrage that successive Israeli wars in Gaza have provoked in the West.

. The views expressed by Lieberman were fairly common across the Middle East during the Obama years. In a period of turmoil, revolution, brutal wars and deep antagonisms between nations and sectarian groups, one common theme – bringing together the many feuding parties – was a belief that US power was on the wane in the Middle East.

The notion that the US under Obama was 'weak' had become a global theme by the end of the Obama years. I heard it everywhere – in Moscow, Beijing, Singapore, Warsaw, Tokyo, even in Paris. But the origins of that charge of weakness were rooted in what the Obama administration had done and – more significantly – had not done in the Middle East. It was Obama's reluctance to use military power in the Middle East and to enforce his self-proclaimed 'red lines' – particularly over the use of chemical weapons that had underpinned the idea of a 'weak Obama' and an 'America in retreat'. As a result, even the architects of America's pivot to Asia felt that the US had no option but to reassert its 'toughness' in the Middle East – even if this involved continuing to waste time and resources on the region. Kurt Campbell, the intellectual architect of the pivot, wrote that 'How the US fares in the rest of the world has critical implications for its long-term role in Asia. Any effort to cut and run from the hard times that currently hang over the Middle East . . . would have negative consequences for US staying power and security commitments in Asia as a whole.'[11]

To be fair to President Obama, his reluctance to use force in the Middle East was both entirely consistent with the platform on which he had originally run for the presidency, and almost certainly wise. As the president realised – and his critics seemed to have forgotten – American military might had been remarkably effective in winning battlefield victories in the Middle East and remarkably ineffective in creating lasting political stability. This was a lesson that was learnt not just by Obama. Robert Gates, the president's first and most thoughtful Secretary of State for Defense, was by no means uncritical of Obama. But it was he who said that any future Defense Secretary who recommended that ground troops should be deployed in the Middle East or Asia would need 'his head examined'.[12]

Yet the way in which Obama had resisted the pressure to intervene militarily in the Middle East created the impression that the world's pre-eminent power was now deeply reluctant to deploy military force. Given that the world's security system was constructed around American alliances, red lines and security guarantees, this was a potentially dangerous idea. It risked encouraging powers that disliked a US-dominated world – in particular China and Russia – to see if they could get away with challenging American power.

What was often missed, however, in the lamentations about American lack of resolve in the Middle East was the even greater absence of the other pillar of Western power – the European Union. The political order that was unravelling in the Middle East in 2015, in the wake of the Arab Spring, was one that had been constructed by European colonialists almost a century earlier through the Sykes–Picot agreement of 1916.

It is also Europe that is threatened much more directly than the US by the collapse of the modern Middle East. There were many more European citizens than Americans who had signed up to fight as jihadists with ISIL. The long-standing fear of European security agencies – that jihadist fighters would return to Europe from Syria and then commit terrorist attacks – were finally borne out in two separate terror attacks in Paris, in January and November 2015. The refugees flowing out of Syria were, by that time, also arriving in increasing numbers on the shores of the European Union. In 2015 over 1.8 million would-be refugees from the rest of the world entered the European Union – with Germany alone receiving 1.1 million. The largest single group came from Syria – with Iraq, Afghanistan and Iran also providing sizeable contingents.

The refugee flows into Europe are a political and humanitarian problem in the here and now. But they also represent a historic reversal of the migration patterns, established during the centuries when European powers dominated the world.

In the colonial era Europe practised a sort of demographic imperialism, with white Europeans emigrating to the four corners of the world. In North America and Australasia, indigenous populations were subdued and often killed, and whole continents were turned into offshoots of Europe. Colonies all over the world were settled by European immigrants, while at the same time several millions were forcibly migrated from Africa to the New World as slaves. In 1900, at the height of the imperial era, European countries represented about 25% of the world population and Europe was still sending settlers all over the world. By 2015, by contrast, the roughly 500 million people in the twenty-eight nations of the EU accounted for just 7% of world population. Without immigration, the populations of countries like Germany and Italy would fall steadily. By contrast, the populations of the Middle East and Africa are booming – with citizens that are, on average, younger and poorer than Europeans. The population of Egypt, for example, doubled from 40 million to more than 80 million between 1975 and 2015. The population of Africa, which is currently more than 1 billion, is projected by the UN to be over 2.5 billion by 2050. Even without the current wars across the Middle East, these demographic and economic pressures will ensure that immigration into Europe from the Greater Middle East and Africa will be a vexed issue for many years to come.

And yet while the Europeans have even more at stake in the remaking of the Middle East than the Americans, they have proved even less effective in responding to the turmoil unleashed by the Arab Spring. In a flush of enthusiasm, Britain and France played the largest role in the air campaign against Libya in 2011. But when post-Gaddafi Libya collapsed into near anarchy – with the internationally recognised government driven out of Tripoli in 2013 and forced to meet on a cruise ship off the Libyan coast – the French and British governments relapsed into something like embarrassed silence. The only real sign that they had learnt the lesson of the failures of Libyan and Iraqi interventions was in their initial reluctance to join the American bombing campaign in Syria.

For some of the more thoughtful European policymakers, however, the state of the Middle East was a chastening lesson about diminishing European power. Pierre Vimont, a veteran French diplomat who served as the EU's senior diplomatic official from 2010–14, reflected that 'Europe's reaction to the Arab Spring was totally underpowered. We tried a 1990s solution. But we're now in a more competitive world. These countries have options beyond Europe.'[13] What Vimont meant was that in the 1990s, after the Berlin Wall had collapsed, the EU had had the luxury of moving slowly and deliberately in eastern Europe, and conditioning aid and assistance on thoroughgoing reform. But a generation later, by the time of the Arab Spring, Europe was in the midst of a profound economic crisis and there were other powers competing for space in the Middle East – from radical jihadists, to fabulously wealthy Gulf States, rising Asian nations and a resurgent Russia. As Vimont noted, with more than a touch of despair, 'We Europeans are nowhere. We don't know what we want to do.' The time when 'the West' could simply impose a blueprint on the Middle East was long gone.

The fate of the Middle East in the Obama years illustrated an important point about Easternisation. America's relative decline is just part of a bigger phenomenon – which is the relative decline of Western power as a whole. As America has struggled with the burdens of being the 'sole superpower', it has naturally looked across the

Atlantic for support and 'burden-sharing' from its fellow democracies in Europe. And yet the European powers are in precipitous decline as global political players – a decline that became increasingly evident during the Obama years.

Europe and its Well-Sealed Windows

Go to most of the capital cities of the European Union and you will be visiting the capital of a former empire. The ruins of the Acropolis in Athens speak of the glories of ancient Greece. In Italy, the Colosseum and the Pantheon are reminders of when the Roman Empire defined the civilised world. In Vienna, the grandeur of the Ringstrasse dates back to the late nineteenth century when the city was still the centre of a great empire, rather than the capital of a nation of 8.5 million people. Madrid was once the headquarters of an empire that controlled most of Latin America. Lisbon contains statues of Henry the Navigator, Vasco da Gama and Magellan, the patron and explorers who set out to discover the New World and laid the foundation for a global empire. Ceremonial marches in Paris still end at the Arc de Triomphe, which commemorates the victories of Napoleon's armies. Brussels, now the capital of the European Union, was once the capital of the Belgian Empire and much of the city's inherited wealth stems from the colonisation of the Congo. As for London, my parents' generation grew up in a world where large parts of world maps, including India, were still coloured pink – to signify that they were parts of the British Empire.

By 2009, when an economic crisis erupted in Europe, the age of European imperialism in Asia and elsewhere had been over for roughly half a century. Most Europeans were not, however, prepared for the idea that the slide in Europe's global power might have further to go – accelerated by the economic shock that hit the continent in the early twenty-first century. It was not simply that Europe's voice would count less in the world. The real threat was that Europe's desire to exist as an island of prosperity and political decency in a turbulent world would gradually be put at risk by a loss of political power.

The process of Easternisation means not just that Europe no longer controls large swathes of the globe. That has been the case for decades. It also means that Europe is increasingly vulnerable to political, social and economic trends in the rest of the world that it cannot control – but which pose direct and indirect threats to European stability, prosperity and even peace.

Different parts of the world pose different sorts of challenge and threat. Even before the financial crisis of 2008, Europe had been struggling with low growth and high unemployment. The prolonged and intractable nature of these problems means that more and more economists are giving voice to the idea that competition with low-cost producers in Asia, in particular China, has contributed to the European economic malaise. This is a notion that was once shunned by orthodox economists, but that is becoming increasingly mainstream.

The sense of gloom was particularly acute in southern European countries, which were hit by an acute debt crisis, in the years after the financial plunge of 2009. In countries such as Spain and Ireland, banks had to be rescued leading to a surge in public debt, cuts in government spending and soaring unemployment. The poster child for the European debt crisis was Greece. After it emerged in 2009 that the Greek government had been covering up the extent of its debts, the country lost the confidence of international investors. The Greeks – like the Portuguese and Irish – were compelled to accept official bailouts from the rest of the European Union and from the IMF.

Italy avoided a bailout. And yet the problems of Italy demonstrated that Europe's economic challenges were not simply to do with debt. They also reflected the difficulty Europeans would have in sustaining high living standards and generous welfare states, in a world in which European workers had to compete directly with much less well-paid Asian workers. In the five years after the financial crisis, Italy lost 25% of its industrial capacity. The problem was not just the collapse in European demand caused by a deep recession. It was also that Italian manufacturers, the traditional backbone of the economy, were finding it increasingly hard to compete with competitors in Asia. Ferdinando Giugliano, an Italian economist,[1] told me an anecdote that captured the phenomenon. A neighbour of his in Naples had run a factory making gloves – the kind of small, artisanal manufacturing in which Italy had traditionally excelled. One by one, the factory had lost its clients to cheaper Chinese-made gloves until it was reliant on a single, large customer, the Italian military. But eventually, even Italy's armed forces – under increasing budgetary pressure – reluctantly decided that they too could no longer afford to always 'buy Italian'. The Neapolitan glove factory was forced to lay off most of its staff.

Some of Italy's most successful businesspeople were coming to the reluctant conclusion that long-term trends were moving against the country. In the early stages of the financial crisis, I sat down in Milan with Carlo De Benedetti, who had been one of Italy's leading industrialists through much of the post-war period. De Benedetti sketched out for me how vulnerable a heavily indebted Italy was to any rise in interest rates and how depressed the country seemed. Then he added, 'Now, when I go to China, I'm reminded of how Italy was in the 1950s. That sense of optimism as families get their first television, their first washing machine, their first car.'[2]

Yet Italy still looks like a promised land when viewed from the much poorer nations on the other side of the Mediterranean. In the first six months of 2014, as the Middle East disintegrated, over 100,000 refugees arrived in Italy by sea. For a country that was entering its sixth year of recession, the extra burden was far from welcome. There, as elsewhere in Europe, political parties that peddled in anti-immigrant rhetoric are gaining steadily in support. The blowback from the turbulence and war in the Middle East has increased the sense of social and political crisis within Europe.

The disintegrating frontiers of the modern Middle East date back to the heyday of European colonialism, in particular the agreement of 1916, in which Britain and France drew up the borders of the modern states of Syria, Iraq and Lebanon. A century later, however, European powers have definitively lost the ability to impose political order on the Middle East. The British and French first discovered this as long ago as 1956, when they made a failed attempt to depose the Egyptian leader, Gamal Abdel Nasser. In 2011, the same two nations led a Western intervention in Libya, in an effort to prevent the Gaddafi regime massacring its opponents in the city of Benghazi. This time, the British and the French received crucial support from the Americans and other Nato allies – and did succeed in overthrowing a Middle Eastern leader. But the Europeans' reluctance to put troops on the ground after the fall of Gaddafi meant that they left behind a political vacuum, which turned into a failed state. Most of the refugees who arrived in Italy in 2014 had set off from a lawless Libya.

Failed states in the Middle East, in turn, created havens for jihadist movements intent on taking the fight to Europe itself. Five years after the fall of Gaddafi, the jihadists of Islamic State had established a substantial enclave in Libya. Thousands of European Muslims have travelled to Syria or elsewhere in the Middle East to join Islamic State – and tracking the movements of these EU-passport holders has become a major preoccupation of Western security agencies.

The terrorist threat has, in turn, heightened the controversy over mass migration into Europe from Africa, South Asia and the Middle

East. This immigration – legal and illegal – is changing the character of European societies and politics. Europe's policy of open borders and free migration within the EU meant that refugees arriving in southern Europe were quickly able to move towards the stronger economies in the north. The impact on Germany, in particular, was extraordinary. The country received 77,651 applicants for political asylum in 2012; 127,000 in 2013; 203,000 in 2014 and over 1 million in 2015.[3] By the summer of 2015, the 'migrant crisis' had become the dominant political issue in Germany and across the EU. Germans initially took pride in the warm welcome that ordinary citizens offered to Syrian refugees. Yet the sheer numbers arriving – and the emergence of far-right and anti-immigration parties in neighbouring nations such as the Netherlands, France and Denmark – raised obvious questions about how long this warm German welcome could last. It also immediately raised tensions within the EU, as Germany attempted to share the refugee burden by attempting to impose mandatory quotas on its reluctant eastern EU neighbours.

Within Germany itself, the refugee crisis undermined the political position of the woman who, for most of the previous decade, had been the most successful and powerful politician in Europe – Chancellor Angela Merkel. Asked to pick an image that exemplified modern Germany, Chancellor Merkel had once tellingly replied, 'I think of well-sealed windows. No other country can make such well-sealed and nice windows.'[4] Yet even Germany's well-sealed windows were ultimately not enough to insulate the country from the destruction and violence in the Middle East. When hundreds of thousands of refugees from Syria, Iraq, Afghanistan and elsewhere began to arrive in Germany, it became clear that a rejection of militarism and power-politics could not be a complete answer to the international challenges facing the Berlin government. As Leon Trotsky once put it, 'You may not be interested in war. But war is interested in you.'

Germany's yearning for a quiet life, insulated from the world's troubles, is understandable, given the country's desire to put the horrors of the twentieth century behind it. And yet the character of modern Germany is inevitably shaped by memories of the Nazi past – which have bequeathed a deep and lasting suspicion of the use of military force. That has made Germany an important part of the story of a more reticent West, in an Easternising world.

The character and aspirations of modern Germany are reflected in the architecture of modern Berlin. The chancellor's office looks like a giant, glass eyeball – staring out at the Berlin railway station and across a vast expanse of lawn to the redesigned Reichstag, the seat of the German Parliament. But while the Reichstag is a building redolent of history – the site of the fire that allowed Hitler to consolidate power in 1933 and of the final Russian seizure of Berlin in 1945 – the new Chancellery is meant to signify a fresh start. Its glass walls signify transparency. Its clean wood-floored corridors, muted colours and quiet, open spaces – so different from the concrete of the Nazi-era buildings – are reminiscent of an upscale Scandinavian hotel. Yet while the style of the modern German government is meant to signify a decisive break with the past, the economic crisis that broke out in Europe in 2008 had placed Germany in an oddly familiar situation – as the strongest power in Europe.

It took a financial crisis to both reveal and accentuate this shift in power to Berlin. It was the German government that was forced to construct and, in large part, fund the bailouts of countries like Greece and Portugal. While the bailout deals were thrashed out at European Union summits in Brussels, all of the twenty-eight nations represented there knew that the key decisions would be made in Berlin, because Germany would be the largest single contributor to the bailout funds. As a result Angela Merkel became the key powerbroker. The result was that Germany – the country with the largest population and biggest economy in the EU – emerged as indisputably the most powerful country within Europe. European unification, it had often been said, was intended to create a 'European Germany', rather than a 'German Europe'. But as most of the EU floundered economically,

German leadership and power within the EU became harder and harder to deny.

Given the fears that the prospect of a powerful Germany can still arouse, it was fortunate that the dominant political figure in Germany in this period was a calm, middle-aged woman. The fact that Merkel's nickname is 'Mutti' (or Mummy) was a perhaps subconscious rebuke to those who feared that another powerful German leader would inevitably aspire to being another Fuhrer (a word that translates both as leader and father). Nonetheless some other EU leaders began to see Merkel as not so much a mother figure, but as a headmistress. In 2012, a leading Greek politician described to me the chilling effect the new headmistress of Europe had on her fellow leaders at gatherings of European conservatives: 'When she walks into the room, everybody falls silent.'

It was not just the debt-plagued countries of southern Europe that became increasingly aware of their dependence on Berlin. As the British struggled to carve out a new deal for themselves within the EU, they became steadily more conscious of how badly they needed Chancellor Merkel's assent. As one senior adviser to David Cameron put it to me, 'I know we have put all our eggs in the German basket. But, frankly, there isn't another basket.' The British hope that Merkel could 'deliver' a new deal for the UK on Europe was exaggerated. Many of the changes that Britain wanted – concerning immigration and welfare, for example – required the consent of all the other twenty-seven members of the EU. But it was certainly true that Germany's support and agreement was an indispensable starting point.

This German pre-eminence was a remarkable break with the traditional European way of doing things which – in the post-war period – had relied on a Franco-German partnership. During the early years of the euro crisis, the pretence of Franco-German equality had been preserved. Journalists were encouraged to use the term 'Merkozy' – a merging of the surnames of Merkel and Nicolas Sarkozy, the then French president – to describe Europe's governing partnership. But, behind the scenes, close observers knew where the real power lay. Jose Manuel Barroso, until 2014 the president of the European Commission, the EU's powerful civil service, was known to remark caustically (and in private) that 'France needs Germany to disguise how weak it is, and Germany needs France to disguise how strong it is.'

With the defeat of Sarkozy in the French presidential elections of 2012, the pretence ended. Francois Hollande, Sarkozy's successor, had campaigned against the policies of economic austerity and budget-cutting favoured by Berlin, and promised to bring them to an end. Yet, predictably, he was unable to persuade the Germans to shift course. The relative weakness of the French economy – plagued by high unemployment, rising debt and a looming sense of social crisis – meant that the government in Paris was in an unprecedentedly weak position, as it sought to bargain with Berlin.

It was the same story for Greece, the country that became the symbol and centre of the euro crisis. One hot summer night in July 2015, I was in Syntagma Square in central Athens, watching the crowds celebrate the result of a referendum in which the Greek people had rejected the latest austerity and bail-out package, demanded by Greece's European creditors. Just a week later, the Greek government was forced to retreat and accept an even tougher package after the Germans had threatened effectively to push Greece out of the European single currency. Many on the left in Europe castigated the Germans – claiming that once again they were bullying the smaller nations of Europe. But this judgement struck me as profoundly unfair. In reality, German taxpayers had, albeit reluctantly, funded easily the largest share of successive European bailouts for Greece, which totalled well over 400 billion euros – a staggering sum to throw at a country of just 11 million people. It is hard to imagine that British or American taxpayers would have been similarly generous, faced with the same situation.

Far from revelling in Germany's resurgent power, many policy-makers in Berlin found the situation profoundly uncomfortable. The post-war generation had been brought up to believe that German aspirations to global leadership had led only to disaster and war. In security affairs, Germany took its lead from the United States and the Atlantic alliance. In Europe, Germany worked in close partnership with France to promote an 'ever closer union' of European nations.

The euro crisis changed all that. The world was now look-ing to Germany for a lead. For it was not just other European nations that cared deeply about how Germany would try to resolve the crisis. Given the fact that the European Union was, taken collectively, the largest economy in the world, policy-makers from Washington to Beijing needed to understand German intentions. Germany's insistence on fiscal austerity and budget-balancing in Europe was a source of deep frustration to many in the Obama administration – which wanted the Germans to do more to stimulate the global economy, through Keynesian-style deficit spending.

The idea of resurgent German power was, of course, bound to ring alarm bells in the rest of Europe. During the height of the cri-sis, cartoons appeared in the Greek media showing Angela Merkel in Nazi uniform. My experience, during frequent visits to Berlin throughout the euro crisis, was that the key aides to Chancellor Merkel were amongst the sharpest, most impressive and most civi-lised diplomats anywhere in the world. They lacked the hints of post-imperial pomposity that still clung to some of their French and British counterparts. Nikolaus Meyer-Landrut, Merkel's chief adviser on Europe, and Emily Haber, the head of the foreign ministry and later the interior ministry, were both the children of former German ambassadors. In sharp contrast to the national stereotype of the humourless German, they could both often be sharply funny, as they juggled with the pressures and absurdities of the euro crisis.

My concern about the top German officials was nothing to do with any latent authoritarianism. It was that they were – if anything – too civilised, too grounded in process and the rule of law, to fully comprehend the ruthlessness of Putin's Russia, the national ambitions of a rising China or the domestic risks of fully honouring Germany's legal commitments to refugees. The near-naivety of some of Merkel's circle struck me during the height of the Ukraine crisis in 2014, when the German chancellor was in almost daily contact with Putin. With apparent incredulity, a senior aide to Merkel complained to me that 'Putin has lied to the chancellor' about Russian military involvement in eastern Ukraine. One was tempted to ask – what did the Germans expect?

The real problem for German leadership in Europe, however, was not naivety. It was that Chancellor Merkel was leading a country that yearned for nothing more than a quiet life. The Germans had learnt the lessons of the twentieth century almost too well. As a result, the idea that the military could be the solution to anything seemed to be almost anathema to the German public. It was true that German troops had served in Afghanistan, but their mission was so couched with 'caveats' (for example, a prohibition on night patrols) that Germany's professional soldiers found the whole experience frustrating and humiliating. When any international crisis broke out – whether over Russia, or Syria or the euro – the first instinct of the German public seemed to be to look the other way. Opinion polls consistently showed the German public far more averse to military intervention than their French, British or American counterparts.

Germany's political and diplomatic leadership felt that they needed to both understand and – to some extent – reflect this public mood. On a visit to the Chancellery in the summer of 2013, a few weeks before the German election which would see Merkel triumphantly returned for a third term in office, I found one of her senior aides politely amused by the foreign interest in German intentions. After we had discussed how German policy to Europe might change after the vote (not much, I was assured), my host smiled broadly and remarked, 'You know it's funny, foreigners want to know what the German election will mean for the Middle East or the future of Europe. But we are debating whether to have a "veggie day" in works canteens.'

That insularity extended well beyond European affairs. As policy-makers in Washington grappled with the implications of the rise of China and the turmoil in the Middle East, the most powerful nation in Europe was more than content to be a bystander. When President Assad used chemical weapons in Syria, there were agonised debates in Washington, Paris and London about whether to respond with military force. There was no such debate in Berlin, where it was simply assumed that Germany would not take part.

In the Cold War era, Germany's reluctance to exercise global leadership had not mattered much because France and Britain remained substantial military and economic powers whose commitment to playing a global security role meant that the 'Western alliance' was a phrase that really meant something. But the financial crisis of 2008 forced deep cuts in both French and British military spending. Add that to the insularity of Germany – the most powerful and populous nation in the EU and the fourth-largest economy in the world – and the emerging picture was of a Europe that was dissolving its ability to play a global role.

The reduction in British and French military strength over the past forty years has been breathtaking. By 2013, Britain's Royal Air Force had just one quarter of the number of combat aircraft that it had in the 1970s. The Royal Navy had nineteen destroyers compared to 69 in 1977. In 1990, the UK had twenty-seven submarines and France had seventeen; by 2015, the two countries had seven and six submarines respectively. Exasperated British military commanders complained that their political masters were increasingly living in a semi-fantasy world in which they ordered military operations in far-flung places like Syria or Libya, ignoring the fact that they had all but abolished the forces they wished to deploy. As one British general complained to me, 'The prime minister wants to use the military. He just doesn't want to pay for it.'

And yet Britain and France remain the only two European nations that even aspire to be global military powers. The French had wisely stood aside from the Iraq War – and had been derided in the US press as 'cheese-eating surrender monkeys' for their pains. Despite the steady downward pressure on French military spending, both President Hollande and President Sarkozy proved willing to deploy the French military in Africa and the Middle East. But French policymakers are well aware that in any major global crisis, American power is indispensable – and they worry that the US is increasingly reluctant to deploy that power. Reflecting on America's role in the world in 2013, Laurent Fabius, the French foreign minister, mused that, 'The United States gives the impression of no longer wanting to get drawn into crises.' Unfortunately, as Fabius added, 'Nobody can take over from the Americans from a military point of view.' With the role of global policeman now vacant, Fabius noted that 'there is a risk of letting major crises fester on their own'.[5]

The cumulative effect of America's growing reticence, Germany's semi-pacifism and defence cuts in Britain and France is that the Nato alliance – the bedrock of Western security since the end of the Second World War – is in disrepair. The sense that Nato's decade-long mission in Afghanistan has effectively failed has further sapped the West's interest in acting collectively around the globe.

Consciously or unconsciously, Europeans are taking a gamble with their security. With the Cold War receding into memory and domestic welfare budgets under pressure, Europe is choosing to disarm. If the continent's immediate environment remains peaceful that might not be a problem. But with an angry Russia to the east, an increasingly inward-looking America to the west, and a Middle East in turmoil to the south, European nations risk discovering that their security gamble has failed, with dangerous consequences.

Meanwhile, in Asia, the picture is very different. Chinese military spending is soaring. India and Saudi Arabia are jostling for the title of the world's largest arms-importer. Even cash-strapped Japan increased its military spending. In 2012, for the first time in over a century, Asian nations spent more money on armaments and troops than European countries. In military affairs, as in business, economics and power politics, the process of Easternisation is well underway.

But there is very little energy or interest in the EU getting involved in the emerging geopolitical struggles in Asia. With so many economic and political problems to cope with close to home, Europeans – once the colonial masters of much of Asia – no longer have much interest in the balance of power in a distant continent. Instead, Asia is seen almost exclusively in economic terms – as an opportunity for European industry and a threat to European jobs.

As a result, many European policymakers looked at America's efforts to 'contain' Chinese power with a degree of detachment that was liable to infuriate their counterparts in Washington. One top German diplomat told me, 'When the Americans talk about China, sooner or later they will say – "Of course, China wants to be number one." It's almost like they have been physically challenged. But we in Europe are not so bothered by that idea.' Looking ahead, my German friend foresaw problems for the West in Asia: 'If the Americans want us to join them in an effort to face down China, I don't think we will follow them. And that could fracture the West.'[6]

The German instinct to stay out of fights in Asia is particularly pronounced given the country's history and the crucial importance of the Chinese market to the country's engineering and machine-tool industries. But the instincts in Paris, London and Rome are not that different. Indeed the politician who best embodied Europe's pragmatic and mercantilist approach to China was George Osborne, who had become Britain's Chancellor of the Exchequer in May 2010, at the age of thirty-eight. The conventional view of Osborne, when he took office, was that he was a staunch Atlanticist. As a student, he had spent time at college in the US and as a politician he had carefully cultivated contacts in the Republican Party. But as chancellor, Osborne became the prime mover behind a British drive to cultivate Xi Jinping's China – even at the cost of antagonising the United States.

As he looked at the future of the global economy, in his first term in office, Osborne became convinced that British interests would increasingly depend on fostering close economic ties with rising Asia – and China in particular. The City of London's role as the capital of global finance is underpinned by the fact that it is a centre for trade in dollars and euros; now, Osborne decided, it needed to position itself to become a centre for trade in the Chinese renminbi, the currency of the future. The British government's ambition to see exports surge also required UK industry to do better in China – the world's largest emerging market. Finally, Osborne wanted to see Xi's government invest some of China's huge foreign reserves in British infrastructure – from nuclear power stations to high-speed rail.

In pursuit of these ambitions, the British decided to roll out 'the reddest of red carpets' for President Xi when he visited London in October 2015.[7] The Chinese leader was invited to give a rare speech to both Houses of Parliament and to stay with the Queen in Buckingham Palace. His invitation to the UK had been hand-delivered by Prince William.

Britain's effusive reception for Xi was all the more pointed given that the Chinese leader's visit took place against a background of high tensions between the US and Chinese navies in the South China Sea. Osborne was privately dismissive of American concerns, telling one confidant that it was inevitable that Beijing would establish a sphere of influence in the South China Sea, adding, semi-flippantly, 'the clue is in the name'. Senior US policymakers, watching Britain's red-carpet welcome for Xi from Washington, were both scornful and aghast. As one US official put it to me, 'What Britain has just said to China is that we know we are a middle power and we accept that you are higher than us in the hierarchy.'[8]

There was an element of truth in this characterisation of Britain's approach to China – and that of the other major European powers. In some respects, a determination to cultivate the rising powers of Asia reflects a pragmatic and clear-eyed adaptation to the way the world is changing. Yet while Europeans would much prefer to concentrate on business, and remain as bystanders in an emerging struggle for power in Asia, that strategy is unlikely to be viable over the long term. Just as the problems of the Middle East burst through Germany's well-sealed windows, so the tensions in distant East Asia will eventually confront the nations of Europe with unavoidable political and strategic choices.

The problem is that the erosion of Europe's own military capabilities has made European nations increasingly dependent on the security guarantees that America provides through Nato. Looking to the US to provide military protection in Europe, while undermining American security policy in East Asia, does not look like a sustainable policy. That is all the more the case now that the countries of the EU are once again facing a military threat from Russia.

Russia Turns East

The European Union's increasing inability to think globally and its aversion to hard power makes a sharp contrast to the renewed international ambitions of Russia. After the collapse of the Soviet Union in 1991, two big ideas shaped the West's approach to Moscow. First, that Russia's global power was in inexorable decline. Second, that the Russian government and people had no option but to look towards western Europe as a model and a partner.

The Ukraine crisis of 2014, however, has undermined both assumptions. Vladimir Putin's Russia is clearly determined to reclaim its status as a world power and is prepared to use military force in pursuit of that end. And increasingly Russia is looking east, not west, for inspiration.

The confrontation between the West and Russia over Ukraine immediately revived memories of the Cold War. There was an 'East–West' conflict throughout that era, and the capital of the East was not Beijing's Tiananmen Square, but Moscow's Red Square – symbolised in the Western mind by the exotic onion domes of St Basil's Cathedral and the annual May Day military parade.

When the Soviet Union collapsed in 1991, Russia looked west for inspiration. The centre of Moscow, which seemed so bleak and alien during the Cold War, began to resemble other European capitals with the same glitzy shops and hotel chains.[1] Russians became a familiar presence in Europe, arriving in large numbers as tourists, businessmen and immigrants. The moment when it first hit me that the Cold War was truly over was when I heard Russian being spoken between a mother and child in a playground in west London in the early 1990s. The Russians, who might as well have lived on another planet during my childhood, were now just another foreign community in the cosmopolitan British capital.

But when I visited Moscow in October 2014 – just weeks before the twenty-fifth anniversary of the fall of the Berlin Wall – Russia was once again moving away from the West. Earlier that year, a revolution in Ukraine had overthrown a pro-Russian government led by President Viktor Yanukovitch. The revolution had been provoked by Yanukovitch's refusal – under heavy Russian pressure – to sign an agreement that would have moved his country towards membership of the European Union. But Russia's apparent victory in preventing Ukraine from moving westwards into the EU swiftly turned into a defeat, as demonstrators filled the centre of Kiev, many waving the EU flag. Yanukovitch first tried violent repression of the demonstrations and then fled the country. His downfall seemed to represent a major strategic defeat for Russia.

Putin, who had been intent on drawing Ukraine into his own rival 'Eurasian Union', was enraged by what he claimed (and probably believed) was a Western-backed coup against Yanukovitch. In the following weeks, Russia moved swiftly to annex Crimea – a part of Ukraine with particularly strong historic ties to Russia and the base for Russia's Black Sea fleet. In response, the EU and the US imposed economic sanctions. Russia had also begun to supply military support to rebel movements in eastern Ukraine, fighting against the new government in Kiev. When, in July 2014, Russian-backed separatists shot down a civilian airliner over eastern Ukraine – killing hundreds of innocent travellers – the West ratcheted up sanctions still further.

By the time I arrived in Russia a few months later, the political atmosphere between Moscow and Washington felt as poisonous as at the height of the Cold War. In the Duma, the Russian Parliament, I visited Vyacheslav Nikonov, the chairman of the Duma's education committee, a prominent supporter of President Putin and a regular on Russian television. Nikonov was descended from Soviet royalty. His grandfather had been Vyacheslav Molotov, Stalin's foreign minister and co-signatory of the notorious Molotov–Ribbentrop Pact, in which Nazi Germany and Soviet Russia had agreed to divide Poland.

Nikonov is also a genuine intellectual, who knows the West well. He is fluent in English, a former professor at CalTech in the US and the author of many books on both Russia and the United States. As we discussed the crisis in Ukraine, however, I found myself transported straight back to the Cold War. 'The American goal is global domination,' I was informed, 'they want to return Ukraine back into a stronghold against Russia.'[2] Similarly, he insisted that there were no Russian troops in Ukraine, as the Western press alleged – the only foreign troops there were Americans and CIA agents. As for the Ukrainian government itself: 'At least five members of that government are neo-Nazis.'

Nikonov's rhetoric echoed what was coming right from the very top. A few weeks later Putin himself told a meeting of Western Russia-watchers that rather than seeking a new balance of power after the Cold War, America had sought to establish a unipolar world, which was 'simply a means of justifying dictatorship over people and countries.'[3]

Behind the angry accusations and Cold War rhetoric, however, Russian intellectuals like Nikonov were developing a more sophisticated and interesting analysis of what had gone wrong between Russia and the West. Nikonov argued that Russia's efforts to join the West after the Cold War had been a fundamental error. Russia was different. It was as much a part of Asia as part of Europe. Culturally, economically and strategically, Russia's future would lie increasingly with the East, not the West. 'We have different roots from the West,' he argued. 'We don't have the Greek–Roman heritage, we have the Mongol heritage, which came from China . . . They established the Chinese tax system and the system of communication that went all the way to the Pacific.' By contrast, according to Nikonov, Russia's relationship with Europe was much more recent: 'Russia never became part of the European system until Peter the Great [the reformist tsar who ruled from 1682 until 1725] and it was always a peripheral part of that system until the nineteenth century. Then, after the Russian Revolution, it was expelled from the Western system for most of the twentieth century.'[4]

In the aftermath of the Ukraine crisis, Nikonov was just one of a number of prominent Russian intellectuals pushing the 'Eurasian' thesis. Another was Alexander Dugin, an extravagantly bearded anti-Western ideologue, who was also a regular on Russian television – raging against the decadence and perfidy of the West and lauding the unique qualities of Russian culture. Dugin's magnum opus, *The Foundations of Geopolitics,* argues that Russia is a victim of a Western conspiracy led by the US and Nato, which aims to contain and break the Russian nation. He argues that Moscow's ultimate goal should be to put the Soviet Union back together again. While many in the West might dismiss this idea as a fantasy, Dugin's work was a set text at Russian military academies and regularly cited by members of Putin's inner circle.[5]

Official Russia, it seemed, had decided to turn its back on the West. This new stance marked a profound break with the strategy pursued by successive Russian governments from the late 1980s onwards. Mikhail Gorbachev, a man praised in the West and reviled in Russia for his role in the peaceful dissolution of the Soviet Empire, had talked of Russia joining a 'common European home'. Boris Yeltsin, Russia's leader through much of the 1990s, had embraced the idea that Russia might one day join the EU or Nato. Even Vladimir Putin had argued in 2000 that 'Russia is part of the European culture . . . And I cannot envisage my own country in isolation from Europe and what we call the civilised world. So it is hard for me to visualise Nato as an enemy.'[6]

The process of estrangement from the West that became so obvious during the Ukraine crisis had, in fact, been underway for a decade and more. It was laid out for me, in Moscow, by Dmitri Trenin – once an intelligence officer in the Soviet army and now, as head of the Moscow office of the Carnegie Endowment, a major American think tank, an important link between Russia and the West. Trenin argued that there had been mistakes and misunderstandings on both sides. Yeltsin had probably been sincere in his desire for Russia to join Nato, but the Russians would have demanded a privileged position in the organisation and would have refused to accept that membership had any consequences for their domestic politics – conditions that were always likely to prove unacceptable to the Americans and Europeans.

But the Americans, according to Trenin, failed to make a real effort to reach out to their old adversaries in the aftermath of the Cold War. Instead, they treated Russia with neglect and disdain. This argument is often dismissed as Russian special pleading by hard-line Western analysts.[7] Yet there is some historical and contemporary evidence for the suggestion that Western leaders were so confident of their victory in the Cold War that they felt little need to accommodate Russian concerns. After the fall of the Berlin Wall, President George H. W. Bush dismissed the idea that Russia might be given some say over a united Germany's future relationship with Nato, telling Chancellor Helmut Kohl of Germany, 'To hell with that. We prevailed and they didn't. We can't let the Soviets clutch victory from the jaws of defeat.'[8]

Even the Obama administration, which went out of its way to try to improve relations with Russia through a 'reset' of US–Russian ties, assumed that America held almost all the cards. At the beginning of Obama's period in office in 2009, I recall being told by a senior US policymaker: 'The Russians keep saying they want to do things fifty-fifty. They have got to be kidding. It's going to be more like ninety-ten.'[9] Russian protests about the 'illegality', as viewed from Moscow, of

Western military intervention in Kosovo in 1999, in Iraq in 2003 and in Libya in 2011 were brushed aside in Washington as self-interested special pleading that could be safely ignored. For a Russia that had felt itself deeply diminished by the collapse of the Soviet Union, every slight from the United States – whether intentional or not – was keenly felt. President Obama probably did genuinely mean to sting when – in the midst of the Ukraine crisis – he referred to Russia as a 'regional power'. In a later speech to the UN, when the US president named Russian aggression in the Ukraine alongside Islamic State and the Ebola virus as major threats to global security, his words were treated in Moscow as a grave and demeaning insult. As far as the Americans were concerned, however, Obama was simply listing the biggest security issues facing the world, as seen from Washington.

The fact that America treated Russia with a degree of disdain in the twenty years after the collapse of the Soviet Union should not imply that the fault for Russia's estrangement from the West lies solely, or even largely, in Washington and Brussels. During the Putin years, Russia took a series of actions that any US or EU administration – no matter how understanding – would have struggled to accommodate. These ranged from the deadly poisoning of the former Russian agent Alexander Litvinenko in London in 2006, to the partial invasion of Georgia in 2008 and the harassment and imprisonment of opposition forces and civil-society activists within Russia itself. Indeed one plausible interpretation of President Putin's actions was that all his talk of American aggression and Ukrainian fascism was largely an elaborate smokescreen to disguise the real motivation behind his actions – a deep fear that his regime was vulnerable to revolutionary change of the sort that had overwhelmed Ukraine in the Orange Revolution of 2004 and then again, a decade later, in 2014.

As a former intelligence operative himself, Putin was probably genuinely convinced that Western intelligence was plotting against him, and that uprisings in Ukraine were merely a template for eventual 'regime change' in Moscow itself. And, at times, that regime change seemed close at hand. On a visit to Moscow in January 2012, I had walked through the freezing streets with thousands of Muscovites demonstrating against the return of President Putin to the Kremlin for a third term, as well as ballot-rigging in parliamentary elections. It was just after the fall of the Gaddafi regime in Libya in 2011, which had been precipitated by a Nato bombing campaign. Some of the demonstrators carried a giant banner that proclaimed 'Putin = Gaddafi'. Since Gaddafi had recently been killed, Putin might have felt an understandable tinge of alarm at that sight.

To justify repression at home, it was hugely in Putin's interests to blame the domestic opposition to his government on foreign conspiracies, aimed at undermining Russian sovereignty. Everybody the Kremlin feared – from domestic civil-society groups to the 'fascists' in Ukraine – could be portrayed as the tools of CIA agents in Washington. But mixed in with all this self-interest, there was also undoubtedly an affronted and defensive Russian nationalism that mourned all the territories lost after the collapse of the Soviet Union – an event that Putin had famously described as 'the greatest geopolitical catastrophe of the twentieth century'. That aggrieved and resurgent nationalism proved to be, in turn, very popular at home. When Putin gave a speech to the Duma in the aftermath of the annexation (or, as he saw it, return) of Crimea, many Duma members wept with emotion – and the Russian president's approval ratings in the opinion polls reached 85%.

Putin's rage and humiliation at Russia's treatment by the West in the aftermath of the Cold War – and his determination to look east as a result – repeated a deep pattern in Russian history. In the nineteenth and twentieth centuries, Russian intellectuals had tended to rediscover their country's Asian roots at moments when they felt spurned or humiliated by the West. As the historian Orlando Figes writes, Russian intellectuals 'craved to be accepted as equals by the West, to enter and to become part of the mainstream of European life. But when they were rejected or they felt that Russia's values had been underestimated by the West, even the most Westernised of Russia's intellectuals were inclined to be resentful and to lurch towards a chauvinistic pride in their country's threatening Asiatic size.'[10]

Periods of infatuation with the West, which could last for decades, alternated with deep disillusionment and the rediscovery of the idea of Russia as an Asian or, at least, Eurasian country. In the period before the Napoleonic Wars, the Russian elite spoke French to each other – but Francophilia disappeared in Russia after the great patriotic war against Napoleon in 1812. In the mid-nineteenth century, Russian reformists once again looked to Europe for inspiration. But the Crimean War from 1853–56, in which Russia fought Britain and France, once again led to a widespread sense in Russia that the West had betrayed their nation. By contrast, Russia's successful expansion into Central Asia during the mid-nineteenth century convinced many intellectuals that their country's true destiny lay in the East. In 1881, Dostoevsky advised his readers: 'We must cast aside our servile fear that Europe will call us Asiatic barbarians and say that we are more Asian than European . . . In Europe we were hangers-on and slaves, while in Asia we shall be the masters.'[11]

The 'Eurasian' theories that became popular in Russia, as President Putin's rage against the West mounted, tapped into deep historical traditions, but they also appealed to some modern trends and ideas. The Moscow intellectuals developing 'Eurasianist' ideas in the Putin era shared certain assumptions with the neo-Confucianists in Beijing, who were helping to shape the ideology of the Xi Jinping era. In particular, Russia's fear of the West was combined with contempt – and repeated assertions of Western moral and economic weakness. Like the Chinese, the Russians liked to dwell on what they saw as the weaknesses and pathologies of Western democracies – with everything from gay marriage to the American budget deficit cited in evidence. In the midst of the Ukraine crisis of 2014 Sergey Karaganov, a prominent academic and economist, asserted that 'Russia is far stronger and the West far weaker than many imagine.' The Western alliance was now 'a directionless gaggle, beset with economic insecurities and losing sight of its moral convictions. America and its allies once held the future in their hands but, at the beginning of this Asian century, they have let it slip through their fingers.'[12] When I spoke to Vyacheslav Nikonov in the Duma that same year, I found him almost exultant at the news of the IMF's announcement that China was now the world's largest economy. This, he assured me, 'changed everything'.

If the West was indeed in terminal decline and the future was Asian, it made perfect sense for Russia to look east and towards China. By 2014, it was not just the Obama administration that was intent on performing a 'pivot' to Asia - Putin's Russia decided to perform a similar manoeuvre and for similar reasons: a sense that the future of the world would increasingly be dictated by the economic power of Asia. Fyudor Lukyanov, editor of the influential journal *Russia in Global Affairs,* wrote that 'The Atlantic is no longer the sole centre of world events and engine of global progress. The Pacific and, to a degree, the Indian Ocean are taking over the main stage of world development.'[13] Vladislav Inozemtsev, a professor at Moscow State University, noted that 'Russian policymakers . . . have fallen in love with the idea of a push to the East.'[14]

Putin's plans for a Eurasian Union – based on the states of the former Soviet Union – were badly damaged by the 'loss' of Ukraine, which, in both geographical and economic terms, was the most substantial potential partner. But the imposition of Western sanctions in the aftermath of the crisis gave added urgency to Russia's own 'pivot' to Asia. In May 2014, Putin paid a state visit to China. The strategic closeness between China and Russia was emphasised by joint naval exercises staged by the two countries in the East China Sea that year, and in the Mediterranean the following year. But the core business of the visit was to do with economics and energy. After nearly a decade of negotiations, China and Russia signed a deal to build a pipeline to pump gas from Siberia to China. As the Chinese were wont to put it, this was a 'win-win' deal. For energy-hungry China, a secure supply of Russian gas fuelled the economy, while lessening dependence on highly polluting coal, and on oil and gas that had to travel to China through vulnerable sea routes. For Russia – which in a typical year gains 50% or more of its export revenues from energy – it was crucial to diversify its customer base. Europe remained easily the largest market for Russian oil and gas, and most of Russia's pipeline network pointed west. But with Russia's relations with the EU in crisis, that was a risky situation for both sides. Signing an energy and pipeline deal with China gave Russia a huge alternative outlet for its energy supplies.[15]

But at what price? Although the precise details of the Russia–China energy deal remained a commercial secret, it was widely believed that China had taken advantage of Russia's weakened situation to drive an exceptionally hard bargain, forcing the Russians to agree to a price for their gas that they would have rejected under other circumstances.

The gas deal raised a broader issue about Russia's own pivot to Asia. Some strategic thinkers in the West – and even in Russia itself – argued that Putin's anger with the United States had led him to make a fundamental error of judgement. In the long run, they argued, the real strategic threat to Russia was not an ageing and increasingly pacifist European Union, or a preoccupied and distant United States – it was a rising China. The argument was that geographic and economic imperatives would inevitably make China a threat to the sparsely populated Russian far east.

Russia is the world's largest country, spanning eleven time zones. The flying time from Moscow to Vladivostok on Russia's Pacific coast is over eight hours (compared to the six hours between New York and Los Angeles). Yet, Russia is also very sparsely populated and its population of 150 million is falling – partly because of low birth rates and the fact that Russian male life expectancy is just sixty-two. The Russian far east, where much of the country's energy reserves lie, is particularly sparsely populated with just 7.4 million people living in the entire region, compared to the 110 million people living in north-eastern China and the nearly 1.4 billion people living in China as a whole. The governor of Primorskiy Kray, in the Russian far east, was sufficiently alarmed by the situation that in 2014 he appealed, vainly, for a transfer of 5 million Russians from the west of the country.[16]

Russia's unease is only heightened by the knowledge that the country's sheer size is the product of a history of imperial expansion at the expense of its Asian neighbours, including China. In the 1600s, Russia's land surface almost trebled, as the country expanded beyond the Ural mountains.[17] By the eighteenth and nineteenth centuries Russia had become, in the words of the historian John Darwin, 'after Britain, the second greatest imperial power in Asia and a colossal colonialist'. Tsarist Russia played a crucial role in the 'demolition of the old China-centred world order in East Asia'.[18] Much of the Russian far east, including Vladivostok, was once Chinese and was only ceded to Russia through the treaties of Aigun and Peking in 1858 and 1860: two of the notorious 'unequal treaties' of the Qing era that now make up so much of the mythology of modern Chinese nationalism.[19]

Some determinists argue that this combination of population and economic pressures – combined with historical grievances – make it inevitable that China will one day lay claim to Russia's energy-rich east. But Russia's new Eurasianists dismiss this idea. They point out that China settled its border disputes with Russia through an agreement reached in 1999 – in stark contrast to China's continuing territorial rows with Japan, India and much of South East Asia. During our talk at the Duma, Vyacheslav Nikonov dismissed the idea of an eventual Chinese threat to Russia, arguing that China has always looked east and out to sea, rather than north towards Siberia. Indeed, Nikonov argued, the Chinese have regarded their northern border not as an opportunity but as a threat – hence the construction of the Great Wall of China.

But while Nikonov and his allies might be right to downplay the idea that China would ever contemplate invading Russia, which is the country with the second-largest arsenal of nuclear weapons in the world, a more informal 'invasion' is already taking place through mass

Chinese immigration into the Russian east, driven by trade and investment. Cities like Vladivostok are taking on an increasingly East Asian air, as Chinese immigration and businesses reshape their societies. Exact numbers are hard to come by, but in 2014, one senior Russian official spoke of over 1 million Chinese illegal immigrants entering Russia over the past year.[20] Even if immigration continued at the rate of 500,000 a year, it would give the Russian far east an ethnic Chinese majority within fifteen years. Some Russian analysts argue that these figures are wild exaggerations, but Putin appeared to side with the alarmists, when after the Apec summit in 2012 he remarked: 'If we do not in the near future take practical steps to develop the far east, in a few decades Russians will be speaking Chinese, Japanese or Korean.'[21]

The size and dynamism of the Chinese economy also had profound implications for Putin's hopes of recreating a Russian sphere of influence on the territory of the former Soviet Union. The countries that Putin envisaged joining his Eurasian Union included all the Central Asian nations that were once part of the USSR. Kazakhstan was the first Central Asian state to sign up – with Tajikistan and Kyrgyzstan as possible later entrants. But even the Kazakhs, whose vast country is itself the size of the entire EU, were uneasy about the political implications of Putin's dream. As a recently independent country, they had cause to fear being drawn back into Moscow's orbit – fears that were only stoked by Putin's apparently casual remarks that Kazakhstan's political future might be reopened when Nursultan Nazarbaev, who has governed the country since the break-up of the USSR, finally dies.

The Kazakhs reportedly insisted that the new body, which came into being in 2015 (with Belarus as its third member), should be called the Eurasian Economic Union, to emphasise that it is not intended to be a political organisation. However, the growing economic power of China raised questions about whether Putin's Eurasian Union made sense, even as an economic unit. All the Central Asian countries that Russia envisaged joining the union (with the sole exception of

Uzbekistan) do considerably more trade with China than with Russia. The Chinese government, under Xi Jinping, compounded the problem by making the development of a 'new Silk Road' across Central Asia all the way to Europe a central point of Chinese foreign and economic policy. Whatever the geopolitical vision of Putin, Russia's relatively moribund economy simply could not compete with the size and energy of China.

The potential clash between the ambitions of Russia and China was underlined by separate appearances by the Russian and Chinese leaders in Kazakhstan, pushing their rival visions for the region. In September 2013, Xi laid out his vision for the Silk Road Economic Belt in a speech in Astana, the bleak and windswept new capital of Kazakhstan. A few months later, Putin was in the same city, signing the founding treaty of the Eurasian Economic Union.[22] Officially, China and Russia were keen to stress that their two visions for Central Asia need not clash with each other. But it was hard to avoid the feeling that Russia's 'backyard' was turning into China's backyard, despite the best efforts of the Kremlin.

While China made the economic running, however, by 2014 Putin was emerging as the most prominent international opponent of the US-led world order. His increasingly assertive and anti-American rhetoric made him the spokesman for those nations who were unhappy with a US-dominated world order. China, for all its growing might and assertiveness, was only willing to confront the United States on issues that it regarded as 'core interests' – usually involving disputed territorial claims in East Asia. The Chinese were much less interested than the Russians in attempting to organise opposition to US foreign policy at a global level. This was reflected even at the United Nations where, despite the fact that China is now the second-largest financial contributor to the UN (after the US), Western diplomats noticed that the Chinese usually continued to follow the Russian lead on most major international issues – such as the nuclear negotiations with Iran, or the Syrian peace talks.

Frustrated by Beijing's comparative reticence, some Chinese nationalists began to express open admiration for Putin and his willingness to confront America.[23] After the annexation of Crimea, an admiring biography of Putin made the best seller lists in China, and approval ratings for Russia shot up in Chinese opinion polls.

The emergence of Russia as the most aggressive challenger to the US-led world order made some in Washington openly question the logic behind America's pivot to Asia. Some recalled that Mitt Romney, the Republican presidential candidate in 2012, had been derided by Barack Obama for calling Russia the 'greatest geopolitical threat' to the US. Republicans argued that Romney had been right all along. Even some Obama aides wondered whether the US had been looking in the wrong direction. Jeremy Shapiro, who worked at the Policy Planning department in the State Department during Obama's first term, told me 'We spent so much time thinking about how to cope with a rising power like China, that we forgot that a declining power, like Russia, can do a lot of damage on the way down.'[24] Russia's annexation of Crimea in March 2014 electrified the policy debate in Washington. At a conference I attended that week at the Center for Strategic and International Studies, emboldened specialists on Russia and Europe denounced the whole idea of America's 'pivot to Asia' as a mistake and a delusion – and were greeted with cheers and applause. The designers of the pivot were left to argue that their focus on China and Asia was always driven by a focus on long-term economic and strategic trends – none of which were invalidated by a flare-up in Ukraine. Kurt Campbell, one of the policymakers most associated with the pivot, dismissed the Washington policy elite's sudden obsession with Russia and Ukraine as 'like kids chasing after a football'.[25]

But the argument about whether a crisis with Russia invalidated America's 'pivot to Asia' missed the point. Russia's alienation from the West is part of the same phenomenon as China's increasing power and assertiveness. Both are signals that the world that had come into being in 1989, with the fall of the Berlin Wall, is increasingly under challenge. That world had been characterised by unchallenged American dominance of the global system. Now, the relative decline of US economic and political power – allied to the much more rapid decline of European power – is encouraging rival nations to explore whether US dominance can be challenged and whether, in this new world, there are also strategic and ideological alternatives to the paths promoted in Washington and Brussels.

Kurt Campbell is right that the most significant long-term manifestation of this challenge to the West will be the rise of China. But by 2014 Vladimir Putin's Russia had positioned itself as the most aggressive, vocal and potentially dangerous short-term challenger to the West.

The challenges to the US-led global order from Russia and China have also opened up new strategic, economic and ideological debates in nations hitherto regarded as heading ineluctably westwards. Foremost amongst these are Turkey, Hungary and Ukraine itself.

12

Borderlands

M ost politicians try to say something uplifting when they take office. Arseniy Yatseniuk took a different approach. Accepting the post of interim prime minister of Ukraine in February 2014, he said 'Welcome to hell.'

Sitting in his office in Kiev, a couple of months later, I asked him if the job had proved as hellish as anticipated. Yatseniuk, a gaunt, balding forty-year-old, removed his glasses and rubbed his face wearily – 'Worse,' he said. 'We face the Russian military, Russian-backed terrorism, the economy is insolvent, our own military has been dismantled, the police are disorientated. The last government stole everything they could.'[1]

The day after our conversation, the Ukrainian government responded to this desperate situation by launching an offensive to try to retake territory in the east of the country that had fallen under the control of Russian-backed separatists – the groups that Yatseniuk referred to as terrorists. The authorities in Kiev felt that if they did not fight back, they risked losing large parts of their country by default.

Ukraine's misfortune was that, in the era of Easternisation, it had found itself on the borderlands between East and West. The rupture in relations between Russia and the West and Russia's decision to execute its own 'pivot' to Asia meant that Ukraine was at risk of being ripped apart – with Russia pulling it east and the European Union and the US pulling it west.

The emergence of this conflict shows how, twenty-five years after the fall of the Berlin Wall, the assumptions of the post Cold War era are being overturned. For more than a generation it had been assumed that Ukraine was heading inexorably west. Its goal was to establish the economic and political preconditions – a free-market economy and a functioning democracy – that would allow the country eventually to join the European Union. It was clear that Russia might well object to Ukraine joining Nato, but eventual EU membership seemed uncontroversial. That assumption was disproved by the outbreak of war in 2014. Ukraine's Western destiny was suddenly very much in doubt, as Russia fought to assert its own 'sphere of influence' over the countries of the former Soviet Union. Pro-EU Ukrainian politicians felt that they were engaged in an existential struggle. As I left his office in May 2014, Yatseniuk's parting words were 'One thing is clear, we must be part of the West.'

The Ukrainian dilemma is particularly dramatic. But it is not unique. In fact, the era of Easternisation has reopened the question of the 'Western destinies' of several countries that lie on the borderlands between the new East and the old West. Turkey and Hungary are other prime examples. The emergence of strong leaders with authoritarian tendencies – in the shape of Recep Tayyip Erdogan, the prime minister and then president of Turkey, and Viktor Orban, prime minister of Hungary – saw these two countries quite deliberately begin to turn their backs on the West.

Their decisions reflected global economic, political and ideological trends. The fact that the West no longer dominates the world economy in the way that it did, even in 1990, has opened up new strategic choices for many countries. Turkish companies, for example, have prospered by expanding rapidly in Russia, the Gulf States and Central Asia. The West is no longer the only option. The same is true in the realm of ideas. The rise of Asia, the geopolitical boldness of Vladimir Putin and the economic troubles of the US and Europe have all made it easier for political leaders with authoritarian tendencies – such as Orban and Erdogan – to look for new ideological models, outside the West.

The world leader most willing to confront the West during the Obama era was Putin. The war he launched in Ukraine quickly became a cause célèbre and an international political litmus test, a little like the Spanish civil war of the 1930s. The Russian government noted with satisfaction that many non-Western democracies – in particular India, South Africa and Brazil – refrained from condemning Russia's annexation of Crimea at the United Nations. Even within Europe, the far right and the far left were openly sympathetic to the Putin regime in Russia, as a means of signalling their disgust with the status quo in the West. Politicians such as France's far-right leader, Marine Le Pen, and the leaders of Germany's hard-left party, Die Linke, embraced the Russian argument that Ukraine was a deeply divided country, many of whose citizens looked to Russia for protection.

Paradoxically, even as Russia sought support from the far right in Europe, the Russian media pumped out the message that the government in Kiev was run by 'fascists' and anti-Semites – said to be the direct descendants of those Ukrainian partisans who fought with the Nazis against Stalin's Russia. That message was widely transmitted to Russian-speakers in eastern Ukraine and also found a receptive audience in parts of the EU.

To try to assess the accusations that the new Ukraine was lurching towards neo-fascism, I paid a visit in May 2014 to Victor Pinchuk, Ukraine's most prominent Jewish businessman. Sitting in a pavilion by an artificial lake in his vast estate outside Kiev, surrounded by works of art by the likes of Damien Hirst, Pinchuk gave short shrift to allegations that the new government in Ukraine was linked to neo-Nazism. 'Its bullshit,' he told me succinctly. Certainly his fortunes seemed little affected by the arrival of a new regime in Ukraine – although his businesses, which profited from Russian–Ukrainian trade, were sure to be affected in time.

What was true, however, was that the red and black flag of wartime Ukrainian nationalism was very visible on the barricades that remained in Kiev's Independence Square. Some of the volunteer battalions fighting the Russians in the east also used imagery from the 1930s that played right into the hands of Russian propagandists. One American–Ukrainian fighting with the Azov battalion out in the east assured me that there were no neo-Nazis in his battalion, as the Russians alleged, but added vaguely, 'There are quite a few sun-worshippers and pagans.' Since paganism is sometimes associated with white-supremacist movements in the US and Europe, this was not a completely reassuring statement. What about reports that some members of his battalion had worn Nazi insignia, I asked? My interviewee's response was again not entirely convincing: 'A couple of the guys had the SS sign on their helmets. But they said they didn't know what it was – they just knew it drove the Russians crazy!'[2]

Russian allegations of corruption, mismanagement, brutality and far-right influence in Ukraine had just enough substance to them to help Moscow in its information war with the West. But amidst the propaganda battle, it is important to remember some basic facts. While there clearly is a cultural divide between eastern and western Ukraine, 91% of the country's citizens voted to be an independent nation in 1991. Millions of Ukrainians died in the Stalin-imposed famines of the 1930s, which gives modern Ukrainians good grounds to be suspicious of Russian offers of 'protection'. And when thousands of Ukrainians demonstrated in Kiev in 2014 – and over a hundred died – they were not demanding a 'fascist' government. Instead they were calling for an end to corruption and eventual membership of the European Union. The EU flags that fluttered over Kiev's Maidan (the central square) were a testimony to the fact that the revolutionaries' gaze was towards the West – with Brussels as an unlikely Mecca.

The real struggle, however, was not about whether the soul of Ukraine ultimately belonged to East or West. It was about something much more brutal and basic: power. The Russian argument is essentially that, in the early twenty first century, international relations should be ordered as they had been through much of the twentieth century and before. In that world, great powers granted each other 'spheres of influence'. Wars were avoided by informal understandings between the big powers that they had a veto over what happened in their neighbourhoods. During the Cold War, Russia's sphere of influence had extended all the way to Berlin. Now Russia was fighting in Crimea and the east to ensure that, at least, it continued to hold sway in Ukraine.

Moscow's argument about spheres of influence was one that found a clear echo in Beijing – where the Chinese government is also trying to establish a national sphere of influence, in the South and East China Seas. But the Chinese view of Russia's annexation of Crimea is complicated. Russia's use of a referendum to legitimise the transfer of territory from one country to another potentially set a dangerous precedent, where China was concerned. What if, one day, Taiwan or Tibet or Xinjiang claim the right to hold a similar vote?

The Chinese were much more unambiguously on Russia's side when it came to the original uprising in Kiev, for China also resented Western interference and democratic evangelism in East Asia. When student uprisings took place in Hong Kong in September 2014, the Russians were quick to argue that this was another Western-sponsored 'colour revolution' in the making – on the model of the Ukrainian uprising earlier in the year. This argument swiftly found favour in the official Chinese media.

Guarded sympathy for Russia's arguments about spheres of influence extended beyond the apparatchiks of Beijing. In Asia's cautious, capitalist circles, the West's encouragement of Ukraine's democratic and European aspirations was often condemned as unrealistic and irresponsible. Lee Hsien Loong, the Singaporean prime minister, suggested to me that he understood the West's sympathy for the demonstrators in Kiev's Maidan: 'You can understand the emotional sympathies; they share your values . . . these are idealistic and enthusiastic revolutionaries: in a way, you think back to *Les Mis*.' But Lee also clearly thought Western policymakers had been irresponsible in encouraging the demonstrators: 'Can you take responsibility for the consequences and when it comes to grief will you be there? You can't be there, you've got so many other interests to protect . . . So you have to calculate the whole account.'[3] The same idea was put in rather more colourful language by Ronnie Chan, a Hong Kong property tycoon and philanthropist, appearing at a Pinchuk-sponsored conference in Ukraine later that year. In tones that were both self-deprecating and exasperated, Chan urged the Ukrainians to face the fact that they would always have to accommodate Russian power: 'I am five foot three and I'm ugly,' he said. 'I've had to deal with it. You have also got to deal with facts.'

This kind of brutal realpolitik was little more than a statement of the obvious for many powerful Asians, who often regarded American talk of 'universal values' or 'freedom' as either cynical or deluded. For men like Lee Hsien Loong and Ronnie Chan, who hailed from rich but small places – Singapore and Hong Kong – it seemed self-evident that survival meant maintaining a keen awareness of the sensibilities and preferences of powerful neighbours. A quixotic battle against the regional giant – whether China or Russia – held little appeal.

Beyond that, there were many in Asia – and even in the West – who reacted to Putin's annexation of Crimea with admiration. In China, the Russian leader was widely praised in the blogosphere as a strong man who was capable of standing up to America. The Pew Research Center found that popular admiration for Russia had grown in China following the country's confrontation with the West over Ukraine – rising to 66% in July 2014, from 47% a year earlier. The *Global Times*, a nationalist newspaper, captured the mood when it quoted Wang Haiyun, a Chinese major general, who argued that 'Putin is a bold and decisive leader of a great power, who is good at achieving victory in a danger-ous situation.'[4]

Indeed one phenomenon of the later Obama years was the re-emergence of a fashion for political 'strong men' as leaders – particularly in Asia. Russia had Putin, China had President Xi Jinping, India had Narendra Modi and Japan had Shinzo Abe, all politicians who – in different ways – thrived on the cult of the strong leader. By contrast, Obama's cerebral style was derided by his political opponents at home as evidence of weakness.

Some of the new generation of 'strong leaders' to emerge were in countries that had traditionally been regarded as firmly in the Western camp. Turkey had joined Nato in 1952 and was, throughout the Cold War, a vital, if prickly, bulwark against the Soviet Union. After the collapse of the USSR, Turkey took on a different, but still crucial role, in the Western alliance. As a large, secular Muslim country, a success-ful economy, a democracy and a member of Nato, Turkey was widely regarded in Washington and Brussels as a role model for the rest of the Middle East. Here was a country, it was argued, that offered proof positive that there was no inevitable 'clash of civilisations' between the Muslim world and the West.

Obama felt so strongly about Turkey's role as a pivotal and sym-bolic power that he made his first big speech overseas, as president, in the Turkish capital, Ankara. In his first term in office, he spoke more frequently to Recep Tayyip Erdogan, the Turkish prime minister, than to any other foreign leader.[5]

Erdogan is a new sort of Turkish leader. A devoutly religious man, he had spent much of his career at odds with the country's secular and military establishment – and had indeed even been briefly imprisoned. But that only increased his potential significance in the eyes of Obama and other Erdogan fans in the West. If the Turkish prime minister could demonstrate that a devout Muslim could lead a country – while main-taining its democratic, capitalist, pro-Western orientation – then Turkey's potential significance as a role model only became more pronounced.

Erdogan first became prime minister in 2003. I encountered him shortly afterwards, at a press conference in Brussels, where he pressed Turkey's traditional claim to join the EU – a goal that Turkey had been pursuing unsuccessfully since the early 1960s. The desire to join the EU was a fundamental affirmation of Turkey's orientation towards the West – a path that the country had first been put upon by the Turkish republic's founding father, Kemal Ataturk. As Erdogan's period in office unfolded, however, it became clear that the new Turkish leader had foreign-policy aspirations that extended well beyond membership of the European Union – and indeed harked back to the old Ottoman Empire. Ahmet Davutoglu, Erdogan's foreign minister, gave an insight into these ambitions in a speech in Sarajevo in 2009, when he grandiloquently proclaimed: 'As in the sixteenth century, which saw the Ottoman Balkans as the centre of world politics, we will make the Balkans, the Caucasus and the Middle East, the centre of world politics in the future.'[6] It was not a coincidence that these areas were the lands of the former Ottoman Empire.

The uprisings across the Arab world that began in 2011 gave Erdogan and his entourage in the ruling AKP party an opportunity to indulge their dreams of regional leadership. As a devout Muslim, Erdogan embraced the rise of political Islam in the Sunni world – and, in particular, the emergence of a Muslim Brotherhood government in Egypt. Erdogan's emotional condemnations of Israel also signalled his willingness to distance himself from his American allies, while courting favour in the non-Western world and on the fabled 'Arab street'. For a while, this Turkish drive for regional influence seemed to be going well. When Erdogan visited Egypt in September 2011, a few months after the revolution, he was greeted by 20,000 people at Cairo airport.

The overthrow of the Muslim Brotherhood in Cairo and a bitter falling-out between Erdogan and the Assad regime in neighbouring Syria complicated Erdogan's drive for regional influence. But it did nothing to reconcile Turkey with the the West. On the contrary,

Erdogan took an increasingly sceptical attitude to both the US and the European Union. There were many good reasons for Turks to feel fed up with Brussels. Being kept in the antechamber of the EU for more than fifty years was humiliating. Even though it was true that Turkey met neither the political nor the economic criteria for membership, the Turks felt – with reason – that Europe's curmudgeonly attitude to Turkey's application also reflected a cultural prejudice and a fear of mass migration from a relatively poor, Muslim country.

But Erdogan and his supporters in Turkey were also disillusioned with Europe for reasons that went well beyond hurt pride. The AKP's reassertion of conservative cultural values on issues such as women's right and gay issues clashed with the increasing liberalism of western Europe. When the EU plunged into a deep economic crisis in 2009, Turks also began to contrast the rapid growth rates of Turkey and Asia with the apparent decline of the richer, but sclerotic West. As Sinan Ulgen, one of Turkey's sharpest political analysts, explained, 'Political Islamists now tend to view the West in general, and Europe in particular, as a civilisation in political, economic, social and moral decline.'[7]

As the Erdogan years unfolded, so clashes between Turkey and the West multiplied. The Arab Spring merely added fuel to the fire. Rather than being a beacon of Western-style liberalism for an Arab world in ferment, Turkey under Erdogan became a fulcrum for Muslim denunciation of Western inaction over the unfolding tragedy of the civil war in Syria. Erdogan's own rhetoric also became increasingly overheated. One fairly typical remark was made in late 2014; as the death toll in Syria mounted, Mr Erdogan told his people: 'Believe me they [the West] don't like us . . . They look like friends, but they want us dead. They like seeing our children die.'[8]

Behind the emotional arguments about the Middle East, a broader divergence was occuring. Under Erdogan, Turkey had embarked on a process of Easternisation. The implications extended well beyond geopolitics. Indeed Erdogan's policy of Easternisation represented a fundamental challenge to Turkey's governing ideology – an ideology that had been instilled into the Turkish republic by Ataturk. His self-appointed mission, after the First World War, was to construct a new Turkish state on the ruins of the Ottoman Empire. For Ataturk, modernisation and national survival involved embracing the West and abolishing Ottoman cultural practices. The new Turkey was to be a secular state. The military took a close and often repressive interest in the political activities of Islamists. Even the Turkish language was changed. The traditional Ottoman script was junked in favour of the Roman alphabet.

For Erdogan, the militant secularism of Ataturk's Turkey was offensive. Fairly swiftly, Erdogan set about challenging aspects of Ataturk's legacy. A ban on women wearing headscarves in universities was abolished. Religious schools were encouraged, as was the teaching of the old Ottoman script. Some of these moves could be interpreted as an expansion of civil liberties, to allow more freedom for Turkey's devout masses to practise their religion. But Erdogan's greater indulgence to Islam was combined with a restriction of some of the civil liberties that were dear to Turkey's secular liberals. On several visits to Turkey during the Erdogan years, it became clear to me that many of my colleagues in the Turkish media were living in a climate of fear. This was hardly surprising, since there were said to be more journalists in jail in Erdogan's Turkey than in Communist China.[9]

In 2013, the anxieties of Turkey's pro-Western liberals spilled over onto the streets. It was plans to redevelop Gezi Park, a block-sized patch of green just off Taksim Square, Istanbul's symbolic heart, that provoked the original protests. Once again, beneath the Gezi dispute was a culture clash between secularists and Islamists. Erdogan's plan for the park was to build a replica of an Ottoman barracks that once stood there, and that was the base for a rebellion by Islamist officers in 1909 – before being razed by the secular republic. The prime minister also wanted to rip down the massive Ataturk cultural centre just up the road in Taksim, and replace it with a neo-baroque opera house. And he also proposed that a mosque should be built on Taksim. To many of his opponents, these suggestions all looked like part of a co-ordinated attack on Turkish secularism.

The Taksim protests revealed a deep division between Turkey's pro-Western urban elites, and the Easternisers led by Erdogan. In America, the cultural divide that defines politics is between red and blue states. In Turkey, the divide is between 'black' and 'white' Turks. This is not a reference to skin colour, but to social attitudes and class. The 'white' Turks tend to be secular, relatively well-off and more urban. The 'black' Turks are pious Muslims and tend to be poorer and more provincial. Think of the scorn and mutual mistrust between red and blue America – then triple it – and you will have an idea of the depth of the divide that separated the two camps in Turkey's culture wars.

The demonstrations in central Istanbul were very largely the preserve of the white Turks. One hot summer evening in 2013, I joined several thousand people gathered in Taksim Square at a protest provoked by the release on bail of a policeman who had shot dead a demonstrator in Ankara. The crowd in Taksim would have blended right in with the 'Occupy Wall Street' demonstrators at Zuccotti Park in New York or a student demo in Paris. There were red flags for the hard left, rainbow flags for the gays, green flags for the environmentalists, many students, and a few professionals who seemed to have come from the office. The young women, who often led the chants, were typically wearing shorts or vests. Some sat on their boyfriends' shoulders, with their dark glasses perched fashionably on their heads. The only woman in a headscarf I saw was an old lady, on the fringe of the crowd, who was selling water to the demonstrators.

The ruling AKP party – against which many of the chants were aimed – is run by pious Muslims. The wives of both Erdogan himself and his predecessor as president, Abdullah Gul, wear headscarves. The crowd in Taksim was dominated by the secular, urban middle classes. The core vote for Erdogan is more devout and more socially conservative. It was these loyalists the prime minister was appealing to when he condemned the demonstrators as looters and tools of a foreign plot and claimed that they had drunk beer in an Istanbul mosque.

Alcohol is another front in Turkey's culture wars. About a week before the Gezi demonstrations broke out, the Turkish Parliament passed a new law that forbade the sale of alcohol from any outlet within a hundred metres of either a mosque or a school. Nobody was quite sure how strictly the new law would be interpreted – and whether there would be exceptions for the tourist trade, or for stores that were already licensed to sell the demon drink. But, since there are rather a lot of mosques and schools in Istanbul, the implications were potentially drastic. For the 'white Turks', one of the great joys of summer in Istanbul is to sit out overlooking the Bosphorus, sipping a beer or a glass of white wine. The real alarmists thought that Erdogan – who regularly targets Istanbul's whisky-sipping, Bosphorus-gazing elite – had that simple pleasure in his sights.

For all his fiery rhetoric, Erdogan was still inclined to proceed cautiously. His heart was with the Islamic world and his geopolitical ambitions also inclined him to look east. But hard-headed business interests also mattered. Emerging markets have opened up important new opportunities for Turkish companies, but the country still does a lot of trade with Europe and it has a booming tourist business to protect. So, Turkey under Erdogan attempted to strike a balance between East and West – an idea that had a certain logic, given its geographical position straddling Asia and Europe.

Yet even the idea of a balance between East and West was a significant departure. For generations, Turkey was a country that had looked one way only – towards the West. The East, for the Ataturk secularists, represented only backwardness and poverty. In the twenty-first century that attitude no longer held sway. For all his anger, emotion and occasional hypocrisy, Erdogan was an emblem of Turkey's adjustment to a more Easternised world.

Turkey's pivot East made sense, in some ways, given the country's Muslim heritage. What was more surprising during the Obama years was that even some countries inside the European Union – the second pillar of the Western world – had begun to look east. Foremost amongst these was Hungary, under a charismatic, controversial and authoritarian leader – Viktor Orban.

When I had visited Hungary in the run-up to the country's accession to the European Union in 2004, Orban was still something of a hero to Western conservatives. He had emerged as a dashing young student leader during the downfall of Communism in 1989, and was an economic and political liberal who expressed admiration for Thatcher and Reagan. His press in the West was laudatory. But what many of Orban's Western admirers initially missed was that he was also a nationalist – who like many Hungarian right-wingers was still mourning the lands that Hungary had lost in the aftermath of the First World War. As Orban dug himself into power, it became increasingly apparent that winning the internal power struggle with his domestic political opponents – and appealing to local nationalists – was more important to him than obeying liberal pieties, even if those pieties were enshrined in the European Union laws that Hungary had signed up to.

Hungary under Orban took on an increasingly authoritarian tone, with new laws restricting the freedom of the media and favouring the political and commercial interests of Orban's supporters. As a result, relations between Budapest and Brussels became increasingly fraught.

The unfavourable attention that Hungary was attracting in Brussels in turn upset and enraged Orban. Like Turkey's President Erdogan, the Hungarian leader began to indulge in increasingly anti-Western rhetoric – taking the weakness of the European economy, in the post-crisis years, as a symbol that the West itself was decadent and in decline. Orban hailed instead the authoritarian model of development visible in Asia as the model of the future. In a controversial speech in 2014, the Hungarian leader suggested that 'liberal, democratic states cannot remain globally competitive', and added: 'Today the world tries to understand systems that are not Western, not liberal, maybe not even democratic. Yet they are successful.' His own goal, he suggested, was to build an 'illiberal state, based on national foundations'.[10] The prime minister cited Singapore, China and Turkey as possible inspirations. All three control the media and the political opposition in ways that are unacceptable in the EU. All three believe in government direction of the economy. And China and Turkey also indulge in a strongly nationalist political discourse that clearly appeals to Orban but that is frowned upon in Brussels.

Hungary's trajectory under Viktor Orban was greeted with dismay in Washington, Brussels and Berlin. One senior German official described the Hungarian leader to me as 'our little Balkan Putin'.[11] Yet the European Union seemed powerless to drag Hungary back into line. Instead, in 2015, when Europe suddenly found itself struggling to cope with an inflow of over a million refugees from the Middle East and Africa, Viktor Orban's decisive and authoritarian style began to attract admiration from conservatives in western Europe and even the United States.

In an effort to bar the refugees' route north to Germany – which crossed Hungarian territory – Orban authorised the building of tall, razor-wire fences along the Hungarian border, patrolled by armed guards. Liberals in western Europe were appalled and condemned Orban's behaviour as brutal and illegal. Horror at the television pictures of ill-treated refugees, coming out of Hungary in the summer of 2015, encouraged Angela Merkel to open Germany's doors to refugees. But Orban became something of a hero to conservatives in Germany and the rest of the EU, who saw him as a man of action, willing to take tough decisions in the interests of his country. In the summer of 2015, Orban was feted at a conference of Germany's Christian Social Union, Merkel's coalition partners. And he was also a close ally and role model for the nationalist and conservative political parties that won power in Poland in late 2015. That change in political direction in Poland was followed by Orban-like manipulation of the state-run media and the courts. Poland's new direction illustrated that Viktor Orban's Hungary could no longer be dismissed as an isolated aberration by the rest of

Europe. Instead, just as Orban looked to Xi's China as an inspiration, so conservative forces in Europe were now looking to Orban as a potential role model.

Orban is a sufficiently subtle political operative to avoid directly racist rhetoric and to know the value of sending out mixed political signals. But more overtly racist forces are resurfacing in both eastern and western Europe – and, once again, Hungary is to the fore. As well as Orban's Fidesz, the country is home to a flamboyant far-right party called Jobbik, which campaigns against 'Israeli influence' in Hungary – and which now has a significant presence in the Hungarian Parliament. Krisztina Morvai, one of the party's most prominent figures, has had a career that symbolises the disappointed hopes of the West. After the downfall of the Soviet Empire in 1989, she became the first central European recipient of a UK government academic scholarship – which was personally presented to her by Margaret Thatcher. It was a rather bitter irony that this protégé of western Europe should emerge as the leader of a far-right movement. When I met Morvai in Budapest in 2009, she outright rejected the idea that she was some kind of proto-fascist. But she was disturbingly evasive in her discussion of violence against gypsies by right-wing paramilitaries, and strikingly emotional in her denunciations of Israeli business influence in Hungary.

In their different ways, the fates of Hungary, Turkey and Ukraine in the years after the financial crisis of 2008 illustrated the waning power of the European Union as a pole of attraction and as a force for Westernisation. The period that I spent living in Brussels from 2001–5 was, in retrospect, the heyday of EU power. The European economy looked strong. A European single currency was launched to widespread acclaim. Countries were queuing to join the EU, which seemed to hold out the promise of prosperity and good governance. Those EU hopefuls included Hungary, Ukraine and Turkey.

A decade later things had changed. Economic crisis had sapped the credibility of the European Union. Hungary was inside the club, but breaking its rules with abandon – and looking to Asia rather than to Brussels for inspiration. In foreign affairs and domestic politics, Turkey was increasingly looking east rather than west. As for Ukraine, its political elite and much of its population still yearned to 'join Europe'. But Europe was too weak to pull Ukraine aboard. Instead, the country was floundering and sinking – torn between an angry Russia and an uncertain West.

13

Africa and the Americas – China Beyond its Backyard

When Barack Obama appeared before the leaders of the African Union in July 2015, it was a moment freighted with symbolism and emotion. The US president proclaimed, 'I stand before you as a proud American,' gave a lengthy pause and then added, 'I also stand before you as the son of an African.'[1] His audience cheered and whooped.

The personal and political connection between America and Africa, epitomised by Obama, should give the US a huge advantage in building a special relationship with the African continent. But the building that Obama was speaking in told a different story. The new African Union headquarters in Addis Ababa, the capital of Ethiopia, had been funded entirely by a $200 million grant from China. At a hundred metres tall, with a vast conference centre attached, the AU building dominates the Addis skyline. The city is also home to the first urban metro system built in sub-Saharan Africa – which was constructed, funded and operated by a Chinese company. These developments were testament both to the rapid development of Ethiopia and to the close ties between emerging African economies and China.[2]

Even in 2015, many Western images of Ethiopia remained stuck in 1984, when the Ethiopian famine caused hundreds of thousands of deaths and provoked the Live Aid concerts that caught the imagination of a generation of young people. But by 2015, when Obama became the first US president to visit Ethiopia, those images of famine and despair were seriously out of date. Indeed the Ethiopian economy grew by an average of over 10% a year between 2004 and 2014 — and the World Bank predicts that it will continue to be one of the world's fastest-growing economies over the following five years.

The idea of Africa as an economic dynamo is still something of a novelty in the West. As recently as the year 2000 *The Economist* ran a cover story on Africa entitled 'The Hopeless Continent'. The magazine noted that 45% of Africans were living in poverty, that corruption and misgovernment were endemic across the continent and that 'wars still rage from north to south to east to west'. It concluded gloomily that 'It begins to look as if the world might just give up on the entire continent.'[3]

The bluntness of *The Economist*'s verdict provoked controversy. But, in reality, the magazine was simply giving public expression to a very widespread sentiment in the US and Europe: after the Ethiopian famine, the Rwandan genocide, the civil wars in Somalia and Congo, and Zimbabwe's descent into despotism, it was hard to find much optimism about Africa in Washington or London.

But 'the world' was not giving up on Africa — just the Western world. The view from China was rather different. In 2000, the same year that *The Economist* ran its cover story, the Chinese government convened the first ever China–Africa forum in Beijing, bringing together African and Chinese leaders to discuss investment opportunities in the 'hopeless continent'.

Where many in the West saw only despair and disappointment in Africa, the Chinese had spotted opportunity. China's rapidly growing industrial economy needed raw materials and Africa was rich in those. Many African nations badly needed new infrastructure and Chinese construction companies were looking for opportunities. The speed of China's rise from poverty also meant that Chinese businesspeople and workers were less likely to be dismayed by African conditions than their more cosseted Western counterparts: dirt roads, hungry people and corrupt bureaucrats were familiar enough in China itself. As one Chinese official put it, 'Africa does not frighten us.'[4]

Over the course of the next decade, Chinese trade and investment poured into Africa and helped to transform international perceptions of the continent's prospects. China's two-way trade with Africa grew twentyfold between 2000 and 2010, from $10 billion a year to $200 billion. That made China comfortably Africa's largest trading partner.[5] The biggest deals usually involved the minerals and natural resources that the Chinese economy was hungry for. The examples were legion – they included the Chinese National Petroleum Corporation's purchase of 20% of a natural-gas field in Mozambique for $4.2 billion;[6] a $23 billion deal for China to build three oil refineries and a fuel complex in Nigeria; the construction of the $1.8 billion Merowe Dam on the Nile in Sudan, the largest hydropower project in Africa; and a $24 billion project to transform Lamu port in Kenya.[7]

The impact of Chinese investment was visible all over the continent. Within a decade, China claimed to have built forty-two stadiums and fifty-two hospitals on the African continent – often as part of deals that secured access to natural resources. These giant projects were also a source of prestige for China and a reminder of its growing power.[8] The Oxford academic Chris Alden remarked that 'China is increasingly replacing the West as the new face of globalisation in Africa.'[9]

China's growing presence in Africa was not just a matter of buildings, roads and investment – it was also about people. Chinese faces were increasingly visible across the continent, from boardrooms to market stalls. By 2010, it was widely estimated that there were around a million Chinese immigrants resident in Africa — although in truth, nobody could be sure of the real figure. Sometimes it took an anecdote or an incident to dramatise the new situation. In 2011, as Libya collapsed into civil strife following the overthrow of the Gaddafi regime, the Chinese government organised a naval mission to rescue its citizens stranded in Libya. I was at a lunch at the Japanese embassy in London at the time, and remember the shock of my Japanese hosts to discover that there were 30,000 Chinese people working in Libya — and that the Chinese government was capable of organising a naval mission in the Mediterranean to rescue them.

The growth of Chinese influence in Africa has also raised eyebrows in Washington, as well as Tokyo, for understandable reasons. For China's growing influence in Africa is the most prominent example of China emerging as a truly global power — with an economic and diplomatic reach that extends well beyond its own Asian hinterland.

Western powers had got used to regarding the African continent as part of their 'zone of influence'. The 'Scramble for Africa' of the 1880s had divided the continent up as the colonial fiefdoms of various European powers — with the British and French to the fore, and the Portuguese, Germans and Belgians also prominent. Even after decolonisation, European powers assumed that they had a special role to play in Africa. The French still jealously guard their influence in 'la Francophonie' — the French-speaking former colonies in West Africa. The British nurture their ties and investments with the nineteen Commonwealth nations in Africa, including regional powers such as Nigeria, Kenya and South Africa. Portugal remained an imperial power in Mozambique and Angola until the 1970s, and as the Portuguese economy has slumped in recent years, many members of the Portuguese middle class have returned to Angola, in particular, in search of work. The United States also has its special ties to Africa, through the African American community. Beyond that, Africa was also contested ground in the Cold War. In the 1970s, the US fought a proxy war with the Soviet Union in Africa, with the two superpowers intervening to back rival sides in the Angolan civil war.

For all these reasons China's growing and visible presence in Africa came as something of a shock to many in the West. Yet, in truth, Western companies and governments had simply not moved with the speed and daring of their Chinese counterparts. As Kofi Annan, the Ghanaian former Secretary General of the United Nations put it, 'I ask the West, where were you?'[10]

The expansion of Chinese influence in Latin America, although less commented upon, was in many ways just as remarkable as China's growing presence in Africa. Latin America, after all, was the United States's backyard. The Monroe Doctrine, declared in 1823, had made it US policy to oppose foreign intervention in the Americas. Throughout the Cold War, the US had fought to combat Russian influence in Latin America – acting, often ruthlessly, from Nicaragua to Cuba to Chile.

But in the first decade of the twenty-first century, the influence of China grew with remarkable speed, in a way that the Americans largely missed. That development – combined with the 'pink tide' that saw the rise of a number of left and far-left governments in Latin America, after the turn of the millennium – saw a sharp diminution in Washington's influence in the Americas. In 2015, Michael Reid, a noted regional analyst, could comment that 'The United States arguably has less influence now in Latin America than at any point in the past century.'[11]

Latin American countries, which had previously felt that they would always live in the economic shadow of the US, suddenly found that they had options. On a visit in 2010 to Brazil, Latin America's largest country, I was told bluntly by a senior diplomat that distant China was now more important to Brazil than the US. Reflecting this new reality, the newly elected president, Dilma Rousseff, made a state visit to China in April 2011 – several months before visiting Washington.

The reason was simple: China was now Brazil's largest trading partner – importing almost twice as much from Brazil, by value, as the

United States. And Brazil's economic boom, which had seen real-estate prices in Sao Paulo exceed those in New York, was directly linked to China's hunger for Brazilian soy, sugar, meat, iron and copper. Much as with Africa, China's thirst for natural resources and commodities was the driving force of a remarkable boom in two-way trade. In the decade after 2000, China also became the largest trading partner of Peru and Chile which, like Brazil, are large commodity producers. Between 2000 and 2013, China's trade with Latin America grew from $10 billion to $257 billion a year.[12]

The Brazilians soon discovered, however, that economic dependence on China was a double-edged sword. Even in 2010, the country's manufacturing industries were struggling to compete with cheap Chinese imports and screaming for protection. By 2014, when I revisited the country, Brazil's growth had slowed sharply – largely in response to falling demand for commodities, as Chinese growth slowed. The public mood was restive. When President Rousseff appeared at World Cup matches, she was booed. But even so, Brazil had little option but to humour the Chinese. A summit of the BRICS nations was scheduled in the Brazilian city of Fortaleza to coincide with the World Cup – largely, it was rumoured, because President Xi Jinping was a football fan.

Brazil's membership of the BRICS and the G20 was a symbol of the fact that the country was increasingly being treated as the spokesman for an entire continent – a status that it enjoyed in large part because it has the biggest population in Latin America, with just over 200 million people.[13] Some, particularly in Mexico (Brazil's main regional rival), resent the lazy tendency to regard Brazil as speaking for the continent and argue that Brazil is atypical of Latin America, because of its dependence on commodity exports.

In reality, however, most of the leading Latin American economies – including Argentina, Chile and Peru – are big commodity producers, whose trade with China also boomed in the first decade of the twenty-first century. China's footprints are visible all over America's backyard – even in the Caribbean islands, which are just a short flight from Miami. In the Bahamas, one of America's favourite Caribbean resorts, it is Chinese investors who have funded the largest new hotel on the island – the $3.5 billion Baha Mar convention centre, with 2,200 rooms and the largest casino in the Caribbean. The project has not run smoothly. In early 2016, the huge complex – almost complete, but still empty – filed for bankruptcy. But such a giant project is unlikely to be abandoned – and the Bahamian government claims that Baha Mar alone will eventually account for 12% of their country's GDP.[14]

Setbacks such as these are probably inevitable, given the imperial scale of some of the infrastructure projects that Chinese companies have promised to back in Latin America. One example is a plan for a new canal across Nicaragua that would link the Pacific and Atlantic oceans, at a cost of $50 billion, and so rival the Panama Canal that the US built between 1904 and 1914. Another Chinese-backed project was a proposed new high-speed railway in Mexico. And on a visit to Brazil in 2015, Li Keqiang, the Chinese prime minister, signed an agreement for a new feasibility study for a Trans-Amazon railway to run from Brazil's Atlantic coast to the Pacific coast of Peru.[15]

These projects are not simply commercial in intention. They are intended to send a message of Chinese power and ambition – reminiscent of Britain's commitment to a Cape-to-Cairo route at the height of British imperial ambition. Sceptical observers point out that the announcement of an ambitious Chinese project is not always followed by fulfillment. It is not just the Bahamian hotel project that ran into financial difficulties in 2015,[16] so did the Mexican high-speed railway. There are also reasons to doubt whether the new Nicaraguan canal will ever be completed; or if the Trans-Amazon railway will even make it off the drawing board. And yet these announcements are still significant. They signal that China has the ambition and the finance to consider projects that would transform the infrastructure of a far-off continent in America's backyard.

In both Latin America and Africa, it was China's investment that generated the most excitement and controversy. But a single-minded focus on China obscured the fact that both Africa and Latin America were also attracting significant amounts of capital from the rest of Asia.

India, in particular, is well placed to make the best of new opportunities in Africa. Railway workers and traders from India had migrated to Africa in the early twentieth century – famously, even Gandhi spent twenty years in South Africa as a young man. Until 1999, India did more two-way trade with Africa than China – and family and ethnic ties across the Indian Ocean, as well as relative proximity, gave India a comparative advantage on the continent. The sight of China forging ahead spurred on the Indians. Following the Chinese model, the Indian government held summits with African leaders in 2008 and 2011. Indian companies also poured into Africa. In one emblematic investment, Bharti Airtel invested $10.7 billion on building an Africa-wide mobile-phone network. By 2010, India's two-way trade with Africa stood at $57 billion – just under a third the level of China's.

Some development economists argue that over the coming decades it will be Africa's relationship with India – rather than China – that provides new dynamism to the world economy. The thesis is that as the populations of China, South Korea and Japan age and then shrink, so growth in East Asia will slow. By contrast, India and Africa have much younger populations. Over the long run that might mean that the Indian Ocean rim displaces the Pacific Rim as the most dynamic area in the global economy.[17]

Spooked by the sight of Chinese expansion in Africa and Latin America, Japan has also tried to respond. In January 2014, Shinzo Abe became the first Japanese prime minister to visit the African continent in eight years. Japan was already one of the largest aid donors to Africa – but Abe pledged to also encourage more private-sector investment.[18] Six months later, Abe was on a tour of Latin America – a continent with which Japan had stronger ties. There are thought to be over 300,000 Brazilians of Japanese origin in the city of Sao Paulo alone, while in Peru, the ethnically Japanese Fujimori family has also provided one president and a presidential candidate. Abe's five-nation tour took in Brazil, where he pushed for Japanese involvement in the development of the Sao Paulo subway and the offshore oil industry. In Mexico and Colombia, the Japanese leader signed energy deals, while in Chile he blessed a large Japanese investment in a copper mine.[19] Just as shrewd Latin American countries had once profited from the geopolitical competition between the USSR and the US, so now they found themselves as players in the emerging geopolitical rivalries in East Asia.

For by the time Abe was touring Africa and Latin America, it was clear that both continents were part of an emerging battle for political influence that implicated the US, Europe, Japan, India and – above all – China. It was inevitable that it was China's involvement that sparked the most interest and concern in the West – both because of the scale of Chinese investments and because China, unlike India or Japan, is regarded by the United States as an emerging global rival. Some prominent figures in the West take a largely benign view of China's involvement in Latin America and Africa. As president of the World Bank, Robert Zoellick, who had served in several Republican administrations, maintained a deliberately positive attitude, stressing the benefits brought by Chinese investment.

But many Western commentators are intrigued by the idea that China might replicate old patterns of exploitation that were once patented by the countries of Europe. After all, the pattern of European imperialism had often been that traders (or missionaries) made the first breakthrough, creating conflicts and demands that later led to the imposition of political control from Europe. Even if China never sought a formal political role in Africa, Beijing's role in propping up some of the continent's less attractive regimes – for example in Sudan or Zimbabwe, through financial and diplomatic support – has attracted Western charges of exploitation and political cynicism.

The Chinese are well aware of Western suspicion of their involvement in Africa and are determined to give it short shrift. At a meeting with Chinese academics specialising in Africa, in Beijing in 2008, I was reminded that Westerners – who had once traded Africans as slaves and then colonised their countries – are ill-placed to complain about China's behaviour in Africa. Indeed, I was told, because China itself had suffered at the hands of Western imperialism, it has empathy with the economic and political needs of Africans. Chinese investment was not some form of new imperialism. Instead, it is 'south–south' co-operation. Wang Yi, China's foreign minister, made the same point on a trip to Africa in 2015, when he vowed 'We absolutely will not take the path of Western imperialism.'[20]

China's foreign policy emphasised 'non-interference' in the internal affairs of the African governments it was dealing with – and many African leaders clearly welcomed the contrast with fussy Western 'conditionality'. Western lenders, such as the World Bank or the US government, now routinely demand that African borrowers accept environmental and governance conditions before loans are released. The Chinese have been much less fussy. Abdoulaye Wade, the former president of Senegal, argued that 'China's approach to our needs is simply better adapted than the slow and sometimes patronising post-colonial approach of European investors, donor organisations and non-governmental organisations.'[21]

Critics of China's methods respond that whilst African leaders might be delighted by the deals they could do with the government in Beijing, ordinary Africans were not always such clear beneficiaries. One common complaint is that Chinese firms have often brought in labour from China itself, rather than employing locals. Western journalists also found it relatively easy to find Chinese employers expressing racist attitudes towards Africans that sounded like they could have come from the mouths of Western imperialists.

Like the Brazilians, some Africans also worry that China's relationship with Africa has replicated some of the malign economic characteristics of colonialism, because Africa has sold raw materials and imported higher-value manufactured goods in return. Lamido Sanusi, a respected central-bank governor in Nigeria, has complained that this kind of economic relationship is 'the essence of colonialism' – because it locks African countries into a dependent relationship with China, with China capturing most of the profits.[22]

Yet, as China's economy has changed, the nature of Chinese investments in Africa is also changing. Rising wage costs in China means that many manufacturers are now looking elsewhere for low-cost labour. If President Obama had looked out of the window as he drove into Addis Ababa in 2015, he might have seen a new industrial park near the airport – full of Chinese-backed factories, such as one owned by Huajian, the world's largest shoemaker – which was already employing 4,000 people and had ambitions to grow to 40,000. Little wonder when wages in Ethiopia were ten times lower than those in southern China.[23]

China's growing economic influence has also inevitably become a political issue across Africa. In Zambia in 2011, Michael Sata won a presidential election after campaigning vociferously against the allegedly exploitative nature of Chinese investment in his country. In South Africa, some felt that their country was humiliatingly willing to accommodate China. When the South African government refused to meet the Dalai Lama in 2014 (always a litmus test of a willingness to accommodate Beijing), one influential South African columnist fulminated that 'The Dalai Lama has become a byword for South Africa's grovelling submission to Chinese diktat.'[24]

In Africa, as in Europe, however, most political leaders are willing to adapt pragmatically to Chinese preferences on issues such as the Dalai Lama, in the interests of preserving valuable business ties. Once in office, even Zambia's President Sata quickly made his peace with China – which was, after all, the biggest customer for Zambian copper.[25]

And while there have been complaints about China's political influence, for most governments in Africa and Latin America the arrival of the Chinese and other Asian investors has been a welcome development – politically, as well as economically. For countries and politicians that had chafed at a Western-dominated world, a degree of Easternisation offered interesting new political possibilities.

Luis Inacio da Silva, otherwise known as 'Lula' – who was the charismatic president of Brazil between 2002 and 2010 – was widely regarded in the West as a former radical who had embraced a form of moderate, pro-Western social democracy. But when it came to foreign policy, Lula retained a radical edge, arguing that 'Brazil, Russia, India and China have a fundamental role in creating a new world order.'[26]

The BRICS acronym, once little more than a marketing tool for Goldman Sachs, had taken on a real political life by the end of Lula's period in office – holding regular summits of Brazil, Russia, India and China, and welcoming South Africa to the fold in 2011. Most Western observers have dismissed the BRICS pretensions to form a political counterweight to the West, pointing out that the organisation grouped together democracies and autocracies and economies of vastly different sizes. (The Chinese economy is more than twenty times the size of South Africa's.) Nonetheless, there is some evidence that, at a time of political crisis, the BRICS can take a common position. The Russians were delighted that none of their BRICS partners voted with the US and the EU to condemn Russia's annexation of Crimea, when it was debated at the UN in 2014.

The Americans' knowledge that they are once again competing for influence in Africa and Latin America has prompted some changes in their foreign policy. In 2007, the US set up a military command group focused on Africa, to sit alongside the existing regional commands that were focused on the Pacific, the Middle East, Europe and the Americas. (Slightly bizarrely, 'Africom' was based in Stuttgart.) Its establishment had a lot to do with the emergence of terrorist threats in Africa, but it also reflected an increasing American awareness of the risk of strategic competition emerging in Africa.

The Obama administration has also sought to bolster America's 'soft power' in both Africa and the Americas, as a counter to Chinese economic influence. The revelations that the US had been spying on the telecommunications of President Rousseff of Brazil were a blow, resulting in a cancelled state visit to Washington. But Obama was able to gain some lost ground by re-establishing diplomatic relations with Cuba in 2015, soothing a long-standing sore in US–Latin American relations. The Americans also began to play down their demands for Latin co-operation in the 'war on drugs', as they sought to bolster their position in the Americas.

The question of whether Western policy in Africa and the Americas should change in response to a new competition for influence with China has been posed with increasing urgency during the Obama years. Some policymakers argue, usually sotto voce, that the US and the EU should moderate their rhetoric on issues like governance and democracy, for fear of losing friends and contracts.

On his Africa tour of 2015, however, Obama quite deliberately took the opposite tack. In set-piece speeches in both Kenya and Ethiopia he tackled some of the most sensitive issues in African politics and society – speaking out in favour of gay rights, condemning the 'cancer of corruption' and telling the African Union that 'Nobody should be president for life.'[27] As it happened, the president of the African Union at the time was Robert Mugabe, the despotic ninety-one-year-old president of Zimbabwe who was well into his third decade in office. Mugabe, however, was not present in the audience – some of whom warmly applauded Obama's pro-democracy rhetoric. Obama's message that 'Africa doesn't need strong men, it needs strong institutions' provided a strong contrast to China's stress on personalised diplomacy and 'non-interference' in the domestic affairs of African nations.

For the US to take such a position was a gamble at a time when China's influence was growing so rapidly in both Africa and the Americas. But, taking a longer view, Obama's stress on strong institutions was well judged. For in an age when the world economy is Easternising, the best chance Americans and Europeans have of retaining their global political power lies in the enduring strength of Western institutions.

14

The West's Institutional Advantage

The headquarters of the Society for Worldwide Interbank Financial Telecommunications are set back from a wooded road in the small Belgian town of La Hulpe, just outside Brussels. Anyone driving past would have no reason to think that they were passing by an institution that serves as the switchboard of the world's financial system. The only hint of Swift's importance is the sheer size of the society's building – which is the length of a football field.

Yet Swift emerged unwillingly from suburban anonymity in 2012, when the passage of EU sanctions forced the society to disconnect Iranian banks from its service. At a stroke, Iran was cut off from the global financial system. Within months, the Iranian economy was suffocating – forcing the Islamic Republic to make major concessions in international negotiations over its nuclear programme.

Iran's troubles highlighted the fact that access to the global economy is dependent on the ability to transfer money across borders. Swift provides the technology and protocols that connect international banks. Anybody who has done an international money transfer, requiring a SWIFT code or an IBAN number, will have used its system.

Swift is a privately owned co-operative that is owned and run by its member banks – and its board contains representatives of financial institutions from all over the world, including Russia, China and Japan, as well as the US and Europe. The location of the society's headquarters in Belgium seemed of scant significance until the drive for international sanctions on Iran. At that point, the fact that Swift is subject to European law came into sharp focus. When the EU, pushed hard by the United States, passed sanctions that targeted Iran's links to Swift, the society had little option but to cut off its services.

The devastating effect of the Swift ban was noted all over the world. When the West started imposing sanctions on Russia in the aftermath of the annexation of Crimea, one senior Russian diplomat warned that cutting his country loose from Swift would be regarded as tantamount to a declaration of war.[1] But the Swift episode also had a wider significance. It revealed some of the hidden wiring that makes the global economy work. And it also highlighted how much of this wiring is still centred in the West.

This chapter examines why so much of the world is still wired through the West by looking at some of the key institutions that underpin the global economic and political order. These include high-profile international institutions such as the United Nations, the World Bank and the IMF; but they also include much lower-profile organisations that are often regarded as technical and apolitical in nature – such as Swift or ICANN, the organisation that manages internet domain names, which is based in Los Angeles. Then, there are organisations that seem to have little to do with politics, but whose high international profile means that their control and management have become important gauges of prestige and power. These include the governing bodies for world sport, such as FIFA, which runs international football and is based in Switzerland.

Finally, there is a form of international wiring that goes beyond formal institutions: the forms of money and the laws that are most widely used around the world. The US legal system has a reach that goes well beyond its borders, as FIFA officials discovered when they were arrested in Switzerland and extradited to the US following an FBI corruption investigation. The fact that the dollar is the world's leading reserve currency is, perhaps, the single biggest source of American institutional strength – allowing the US to borrow and trade in its own currency and helping US banks to dominate global finance. As a result, the question of whether the dollar will cede its dominance to the Chinese renminbi (RMB) is of enormous political significance.

The fact that so many institutions – formal and informal – that are critical to the governance of the global economy and international politics are located in the West is a major source of political power. But will this advantage endure in the era of Easternisation?

The answer to that question depends on the significance of economic power in deciding who controls global institutions. If economic might is what ultimately matters, we can expect more of the world's wiring to run through Asia in the future. But it is also possible that other factors are important. History plays a part. The United Nations set up shop in New York in 1946 and has been there ever since. Similarly, the World Bank and the International Monetary Fund have been based in Washington DC ever since their foundation. Although the UN, the IMF and the World Bank are all international institutions, the fact that they are based in America matters – it makes them more susceptible to the ideas and political pressures that surround them.

However, the institutional inertia produced by history cannot be expected to preserve the West's advantage indefinitely If international institutions no longer reflect the realities of the world around them, they will eventually become irrelevant – and the world's most powerful countries will bypass them or set up alternative organisations. The most important non-economic Western edge goes beyond history. It is the West's reputation for the rule of law.

As long as the US and the EU are perceived as running institutions that enforce rules predictably, impartially and swiftly, powerful people and institutions may continue to prefer to use institutions based in the

West. In that case the world's wiring will remain disproportionately located in the Western world, even as the West's share of the global economy shrinks.

However, there is a catch-22 involved in the West's institutional power. Although the fact that so many important institutions are based in the West is indeed a source of political power for the US and the EU, if the West begins to use that political power too overtly then the rest of the world's faith in the impartiality of institutions based in the West will diminish. At that point, the drive to set up alternative structures will accelerate, eroding one of the West's remaining great advantages in the competition for international political power. This question of the use and abuse of Western power is one that links very disparate institutions, from the IMF to ICANN.

The United Nations is without doubt the grandest of all international organisations. Yet its origins in the post-1945 order have handed an increasingly anachronistic advantage to the West. The five permanent members of the UN Security Council are the US, the UK, France, Russia and China – the nations that were deemed to be the victors in the Second World War. Nobody setting up the UN today would give veto powers and permanent membership to middle-ranking European powers such as Britain and France, and not to India, Japan or Germany. Nor would it be feasible to have no African or Latin American country represented on the UNSC.

Successive efforts at Security Council reform have foundered on cross-cutting international vetoes – the Chinese will not countenance Japan joining the UNSC; the Africans cannot agree on a single candidate and nor can the Arabs. China is also quietly opposed to India joining the Security Council and while the British and the French might support a German bid, the rest of the world would not countenance three permanent European members. The result is deadlock – heightening the sense of injustice in India and Brazil, in particular.

And yet the UNSC has just about retained its international legitimacy, courtesy of a historical legacy – the fact that, following Japan's surrender, China was one of the victors of 1945. This has ensured that the world's two largest powers at the beginning of the twenty-first century – the US and China – are represented on the world's most important decision-making body. And that, in turn, makes the anachronism of British, French and even Russian membership less intolerable. The fact that the relatively powerless UN General Assembly is often seen as a forum for anti-Western posturing has damaged the UN's reputation in the US – but paradoxically boosted its international legitimacy elsewhere.

The perception of bias towards the West is even more problematic when it comes to the world's two leading international economic institutions – the IMF and the World Bank. The Bretton Woods institutions – so named because they were conceived at a conference in Bretton Woods, New Hampshire, in 1944 – are based in Washington. By tradition, an American has always headed the World Bank and a European has always headed the IMF. American embarrassment at this state of affairs may have been reflected in their decision to nominate an Asian American, Jim Young-Kim (president of Dartmouth University) as the new head of the World Bank in 2014.

The historical anachronism surrounding the leadership of the Bretton Woods institutions was compounded by the voting weights at the IMF. By 2014, the four largest BRICS (Brazil, Russia, India and China) accounted for 24.5% of global economic output, but had only 10.3% of the votes at the IMF. By contrast, the four largest EU economies (Germany, France, the UK and Italy) accounted for 13.4% of the world economy, but had 17.6% of votes. To correct this obvious and growing anomaly, the IMF and its key members agreed to reform the voting system in 2010, with a 6.2% shift in votes towards dynamic, emerging economies.[2] Yet even this very modest change proved too much to accept for the US Congress, which refused to ratify the changes for five long years.

America's inability to pass IMF reform became a serious embarrassment to the Obama administration. Jack Lew, who served as US

Treasury Secretary from 2013, lamented the regularity with which he found himself having to apologise to other finance ministers for American inaction on IMF reform. A low point was reached at a G20 summit in Brisbane in 2014, when Putin won allies around the table as he criticised US sloth on IMF reform. Eventually, towards the end of 2015, Congress finally endorsed the changes. But by then, significant damage had been done.[3]

China's successful move in 2014 to press ahead with the formation of a BRICS bank and an Asian Infrastructure Investment Bank – both of which were to be based in China – was widely perceived as a reaction to the innate Western bias in the Bretton Woods institutions. The warm international reaction to both new institutions may, in large part, have simply reflected China's growing financial muscle. But it also suggested that perceptions of pro-Western bias at the IMF and the World Bank were widely shared in emerging nations.

The IMF's behaviour in the European financial crisis added fuel to charges of pro-Western bias. Critics in the emerging world pointed out that the IMF had extended loans of €58 billion to Greece, a moderately well-off European country of 11 million people. By contrast, when Indonesia – a country of over 200 million people – was threatened with bankruptcy in 1997, the IMF had extended $23 billion in loans and imposed conditions so severe that they contributed to the downfall of the Suharto regime, which had been in power for over thirty years. The IMF's strictness with Indonesia (symbolised by a famous photo of the then IMF chief, Michel Camdessus, a former French finance minister, standing over President Suharto as he signed the bailout deal) seemed to contrast strongly with its willingness to bend the rules for Greece and the tottering euro project. Critics in the developing world were swift to point to the fact that throughout the Greek crisis, the IMF had been headed by two former French finance ministers: first Dominique Strauss-Kahn and then, when he was forced to resign in disgrace in 2011, Christine Lagarde. The survival of the euro was an issue of the utmost importance for France.

So it was certainly questionable whether IMF bosses so closely connected to the French state could really be impartial, when it came to the euro.

When the IMF's main 'clients' were almost invariably non-Western nations in need of financial assistance, a former French finance minister (such as Jacques de Larosière or Christine Lagarde) could be seen as an impartial source of money, expertise and aid. But when the financial crises were taking place in Europe, Western leadership of the Bretton Woods institutions became increasingly contentious.

This same question of whether the West can still be trusted to run international institutions in an impartial fashion came up again and again in different guises: with Swift, ICANN and FIFA all providing different versions of a similar debate.

Swift's directors were aghast to find themselves used as a tool of Western foreign policy. The organisation relies on providing a global service and could see the cost of appearing to take sides in international political disputes. Swift's chairman Yawar Shah had boasted that 'Neutrality is in Swift's DNA.'[4] Yet when the pressure to isolate Iran grew, Swift was powerless to resist. Although it was ultimately EU law that forced Swift to act, the organisation was also under considerable threat from possible US sanctions. If Swift had refused to act, legislation under consideration in America could have placed its directors on a list of 'Specially Designated Nationals' (the much-feared SDN list), barring them from entry to the United States. That would be an extremely difficult situation to be in for anyone involved in international finance.

In the aftermath of Swift's disconnection of Iran, Lazaro Campos, its former CEO, drew attention to the implications of Western sanctions, warning that 'Global organisations are now a species in extinction. I think that the extraterritorial nature of some of the legislation we're seeing in the US, and now increasingly in Europe, makes it almost impossible for global companies to be global because we end up being a tool for politicians.'[5]

Campos' fears began to be realised in 2014. As talk of a ban on Russia using Swift mounted, so the Russians began to talk more intensively to the Chinese about setting up an alternative international payments system. Reports surfaced that Beijing was working on a China International Payments System (CIPS), which would be a platform for transactions in RMB. The Russians, in turn, made it clear that they were potentially very interested in using CIPS as an alternative to Swift.

The West's use of institutions like Swift for political purposes – while immensely tempting – had the potential to backfire. As Campos complained: 'On the one side the Western world wants the East to come and join the system. But, at the same time they're using, misusing, the system to implement their own geopolitical objectives. We're going to have to choose.'[6]

The realisation that imposing a Swift ban on Russia could have unintended consequences helped to persuade Western governments to keep the option in reserve as the Ukraine crisis mounted. As one White House official put it to me in 2014, 'If you ranked sanctions on a scale of one to ten, Swift would be a ten – and right now we're still only on a three or four.'[7] There were also strategic reasons for encouraging the Russians, the Chinese and others to keep using a Western payments system. As one former US intelligence official explained to me, with a slight smile, 'As long as they use Swift, we can watch what they are doing.'[8]

The obvious implication of this statement – that some financial transactions carried out through Swift can be monitored by Western intelligence agencies – dates back to the reaction to 9/11, when American anti-terrorism legislation had compelled Swift to hand over data on financial transactions that might have a bearing on terrorism. The data that Swift and other financial organisations are compelled to hand over is tightly circumscribed by law to ensure that it is confined to the 'war on terror'. But the 2013 revelations by the American whistleblower Edward Snowden, of the monitoring of phone calls and internet traffic by America's National Security Agency (NSA), inevitably heightened concern about the extent of US electronic surveillance of global communications well beyond the sphere of finance. The Snowden revelations caused political controversy all over the world. The resulting political backlash threatened to fracture the global nature of the internet, as countries reacted against American 'control' of the underlying infrastructure that governed the World Wide Web.

The fact that so much of the administration and technology underpinning the internet is centred in the US reflects the origins of the web as a project sponsored by the US Department of Defense and developed in American universities. One institution that attracted particular fascination and controversy was ICANN, the organisation that assigns the unique names and numbers that identify individual websites across the world – effectively the internet's telephone book.

ICANN's work was originally done by a single individual: Jon Postel of the University of Southern California. In time, Postel was replaced by an institution, but ICANN remained based in Los Angeles and regulated by the US Department of Commerce. As the internet scholar Laura DeNardis points out, ICANN is just one part of the wiring that makes the internet work. Nonetheless, even before the world had heard of Edward Snowden, ICANN had become central to what DeNardis calls an 'international narrative' about 'what is construed to be hegemonic and historic US government control of the internet'.[9] The year before the Snowden scandal broke, Sachin Pilot, India's telecommunications minister, complained: 'Globally internet traffic passes through thirteen root-servers. Nine of them are in the US, two each in Japan and western Europe . . . I believe India and other countries ought to play a much more relevant role in managing traffic flows. The internet is a global resource, whose governance can't be limited to a particular geography.'[10] Within a couple of years, technological development meant that the thirteen root-servers all existed in multiple locations on different continents. However, this technical change did almost nothing to assuage the wave of global concern about US 'control' of the internet stirred up by Snowden.

Demands for some kind of UN control over the internet, which had been rumbling for decades, escalated hugely in the wake of the Snowden revelations about the NSA's global reach. The decision by Dilma Rousseff, the president of Brazil, to cancel a state visit to Washington in protest at discovering that her email had been monitored by the US, was not just a one-off protest. In a later speech to the UN, Rousseff demanded international control of the internet. Meanwhile, the Brazilian government contemplated laws demanding that personal data on Brazilians be stored only on servers within the country's national boundaries. Angela Merkel, another leader whose communications had been snooped on by the NSA, also floated the idea of breaking with American control, talking of the need for a European internet. In Brussels, the European Commission argued that 'Large-scale surveillance and intelligence activities have led to a loss of confidence in the internet and its present governance arrangements.'[11] The American internet giants began to fear – with reason – that this backlash might be used by their European rivals to press for laws, restraining the likes of Google. On the European left, a new acronym began to be used to denote the allegedly sinister power of Silicon Valley – 'GAFA', which stood for Google, Apple, Facebook and Amazon.

China's reaction was less voluble, but potentially even more threatening to US interests. The Snowden revelations broke just two days before the Sunnylands summit between presidents Obama and Xi Jinping in June 2013. The Americans had been planning to put complaints about Chinese cyber espionage at the centre of discussions, but were thrown on the defensive by the NSA scandal. (Some American officials believed that this was no coincidence, noting that Snowden first broke cover in Hong Kong.) In the following year, the Chinese official media began to warn their country's companies against using the products of American computing giants such as IBM, Cisco and

Microsoft – with all three firms reporting significant drops in sales in China.[12] In many respects China's increasingly suspicious treatment of the big US technology companies simply mirrored the extreme wariness with which the Americans had treated Chinese tech firms, in particular, Huawei, one of the world's biggest makers of telecoms equipment. China's increasingly tight censorship of the internet at home – although driven by domestic political concerns – was also now justified increasingly in terms of 'national security'.

The Obama administration's argument that the NSA did not snoop on American citizens was of no help to companies like Google, Facebook and Amazon – which were seeking to build global businesses and saw the whole world as potential customers. In the wake of the Snowden affair, relations between Silicon Valley and the White House deteriorated sharply. Mark Zuckerberg, the founder of Facebook, complained that 'The government blew it', adding, 'Governments around the world are now threatening the security of the internet by passing their own laws that permit intrusion on internet users.'[13] When I visited Silicon Valley in the spring of 2015, it became clear that relations between the Obama administration and companies such as Google and Facebook were far from cordial. In an effort to reassure their customers about the security of their data, the Silicon Valley giants were promising to provide them with new forms of uncrackable encryption. These efforts were greeted with horror by US intelligence agencies who argued that it would mean that communications between terrorists would 'go dark' – putting ordinary citizens at risk. The US government was threatening Silicon Valley with new legislation, which would compel 'GAFA' to hand over customer data.

Despite its impatience with Silicon Valley, the Obama administration also felt the need to try to assuage international concerns about American control of the internet – and made some important concessions. In the wake of the Snowden scandal, the US Department of Commerce announced that it would relinquish regulatory control over ICANN in favour of a more international form of management – with the important caveat that the new system should emphasise control by the private sector, rather than governments. The Obama administration felt that a private-sector model would safeguard the internet against the spectre of control by the United Nations. But conservative critics in the US were not reassured. Newt Gingrich, a prominent Republican, warned that for the US to relinquish control of ICANN was 'very, very dangerous', adding, 'This risks foreign dictatorships defining the internet.'[14]

The fear that the West was losing control of institutions that it once invented was not confined to the internet. The governance of football, the world's most popular sport, had far less economic significance than the governance of the internet – but a higher international profile. In December 2010, FIFA seemed to exemplify the declining clout of the West when it rejected bids to stage the 2018 and 2022 World Cups from England, Spain, the Netherlands, the US and Australia – in favour of Russia and Qatar. Despite deploying the British royal family as lobbyists, England's bid for the 2018 tournament had received a humiliating two votes – trailing in last. Sir Dave Richards, the chairman of England's Premier League, complained bitterly, 'We started the game and wrote the rules and took it to the world. We owned the game . . . Then fifty years later, somebody comes along and they actually stole it.'[15] The British press was full of accusations of corruption at FIFA. But it seemed as if there was nothing to be done.

In May 2015, a couple of days before a FIFA congress in Zurich, my *FT* colleague Simon Kuper wrote that Sepp Blatter, the seventy-nine-year-old Swiss president of FIFA, had 'understood very early that there's a new world order in which Westerners don't matter very much'. The decision to award the World Cups to Russia and Qatar were symbols of that order, and 'Western countries are powerless to change FIFA.'[16]

Yet, a few days later, something happened that undermined assumptions of Western powerlessness. Swiss police, acting on a warrant from the FBI, swooped on the FIFA congress in Zurich, arresting several of the organisation's most senior officials. Within days, the once untouchable Blatter resigned. This was a chain of events that only the US had both the will and the means to set off.[17]

But what was the source of this enduring American power? The answer it seemed was twofold: the US dollar and the US legal system. The FBI were able to build a case that was answerable in America because the bribes that were allegedly paid went through US banks – which, in turn, reflected the central role of the dollar in the global financial system. It was FIFA officials' use of the US banking system that helped to bring them within reach of the American legal system. These powers were not a freak of the FIFA case. The power of the dollar and of American and EU law were also what had enabled the West to co-ordinate sanctions campaigns against Iran and Russia.

The dollar and the law are two powerful forces that mean that, even as the global economy Easternises, much of the world's wiring still runs through the West.

But how long will these advantages last, in a world in which China and other Asian economies are rising fast? The answer will depend on internal developments in Asia and the West – and, above all, in China and the US. Further evidence that the US is inclined to abuse its institutional power to advance its foreign-policy goals will spur further efforts to develop alternative non-Western institutions. However, the success of those efforts will depend on whether the sponsors of these new institutions are able to persuade other countries that their new forums are less open to political manipulation than the old ones, based in the West. For China, in particular, this raises very fundamental issues about the rule of law, in a system in which the Communist Party remains above all other institutions – including the courts.

As things stand, the world's preference for using the legal systems of the West – and of the US and the UK in particular – remains very marked. The widespread use of British common law in international business has led to some arguing that just as America has the world's 'reserve currency', Britain issues the world's 'reserve law'.[18] Britain's ambition to be 'lawyer to the world', in the words of Kenneth Clarke, the Justice Secretary in the first Cameron government, seemed well on the way to fruition with more international commercial disputes arbitrated in London than any other city in the world.[19] In 2012 some 40% of big international businesses reported that they used English law for cross-border deals, with another 22% opting for US law. As a result, in 2015, ninety-one of the hundred largest law firms in the world were either British or American – and almost two-thirds of the litigants in English commercial courts were foreigners.[20]

This global preference for using the British or American legal systems is, in large part, a tribute to these countries' strong reputations for the rule of law. For the emerging economic giants of Asia, it is also a commentary on the deficiencies of their own legal systems. China's system of commercial law was designed by the Communist Party and its courts remain under party supervision. India's democratic system and common-law tradition makes its legal system sound more attractive in theory – but delays in the court system are notorious.

The British and the Americans have good reason to hope that a reputation for efficiency and honesty – combined with the fact that English is the world's business language – will sustain the Anglo-American lock on international law. But there are no grounds for Western complacency. In fact, there are already signs that Asia's growing economic weight is beginning to shift things. Singapore, whose legal system is based on English common law, is gaining an increasing share of the international arbitration business, with Indian firms particularly keen. And Chinese firms are increasingly insisting that legal disputes be arbitrated in Hong Kong – whose legal system is also based on English common law, and is meant to be independent of influence from Beijing.[21] The growing importance of the Chinese market has also increased the power of regulators in Beijing. When Shell bid £47 billion to take over BG (formerly British Gas) in 2015, it found that it needed to get approval from regulators in Beijing and Brasilia, as well as Brussels and Washington.

With the West's global economic dominance slipping into history, the 'soft power' conferred by the Anglo-American world's domination of international law is increasingly crucial to ensuring that the world continues to be 'wired' through the West. However, that means that the West – and especially the US – may pay a heavy price if there is evidence that their institutions are no longer operating in a reliable and fair manner. It is already the case that many international businesses are very wary of the US legal system in particular, citing the aggression of American prosecutors and the reputation of US juries for handing out outlandishly large damage settlements, particularly against foreign corporations. (In 2015, one director of a big European oil firm told me that his company was now more concerned about being ensnared in the US legal system than about the Russian authorities.)

Many sceptical Asians believe that the West – for all its rhetoric about the law and a rules-based international system – is inevitably biased in its own favour. The sheer ruthlessness displayed during the age of imperialism might no longer be on full display, but the US and the EU will always be tempted to abuse their institutional power – whether over the internet, the IMF or the international payments system. Indeed this temptation, they argue, will only grow, as the West's military and economic edge erodes.

Nowhere does this question of Western impartiality (or otherwise) matter more than in the crucial business of money. The connection between global political power and the global use of a currency is well established. As Robert Mundell, a Nobel laureate in economics, once put it: 'Great powers have great currencies.'[22] During the Roman Empire, Roman coinage was the dominant international currency. When the British Empire was at its height, sterling was the world's leading reserve currency. As the US displaced the UK as the world's leading power, so the dollar displaced sterling.

If the dollar's status is simply a reflection of the size of the US economy, then in time it can be expected that the Chinese renminbi will rival and then displace the dollar as the world's leading reserve currency. This indeed is the argument that was made in 2011 by Arvind Subramanian in his book *Eclipse*. Dr Subramanian, who was soon to move from the Peterson Institute in Washington to the chief economic adviser's office in the Indian finance ministry, constructed an 'index of economic dominance' based on a mixture of trading volumes, capital flows and share of world GDP. His historical analysis led him to argue that 'economic dominance in the broad sense . . . is the key determinant of reserve currency status'[23] and to conclude that 'history suggests that the renminbi could be in a position to rival the dollar within the next ten years'.[24]

Subramanian was not alone in his analysis. The growth in the US national debt, in the wake of the financial crisis that began on Wall Street in 2008, raised fears that America might be tempted to use inflation to make it easier to repay its debts. This fear was particularly pronounced in China, which was the single biggest foreign holder of US Treasury bills. When Tim Geithner, the US Treasury Secretary, told an audience of Chinese students in 2009 that China's dollar assets were 'very safe', he was greeted with mocking laughter. That same year Chinese officials, including the head of China's central bank, began openly calling for the end of the dollar's domination of international finance. That, in turn, raised the spectre that foreigners, in particular the Chinese, might lose their appetite for buying US debt – making the dollar vulnerable to a sudden plunge in value. Professor Jonathan Kirshner of Cornell University, a leading expert on international currencies, argued in 2014 that 'The dollar is vulnerable in ways that are unprecedented since before World War One.'[25] Congress's flirtation with a technical default on the US debt in 2013 merely stoked cynicism about the dollar's future.

As for the Chinese, the attractions of reaching for reserve currency status were obvious. The internationalisation of the RMB would mean that America's 'exorbitant privilege' – borrowing from abroad in its own currency – would now be extended to China. China would no longer be compelled to put most of its national savings into US

Treasuries. And as the RMB became a global reserve currency, China might expect to enjoy some of the international power and status that the mighty greenback had bestowed on the US. By the time Xi Jinping took power in 2012, the talk in big international financial centres like London and Singapore was all about the impending internationalisation of the RMB. In 2015, an important step was taken when the IMF announced that the RMB would join the small basket of currencies on which it based its Special Drawing Rights (a kind of international currency). The inclusion of the Chinese 'redback' alongside the American 'greenback', the pound, the yen and the euro was an important symbolic step that was likely to encourage foreigners to hold more of their reserves in Chinese currency.

But there is still a catch. For the Chinese currency ever to aspire to be a true global currency, China would have to dismantle the controls that restrict the amounts of currency that people can move in and out of China. Without the guarantee that they can enjoy immediate access to their money, foreigners have much less reason to keep it in RMB. But a fully convertible currency carries political and economic risks. Politically, it would mean that the all-powerful Communist Party has to relinquish one of its most important controls over the economy. And that control might still be very important. For there is considerable evidence of pent-up demand by rich Chinese citizens wanting to get money out of the People's Republic. This became particularly evident as concerns mounted about the number of rich individuals arrested during Xi Jinping's anti-corruption drive. A complete lifting of capital controls raised the threat of a surge of money leaving China – a threat that was underlined by plunges in the Shanghai stock exchange in the summer of 2015 and at the beginning of 2016.

For believers in the dollar, the threat of capital flight from China points to something more than a problem of technical economic management. It underlines the fact that 'reserve-currency status' is dependent on more than economic factors. Ultimately, a currency gains international confidence because it feels like the safest place for people to store their savings. The desire of many Chinese people to get some of their money out of the country reflects underlying fears about the political stability of China and about the vulnerability of individuals to government action, in a country where the Communist Party stands above the courts.

By contrast, the United States, for all its economic vulnerabilities and political uncertainties, is a country that is governed by the rule of law and that is a stable democracy. America's military power adds a further level of reassurance to nervous foreign investors – who want to be certain that the government they are lending to will still be there in thirty years. Anxieties about the erosion of American power, the vagaries of the US legal system, the long-term solvency of the American state and the rise of political populism in the US mean that this 'package' may not be as attractive as it once was. But 'attraction' is always a relative phenomenon. Compared to unproven Chinese institutions, the 'package of power' underpinning the dollar still looks relatively good. When financial markets take fright, panicking investors still tend to look for 'safety' in dollar assets – even if the origins of the panic are actually to be found in the US itself, as with the collapse of Lehman Brothers in 2008.

The West's institutional edge will help to preserve the global reach of Western nations, even as wealth moves east. But retaining the West's institutional integrity will require tremendous self-discipline on the part of American and European leaders. If Western institutions are used too overtly as a source of political power favouring the US and the EU, they will risk losing their attractiveness to the rest of the world. During the Obama years, the danger signs have mounted as the legitimacy and integrity of Western-dominated institutions – from the IMF to the bodies running the internet – have come under increasing challenge.

It is not just international institutions that will affect the global balance of power. The strength of the major powers' domestic institutions is also critically important. Many Western liberals have long argued that China's challenge to the global order will ultimately founder on the fragility of its domestic political system. They point out that while the method by which the US will select its president twenty years hence is completely predictable, nobody can be sure what political arrangements will prevail in China. The potential fragility of China's economic and political system has come into focus once again during the Xi Jinping years, as the economy has slowed and senior officials have been purged as part of an anti-corruption drive.

Yet, while the West's political institutions seem more stable, it is not obvious that they will always create better outcomes and stronger states. Defenders of the Chinese system point out that China enjoyed a decades-long boom under one-party rule. Over the same period, real wages have stagnated in America and opinion polls have consistently shown declining public faith in political institutions. The Obama years have been punctuated by occasional shutdowns of the federal government, which only add to public disillusionment with Washington. The depth of that disenchantment was illustrated by the unlikely emergence of Donald Trump, a trash-talking television personality and real-estate mogul, as a presidential candidate. European institutions seemed in even worse repair. The combination of the euro crisis and the surge of illegal migrants and refugees into Europe have made the institutions of the European Union look antiquated and inadequate.

The migrant crisis did, however, illustrate an enduring truth. The West's share of the global economy might be shrinking, but Western living standards remain enviable compared to those enjoyed by the rest of the world. The decline of the West did not seem to be uppermost in the minds of the Syrians, Eritreans and others clamouring to get into the EU.

Western living standards are also still exceptionally comfortable, even by the standards of the peaceful and booming nations in East Asia. Even as Asia's share of global output surpassed that of the West, the average American or European remained far richer than the average Chinese or Indian – although the gap is narrowing. In 1980, income per head in Asia was only about one-thirtieth of that in the US. By 2025, according to Australian government projections, income per head in Australia will only be four times higher than the Asian average.[26] But given resource constraints, population pressures and lower productivity, it may be that most Asian nations never fully catch up with the US or the EU, on a per-capita basis. So Western living standards will still seem lavish to most Asians.

This persistent 'lifestyle gap' is likely to have political consequences. If it is blamed on an unfair international system it could be a source of tension between East and West. Restrictive Western attitudes to visas and immigration are already a source of anger in South and East Asia – and matters may get worse, as concerns about terrorism increase the domestic pressure on Western governments to clamp down on immigration. That will matter because while average living standards in emerging Asia will be lower than in the West, the overall economic and political might of the biggest Asian nations will be huge, making their complaints impossible for the West to brush aside. During the twentieth century, the world's richest and most powerful country, the United States, also had the highest average living standards. In the twenty-first century, that connection between personal and national wealth is being broken.

As well as being a potential source of tension, the West's superior living standards are also a significant source of 'soft power' and international prestige. Asia's new rich are often keen to buy properties in Europe and North America and to send their children to be educated in the US and the UK. The cleaner air in Europe and America is often cited as an attraction for people sick of breathing in the smog of Beijing, Jakarta or Delhi.

The West is also widely perceived as 'cleaner' when it comes to government and standards in public life. Across Asia – from democratic India to authoritarian China – popular rage against corruption has become central to political life. There are some parallels with the anti-elite fervour that has been so apparent in the 2016 US presidential election. But international comparisons, such as those carried out by Transparency International, still suggest that Western institutions are relatively clean compared to their counterparts in Asia. Once again, the West enjoys an institutional edge.

These relatively subtle questions of living standards, corruption and institutional power will matter a lot to the global balance of power, if international peace and stability is broadly maintained. But if the kind of dark, violent and anarchic forces that overwhelmed much of the Middle East during the Obama years spread to other parts of the world, then international politics will be shaped by cruder forces – as questions of military power and economic muscle come to the fore.

Conclusion: Beyond East and West

As readers of this book may have gathered, I believe that the crumbling of the Western-dominated world order has increased the chance of conflict – not just in East Asia, but also in the Middle East and in eastern Europe. Indeed, from the viewpoint of the time of writing, in early 2016, the wars in the Middle East and renewed Russian aggression are the most pressing international security issues facing the world.

However, tensions and suspicions between the US and China have also grown steadily more intense in recent years. The fact that this emerging confrontation is between the world's two largest economies means that the survival of a globalised economy is at stake in the Asia-Pacific – much more than in the Middle East or in Ukraine. The US–China rivalry is also now at the centre of a web of dangerous rivalries in the region, which has seen a major arms race take hold in Asia over the last decade. Distracted by internal crises and by turmoil in the Middle East, few politicians in the West are paying attention to the fears and ambitions of nations such as Japan, India, Pakistan, North and South Korea and Indonesia. Yet the increasing concentration of wealth and weaponry in Asia means that if conflicts in the region do break out, they will swiftly have effects all over the world.

In the twenty-first century rivalries between the nations of the Asia-Pacific region will shape global politics – just as the struggles between European nations shaped world affairs for over 500 years, from 1500 onwards. The Easternisation of the global economy means that 'obscure' disputes over uninhabited reefs in the Pacific or the demarcation of the border between India and China now have the potential to shake the world. Complex political struggles within China and India – or even North Korea – will also have consequences that are felt in London and New York.

Power struggles within Asia inevitably have global security implications because the United States remains the most powerful military force in the Pacific. The Obama administration has been determined to maintain America's strategic dominance in the Asia-Pacific region. The Americans understand that the US cannot remain the world's leading power if it cedes its dominant military and diplomatic position within Asia – which is now at the core of the global economy.

Yet, during the Xi Jinping era, it has become increasingly obvious that China is no longer prepared to accept American dominance of China's 'backyard'. At times, Chinese spokesmen have even suggested that the entire US-led world order is no longer fit for purpose. Fu Ying, a former Chinese ambassador to London and confidant of Henry Kissinger, argues that 'The US-led world order is a suit that no longer fits.'[1]

Overturning America's global role is a long-term goal for China. The first step that China is determined to take is to demand that Beijing's definition of its borders and rights, within Asia itself, are accepted by the wider region. This, the Chinese feel, is the very least that an emerging superpower can expect.

The question of whether and how the Americans should resist Chinese ambitions in the Asia-Pacific is likely to be the most critical issue in international relations over the coming decades, since it pits the world's two most powerful nations against each other. There is a pragmatic and 'realist' argument that American resistance is futile and dangerous. The 'realists' believe that the size of the Chinese economy and the power of its military make it inevitable that China will dominate its surrounding region. For the Americans to resist the inevitable would be a route towards a catastrophic war or a humiliating climbdown that would undermine US power all over the world. To avoid either outcome, the realists argue that the US should tacitly grant China a sphere of influence in its region.

This 'realist' argument cannot be lightly dismissed. In the end, however, I am not convinced. If the US were simply motivated by a desire to maintain American global dominance for its own sake, then it would be irresponsible to risk a war with China to sustain US power in the Asia-Pacific region. However, it is clear that most of China's neighbours – including India, Japan, South Korea, most of the nations of South East Asia and Australia – are very uncomfortable with the idea of living in a China-dominated region. The strength of regional support for a strong continued US role in the Asia-Pacific makes America's determination to push back against Chinese hegemony in the Pacific both morally defensible and strategically feasible.

A resolute American stance in the Pacific might then buy time for the internal changes in China that would make Beijing's power seem less threatening to other Asian nations. China's intolerance of internal dissent – and its often ferocious reaction to external criticism – sets much of the rest of Asia on edge. In Hong Kong, which is now part of China but is meant to maintain its own political system, there are growing fears about protections for freedom of speech. Further afield, countries such as Vietnam, the Philippines and even Japan worry that without American protection, they will be powerless to resist pressure from an authoritarian China.

Of course, holding the line in the Asia-Pacific until such time as China changes internally offers no certainties. There can be no guarantee that China will become a more liberal country, even in the medium term: current developments under Xi Jinping point in the opposite direction. Nor can there be any guarantee that a democratic China will be less nationalistic. A generation of young Chinese has been reared on the 'wolf's milk' of nationalism – and the effects of that education will last for generations.

The US itself is also hardly immune to nationalism. Indeed one danger of the American pivot to Asia is that it will eventually lead to a clash between Chinese and American nationalism. The tenor of the 2016 presidential election campaign suggests that a post-Obama America could well swing back towards a more militarised and assertive foreign policy. Donald Trump, who set the tone of the Republican campaign, repeatedly promised to 'make America great again'. Trump's lament that America 'loses all the time', and his promise to rebuild the military and to make sure that the US 'wins' again, certainly promised a more confrontational and nationalistic American approach to the Asia-Pacific region.

And yet there is also a strong undercurrent of isolationism in the rhetoric of both Trump and of Bernie Sanders, the left-wing insurgent in the race for the Democratic nomination. Both Trump and Sanders promised to renegotiate America's international trade agreements – and both take a much more sceptical view of America's global military alliances. Sanders argues that the US should resign from the role of 'world policeman'; Trump demands that Japan and South Korea pay the US for the security guarantees they receive. The popularity of Trump's campaign – and that of Sanders – suggests that there is a strong constituency in the US for a retreat from globalism: repudiating international military and trading commitments. If these trends gather force, then those who lambast Barack Obama for a lack of international engagement might soon become nostalgic for the Obama years.

An America that steps back from its global commitments, such as the Trans-Pacific Partnership or the US–Japan security treaty, would further erode the post Cold War international order. That, in turn, would almost certainly encourage both China and Russia to seek to fill any vacuums left by US power – accelerating the process that has already begun during the Obama years.

This re-emergence of great-power rivalries stands in stark contrast to the original vision of Barack Obama. The forty-fourth US president came to power determined to forge a foreign policy that moved beyond these traditional concerns and instead forged new relationships with Russia, China and the Islamic world – based on identifying common global challenges and developing shared ways of dealing with them. But by Obama's second term in office, Washington had relationships with both Beijing and Moscow that looked very much like traditional great-power rivalry, while the Middle East was in flames.

Yet Obama's original insight – that many of the most serious problems of the twenty-first century are truly global in nature – remains true. The big global issues make international borders and national rivalries seem either irrelevant or dangerously counterproductive. As Western and Asian political leaders look ahead, they should be struck by the extent to which the biggest dangers they and their citizens face are very similar in nature. These challenges include global financial stability, inequality, corruption, cyber security, jihadist terrorism, nuclear proliferation and climate change.

It is important, however, not to be naive about the extent to which these challenges can unite East and West. Potentially, most of them are also a source of bitter division.

The new challenges of cyberspace are an example. Over the course of the Obama era, the security establishments in many Western nations came to rank the threat of cyber theft or cyber attack from China as amongst the biggest national-security challenges they face. Outside the West, however, the Snowden affair heightened suspicions of American 'control' of the internet. But all national governments – in both Asia and the West – are also potentially threatened by the way in which new cyber technologies can empower criminal gangs or terrorists. Dealing with such threats will be extremely difficult, since they raise sensitive questions relating to freedom of expression and espionage. But there is no doubt that these common challenges exist and will ultimately best be dealt with by new forms of international co-operation. The kind of international treaties that govern arms control or the laws of war do not yet exist in cyberspace. Developing them will be one of the biggest diplomatic challenges of the next decade. And yet, the signs are not promising. In fact, the Americans and Europeans continue to report sustained efforts at cyber espionage emanating from China.

Climate change looks potentially more promising as a field for international co-operation. The Obama years started with a debacle at an international climate-change conference in Copenhagen in 2009, where the Western world squared off against a group of developing nations led by China, India and Brazil. Obama's second term, however, was marked by a much more successful and well-managed attempt to achieve an international deal, culminating in the Paris agreement of 2015 in which both China and India agreed to do much more to restrain emissions of greenhouse gases. The Paris deal was preceded by a separate US–China accord, which provided the foundation for a broader international agreement. Important in itself, the climate deal also demonstrated that the US and China – despite their growing rivalry in the Pacific – are still capable of working together on common challenges.

However, critics are also right to point out that the Paris deal, while significant, does not promise to cut emissions fast enough to satisfy mainstream scientific opinion. So climate change remains an issue that should, ideally, unite East and West – but that also has the potential to divide. The developing Asian nations have consistently pointed out that the relatively cosseted lifestyle of Westerners is dependent on levels of energy consumption that are much higher than those enjoyed by Asians.

In the age of global warming, the Indians and Chinese will continue to argue vociferously that there can be no moral reason why Americans and Europeans should have a right to consume far more energy per head than poorer Asians. This is all the more the case given that existing levels of carbon dioxide in the atmosphere reflect the industrialisation of the West in previous eras. These modern-day debates extend the bitterness bequeathed by the West's imperial past. They make it much harder to achieve international agreements that stand a real chance of making the far-reaching economic and environmental changes that might be required to tackle global warming.

But, stepping back from the political fray and the bitterness bequeathed by history, it is also obvious that global warming is a common challenge for humanity. Indeed climate change and water shortages are probably more threatening to South Asia, China and Oceania than to most of Europe or the US. However, the West will not get away without pain. California is already suffering from serious water shortages and the whole of the US is getting used to extreme weather patterns. Meanwhile desertification in Africa, linked to climate change and population growth, is helping to drive the mass immigration into Europe that is now destabilising the EU. The uprising in Syria in 2011 was preceded by four years of devastating drought, which some have linked to climate change. Yemen, another failed state in the Middle East that is wracked by insurgency and war, also suffers from a severe water shortage. So it seems increasingly evident that one kind of transnational problem – climate change – is indirectly linked to another – terrorism.

Geopolitical rivalries in the Middle East, combined with Western unease about human-rights violations in China, India and Russia, have made it harder for the world's major powers to make common cause against jihadist terror. Yet it is also evident that jihadist Islam threatens not just the Middle East, the US and the EU, but also China, India and Russia. Once again, properly seen, this is a common challenge. Further major terror attacks or continuing military success for Islamic State could gradually persuade East and West to make common cause against the jihadist violence that threatens them all.

Concerns about nuclear proliferation have been closely linked to worries about terrorism ever since the ill-fated Iraq War. Nuclear issues also have the potential to divide the great powers. China's irresponsible help to the Pakistani nuclear programme was bitterly resented in both India and the US. North Korea's nuclear weapons programme is also an increasingly serious concern in Washington, as the evidence mounts that the North Korean regime is intent on developing nuclear-tipped ballistic missiles that could threaten the West Coast of the United States. With China apparently unable or unwilling to rein in its client state in North Korea, the US has taken steps to deploy an anti-ballistic missile interceptor in South Korea. Beijing, however, sees the deployment of such a system as threatening the effectiveness of its own nuclear deterrent, and has protested vociferously. As a result, US–Chinese efforts to work together on the common problems posed by a nuclear North Korea are much more fraught than they should be.

However, the Obama years have also offered some evidence that, under the right circumstances, the major powers can still work together on nuclear proliferation. The rising antagonism between Russia and the West did not prevent the Russians playing a constructive role in the Iranian nuclear negotiations.

The most obvious common concern linking the major powers of both East and West is their shared interest in the continuing growth of the global economy. All of the world's largest economies came together in 2008, at the first ever G20 summit, to prevent a global financial crisis turning into a worldwide depression. One thread that links the political discourse in Europe and the US to the debates in China and India is the sense that inequality is a rising problem. Globalisation has helped Asian nations to lift hundreds of millions of people, but it also seems to have contributed to social inequality all over the world. The leaders of both East and West have a shared interest in establishing a more equitable and stable form of globalisation. The mutual economic interests binding Asia to the US and Europe remain the best hope of avoiding conflict. But once again, an issue that has the potential to forge co-operation between East and West is also a potential source of division. The popular revolt against inequality in the US could easily spiral into protectionism – witness Donald Trump's repeated calls for massive tariffs on Chinese goods. If that were to happen, the unravelling of the international trade system would become a major source of international political tension.

When Barack Obama came to power in 2009 his initial goal was to construct a new relationship with China, based on tackling the big global issues that challenge humanity as a whole. President Xi's talk of a 'new type of great-power relations' suggested that he too might be interested in focusing on common challenges such as climate change and financial stability, rather than national rivalries.

The story of the Obama years, however, has pointed in the opposite direction. As I have shown, suspicions between the US and China have grown steadily more intense in recent years. The rise of international tensions in Asia will strengthen the fears of those who believe that 'the Thucydides trap' will eventually spring – and that China, the rising power, will go to war with the United States, the established power. Yet in the age of the internet, nuclear weapons, artificial intelligence and global warming, it seems unduly fatalistic to believe that nations must continue to follow patterns of behaviour that were first observed in ancient Greece. The great political challenge of the twenty-first century will be to manage the process of Easternisation in the common interests of mankind.

Acknowledgements

I would like to thank my *Financial Times* colleagues, Dan Dombey and David Pilling for taking the time and trouble to pore over this book and to point out how it could be improved. Jeremy Shapiro, variously of the State Department, the Brookings Institution and the European Council on Foreign Relations, was so keen to improve my work, that he ended up writing a couple of paragraphs (I'm not saying which ones).

As a columnist for the *FT*, I have benefited hugely from the knowledge and friendship of the paper's network of foreign correspondents. I would particularly like to thank Jamil Anderlini, Tom Mitchell, Lifen Zhang, Leslie Hook and Kathrin Hille in Beijing (Kathrin also helped me in Moscow), Patti Waldmeir in Shanghai, Victor Mallet in Delhi and Simon Mundy in Seoul. In the US, I'd like to thank my colleagues in Washington, New York and San Francisco – in particular Edward Luce, Geoff Dyer (who himself is the author of a fine book on US-Chinese relations), Richard McGregor, Gillian Tett, Demetri Sevastopulo and Richard Waters. I'd like to express my gratitude to Quentin Peel and Stefan Wagstyl in Berlin, Dan Dombey in Istanbul, Tobias Buck in Madrid, John Reed in Jerusalem, Kerin Hope in Athens, Hugh Carnegy and Simon Kuper in Paris, Roman Olearchyk in Kiev and Charles Clover and Courtney Weaver in Moscow, Joe Leahy in Sao Paulo and Andrew England in Johannesburg. All of the above have been generous with their time and ideas. In the UK, I've been lucky to work with excellent editors and colleagues, including Alec Russell, Fred Studemann, Mark Vandevelde, Lionel Barber, Martin Wolf, Philip Stephens and Lucy Kellaway.

I would also like to thank the many think-tanks and research institutes, who have helped me with my work. Particular gratitude is owed to the Berggruen Institute and to Nicolas Berggruen and Dawn Nakagawa, for including me on an eye-opening trip to Beijing. I have also benefited greatly from the twice-yearly meetings of the Daimler Forum and thank the three think-tanks – the Brookings Institution, the Centre for European Reform and the Stiftung Wissenschaft und Politik – that organise these meetings. The European Council on Foreign Relations and the German Marshall Fund have also included me on numerous useful conferences and trips. In Japan, I owe particular thanks to the Keizai Koho Center for inviting me on a superb study tour and to our guide, Isao Tanaka. The Jeju Forum in South Korea have also been thoughtful hosts on several occasions. I would also like to thank the Ditchley Foundation in the UK and the Lowy Institute in Australia for organising two excellent seminars on Asia, held in Oxfordshire and Sydney – thanks in particular are owed to Sir John Holmes of Ditchley and to Michael Fullilove of Lowy. The World Economic Forum in Davos remains a hugely useful meeting, and I'd especially like to thank some of the backroom staff there, including Regula Waltenspuel and Lucy Jay-Kennedy. In the UK, I have benefited from the excellent meetings organised by LSE Ideas, and the work of Nick Kitchen and Mick Cox, as well as the annual Anglo-German meetings, known as the Konigswinter Conference. Various bits of Oxford University, including St. Antony's College, the IR Department and the Blavatnik School, have also generously included me in their activities. Karen O'Donnell at the Leigh Bureau in Dublin has helped me travel the world. Karen Seitz of Fusion Partners also kindly included me in two of her valuable seminars, in Beijing and San Francisco.

As a journalist covering international politics, I have been helped by innumerable people all over the world – too many to mention. But I would like to single out some individuals, who have been especially helpful or patient with me. In the US, this includes Phil Gordon, Joe Nye, Kurt Campbell, Evan Medeiros, Bill Burns, Charles Kupchan, Julie Smith, Derek Chollet, Jim Steinberg, Thomas Wright, Jacob Heilbrunn, Graham Allison, Michael Green and Bonny Glaser. In China, I have again been helped by many people – namely Daniel Bell, Eric Li, Wang Jisi, Zhang Weiwei, Yan Xuetong and Michael Anti. In Tokyo and London, Kuni Miyake, Hideki Asari, Akio Miyajima, Yasumasa Nagamine, Yoichi Funabashi and Daisuke Suchiya all provided valuable insights into Japan. In Delhi, Pratap Bhanu Mehta, Raghuram Rajan, Arvind Subramanian, Shyam Saran, Sanjaya Baru, Shekhar Gupta and Shivshankar Menon all took time to speak to me. In Seoul, I'd particularly like to thank Chung-in Moon and John Delury, and in Taipei, Ketty Chen. In Brazil, Alex Ellis was a generous and helpful host. In Singapore, I was grateful for the help provided by Bilahari Kausikam, Kishore Mahbubani, Malcolm Cook and Tim Huxley. In Australia, thanks are due to Hugh White and Rory Medcalf.

In Europe and the Middle East Thomas Bagger, Nikolaus Meyer-Landrut, Emily Haber, Norbert Rottgen, Volker Perthes and Norman Walter were generous with their time and insights in Berlin. In Paris, I'd like to thank Justin Vaisse, Sophie Pedder, Francois Heisbourg, Henri de Castries and Pierre Levy; and in Italy, Carlo de Benedetti and Ferdinando Giugliano. In Moscow, Demetri Trenin, Yevgenia Albats and Arkady Ostrovsky. In Istanbul, Hakan Altinay, and Sinan Ulgen. In Israel, Mark Regev, Gideon Levy, Ronnie Hope, and Dore Gold. In Cairo, Issandr El Amrani, Tarek Osman and Alaa al Aswany. In the UK, Simon Fraser, Simon McDonald, Edward Mortimer, Mark Leonard, Peter Hill, Kim Darroch, Charles Grant, Robin Niblett, Shashank Joshi, Arne Westad, Martin Jacques, Rana Mitta, Margaret Macmillan, Tim Garton-Ash and Anne Applebaum have all been generous with time and ideas.

I owe huge thanks to my literary agents, Sarah Chalfant and James Pullen, and to my publishers at The Bodley Head, Stuart Williams, Katherine Ailes and Anna-Sophia Watts.

Most of all, I'd like to thank my wife Olivia, and my children – Natasha, Joe, Nat and Adam. They have kept me on my toes with arguments, ideas and questions, they have tolerated my frequent absences, and were always a delight to come home to.

Notes

Unless stated otherwise, the place of publication is London.

PREFACE

1. Ishaan Tharoor, 'China Will Have More Warships Than the US By 2020', *Washington Post*, 15 December 2014.
2. Quoted in Michael Wolff, 'Ringside with Steve Bannon at Trump Tower as the President-Elect's Strategist Plots "An Entirely New Political Movement"', *Hollywood Reporter*, 11 November 2016.
3. Benjamin Haas, 'Steve Bannon: "We're going to war in the South China Sea"', *Guardian*, 2 February 2017.
4. Interview with Donald Trump, *The Economist*, 11 May 2017.

INTRODUCTION

1. The session was organised by the Berggruen Institute of Governance and the group was made up of: Francis Fukuyama, Reid Hoffman, Eric Schmidt, Jared Cohen, Arianna Huffington, Kevin Rudd, Mario Monti, Shaukat Aziz, Juan Luis Cebrian, Nathan Gardels, Fareed Zakaria, Gideon Rachman, Nouriel Roubini, Stephen Schwarzman, Dawn Nakagawa, George Yeo, David Bonderman, Kishore Mahbubani, Paul Keating, Ernesto Zedillo, Felipe Gonzalez, Gordon Brown, Ronnie Chan, Pierre Omidyar, Zheng Bijian, Nicolas Berggruen, Ricardo Lagos, Dambisa Moyo, Aleksei Kudrin, Alain Minc, Wu Jianmin, Feng Wei and Fred Hu.
2. This phrase was, in fact, first popularised by President Jiang Zemin in the 1990s; see Zheng Wang, *Never Forget National Humiliation* (Columbia University Press, New York, 2014), 129.
3. The text of Xi's opening remarks can be found at http://berggruen.org/topics/a-conversation-with-president-xi-at-big-s-understanding-china-conference.
4. Graham Allison, 'Thucydides' Trap Has Been Sprung in the Pacific', *Financial Times*, 21 August 2012.
5. This point is made in John Darwin, *After Tamerlane: The Rise and Fall of Global Empires, 1400–2000* (Penguin, 2008), 24.

6. Ian Morris, *War: What Is It Good For?* (Profile, 2014), 168.
7. *Australia in the Asian Century*, Australian government White Paper, October 2012, 53.
8. *The Economist*, which keeps a watch on this statistic, estimates that this will happen in the early 2020s.
9. 'Dominant and Dangerous', *The Economist*, 3 October 2015.
10. US National Intelligence Council, *Global Trends 2030 – Alternative Worlds*, 4.
11. Ibid., x.
12. Dmitri Trenin, 'Russia Turns Focus to Long-Forgotten East', *Financial Times*, 21 August 2012.

CHAPTER ONE

1. See Darwin, op. cit.
2. Ian Morris, *Why the West Rules – For Now* (Profile Books, 2010), 16.
3. Morris, *War: What Is It Good For?*, op. cit., 168–77.
4. See Darwin, op. cit., 271.
5. Ibid., 355.
6. Pankaj Mishra, *From the Ruins of Empire* (Penguin, 2013), 2–3.
7. Quoted in ibid., 2.
8. The number of people murdered in Nanjing remains disputed. Arne Westad in *Restless Empire* (Basic, 2012) puts the figure at more than 200,000 and most Western historians concur.
9. Darwin, op. cit., 443.
10. Quoted in Tristram Hunt, *Ten Cities That Made an Empire* (Allen Lane, 2014), 4.
11. Mishra, op. cit., 295.
12. Partha Chaterjee, 'Those Fond Memories of the Raj', in *Empire and Nation* (Columbia, New York, 2010). Chaterjee himself argues that 'I think it is something else. The more popular democracy deepens in India, the more its elites yearn for a system in which enlightened gentlemen could decide . . . what was good for the masses.'
13. The history of Bombay as an imperial city is told in Hunt, op. cit.
14. Figures in Yves Tiberghien, 'East Asian Politics in Comparative Perspective', presentation at East China University of Political Science, 28 September 2013.
15. Ibid. The phrase 'the rise of the rest' was coined and popularised by Fareed Zakaria.
16. Danny Quah, *The Global Economy's Shifting Centre of Gravity* (Global Policy, 2011).

CHAPTER TWO

1. Conversation with the author, Davos, January 2014.
2. Joseph Nye, *Is the American Century Over?* (Polity, Cambridge, 2015), 65.
3. Hugh White, *The China Choice* (OUP, Oxford, 2012), 6.
4. Morris, *War – What is it Good For?*, op. cit., 358.
5. John J. Mearsheimer, *The Tragedy of Great Power Politics* (Norton, New York, 2014); claim that China cannot rise peacefully, 403. Other academics to make similar arguments include Professor Christopher Coker of the London School of Economics and Jonathan Holstag of ULB in Brussels.

6. Ibid., 362.
7. Conversation with the author, April 2015.
8. They included Ivo Daalder, who became Obama's first ambassador to Nato, and Philip H. Gordon, who later became Assistant Secretary of State for Europe in the Obama administration and then White House co-ordinator for the Middle East.
9. Some years later, I asked Slocombe if he recalled the exchange. He replied that he did not remember the precise conversation, 'but that's certainly what I would have said under those circumstances'.
10. Justin McCurry, 'Japan reveals record defence budget as tensions with China grow', *Guardian*, 14 January 2015.
11. 'Daily Chart, The Military Balance', *The Economist*, 18 March 2013.
12. Gates quoted in Geoff Dyer, *The Contest of the Century – The New Era of Competition with China* (Allen Lane, 2014), 116.
13. See Robert D. Kaplan, *Asia's Cauldron – The South China Sea and the End of a Stable Pacific* (Ballantine, New York, 2014).
14. See Congressional Research Service, 'China's Naval Modernisation – Implications for US Naval Capabilities', December 2015.
15. Conversation with the author, April 2013.
16. See Dyer, op. cit., 117.
17. Michael O'Hanlon and James Steinberg, 'Going Beyond Air-Sea Battle', *Washington Post,* 3 October 2012.
18. Ibid.
19. Ibid.
20. Ibid.
21. Eyre Crowe quoted in Henry Kissinger, *On China* (Allen Lane, 2011), 519.
22. A group of academics in Harvard have devoted a whole book to the comparison, *The Next Great War*, edited by Richard Rosencrance and Steven Miller (Belfer Center, Harvard, 2015).

CHAPTER THREE

1. Wang Jisi, 'America and China Need Each Other', *Huffington Post*, 12 July 2014.
2. Kissinger, op. cit., 512.
3. Quoted in ibid., 510.
4. Conversation between the author and Chinese officials.
5. Cited in 'The Pacific: A Special Report', *The Economist*, 15 November 2014.
6. 'Chinese Incursion During Xi Jinping's Visit A Mystery', *Times of India*, 4 October 2014.
7. Jamil Anderlini, 'Lame Duck President of a Declining Power Still Inspires the World', *Financial Times*, 11 November 2014.
8. Quoted in Graham Allison and Robert Blackwill, *Lee Kuan Yew* (MIT Press, Cambridge MA, 2013), 3.
9. Quoted in Zheng, op. cit., 103.
10. Liu Mingfu, 'The China Dream' (CNTimes Books, 2015), 1.
11. Ibid., 17.
12. Quoted in Dyer, op. cit., 40.

13. Ibid., 41.
14. Zheng, op. cit., 173.
15. Ibid., 141.
16. Quoted in Shawn Donnan and Geoff Dyer, 'US warns over loss of influence over China bank', *Financial Times*, 17 March 2015.
17. Quoted in Jamil Anderlini, 'Person of the Year: Jack Ma', *Financial Times*, 12 December 2013.
18. Quoted in Gideon Rachman, *Zero-Sum World* (Atlantic, 2010), 178.
19. Conversation with the author, Beijing, April 2013.
20. Wang Jisi, 'US–China Co-Dependency', *American Interest,* April 2014.
21. 'Human rights: Uncivil', *The Economist*, 18 July 2015.
22. Kurt Campbell, 'China at the Summit', *Financial Times*, 12 May 2014.

CHAPTER FOUR

1. Remarks by President Barack Obama to the Australian Parliament, 17 November 2011.
2. Tom Donilon, 'United States and Asia-Pacific in 2013', speech to the Asia Society, November 2013.
3. In true Washington fashion, an unseemly squabble broke out between the White House and the State Department over the intellectual ownership, design and even the name of the pivot or rebalance – with Clinton's State Department struggling for control with Donilon's National Security Council.
4. Conversation with the author, San Francisco, 21 April 2015.
5. Ibid.
6. Conversation with the author, Paris, 2014.
7. Jeffrey Bader, *Obama and China's Rise* (Brookings Institution Press, Washington D. C,. 2012), 53.
8. Ibid., 11.
9. Helene Cooper, 'China Holds Firm on Major Issues in Obama's Visit', *New York Times*, 17 November 2009.
10. Conversation with the author, New Delhi, 12 May 2015.
11. Conversation with the author, Paris, 2014.
12. Ibid.
13. Ibid.
14. Conversation with the author, San Francisco, 21 April 2015.
15. David Lampton, 'A Tipping Point in US-Chinese Relations is Upon Us', http://www.uscnpm.org/blog/2015/05/11/a-tipping-point-in-u-s-china-relations-is-upon-us-part-i/.
16. Conversation with Michael Fullilove of the Lowy Institute.
17. Conversation with State Department official, Washington DC, November 2013.
18. Gideon Rachman, 'Lunch with the *FT*: Bill Burns', *Financial Times*, 6 November 2015.
19. Larry Summers, 'Time US Leadership Woke Up to a New Economic Era', *Financial Times*, 5 April 2015.

20. Quoted in Gerald F. Seib, 'Obama Presses Case for Asian Trade Deal, Warns Failure Would Benefit China', *Wall Street Journal*, 27 April 2015.
21. Shinzo Abe, speech to Congress, 28 April 2015.

CHAPTER FIVE

1. Gideon Rachman, 'Japan offers an unsettling glimpse of all our futures', *Financial Times*, 14 October 2013.
2. Gideon Rachman, 'Lunch with the *FT*: Lee Hsien Loong', *Financial Times*, 11 April 2014.
3. Gideon Rachman, 'A gaffe-prone Japan is a threat to peace in Asia', *Financial Times*, 12 August 2013.
4. Ibid.
5. Private information.

CHAPTER SIX

1. Lee Kuan Yew, *The Singapore Story* (Singapore, 2000).
2. Kaplan, op. cit., 9.
3. Ibid., 20.
4. Conversation with the author, March 2014.
5. Christopher Bayly and Tim Harper, *Forgotten Wars: The End of Britain's Asian Empire* (London, 2008), 10.
6. Ibid., xxvii.
7. Rachman, 'Lunch with the *FT*: Lee Hsien Loong', op. cit.
8. Ibid.
9. Ibid.
10. Bill Hayton, *The South China Sea: The Struggle for Power in Asia* (Yale, New Haven, 2014), 231.
11. Conversation with the author, Paris, April 2014.
12. Kaplan, op. cit., p12.
13. Ibid., 10.
14. The legal arguments are explored in Hayton, op. cit., 210–14.
15. Charles Clover and Geoff Dyer, 'US Struggles for a Strategy to contain China's island-building', *Financial Times*, 7 June 2015.
16. 'US Compares China's South China Sea moves to Russia's in Ukraine', Reuters, 27 June 2015.
17. Conversation with the author, May 2014.
18. 'Vietnam and China, Through A Border Darkly', *The Economist*, 16 August 2014.
19. Ibid.
20. Private information.
21. Banyan, 'Future Tense', *The Economist*, 16 August 2014.
22. Conversation with the author, June 2014.
23. White, op. cit., 177.
24. Malcolm Turnbull, 'Power Shift: Hugh White's *The China Choice*', *The Monthly*, August 2012.

25. Phillip Coorey and Laura Tingle, 'Let Us Know Next Time – How Obama Chided Turnbull over Darwin port sale', *Australian Financial Review*, 15 November 2015.

26. Remarks at a UK–Australia conference at Ditchley Park, May 2014.

CHAPTER SEVEN

1. Arvind Subramanian, *Eclipse: Living in the Shadow of China's Economic Dominance* (PIIE Press, Washington DC, 2011), 4.

2. Interview with the author, Delhi, May 2015.

3. 'India to become world's most populous country around 2028', *Times of India*, 14 June 2014.

4. Interview with the author, Delhi, May 2015.

5. 'India Confident of Overtaking China's Growth Rate', *Financial Times*, 17 May 2015.

6. This figure is based on using real exchange rates. Using purchasing-power measures, the Chinese economy was 2.5 times the size of India's.

7. Interview with the author, Delhi, May 2015.

8. Shashank Joshi, *Indian Power Projection: Ambition, Arms and Influence* (RUSI, Whitehall Paper 85, 2015), 1.

9. Interview with senior Foreign Office official, Paris, April 2014.

10. Interview with the author, Delhi, May 2015.

11. The BRICS was a concept originally dreamed up by Jim O'Neill in 2001, when he was chief economist of Goldman Sachs, as a way of identifying the most exciting and largest emerging markets for investors. The organisation, however, moved from acronym to reality when its foreign ministers began to hold joint meetings in 2006, which was followed by leaders summits that began in 2009. By this time, the BRICS were being marketed as a non-Western alternative to the traditional G7 summits. The political nature of the new organisation made it imperative to include an African nation, so South Africa – which conveniently began with 'S' – was added to the mix.

12. Pankaj Mishra, 'Narendra Modi and the New Face of India', *Guardian*, 16 May 2014.

13. Interview with the author, Delhi, May 2015.

14. Jane Perlez, 'Xi Jinping Heads to Pakistan, Bearing Billions in Infrastructure Aid', *New York Times*, 19 April 2015.

15. 'China gets forty-year management rights on Gwadar port', *Express Tribune*, 15 April 2015.

16. Ibid.

17. Joshi, op. cit., 61.

18. Shivshankar Menon, 'India's Changing Geopolitical Environment', speech, 20 January 2016.

19. Ellen Barry, 'With Much at Stake, Chinese leader visits India', *New York Times*, 17 September 2014.

20. Interview with the author, Abu Dhabi, April 2015.

21. 'US–India Joint Strategic Vision for the Asia-Pacific and Indian Ocean Region', White House, 25 January 2015.

22. Adam Roberts, 'India: A Special Report', *The Economist*, 23 May 2015.

23. 'US says India lynchpin of rebalance strategy', *India Express*, 7 June 2012.
24. Quoted in Shubhajit Roy, 'Day after, China daily says Modi remarks for media hype', *Indian Express*, 3 September 2014.
25. John Authers, 'Diversity Drives Indian Ocean Region', *Financial Times*, 8 May 2015.

CHAPTER EIGHT

1. 'Entangled', *The Economist*, 15 June 2015.
2. Jeffrey Goldberg, 'The Obama Doctrine', *The Atlantic,* April 2016 issue.
3. Interview with the author, Paris, April 2014.
4. 'Susan Rice: That would be a "grave mistake"', *Associated Press*, 23 February 2014.
5. Clyde Prestowitz, 'Obama's Asian allies need to give something back', *Financial Times*, 23 April 2014.
6. Chris Parsons, 'Obama argues against use of force to solve global conflict', *Los Angeles Times*, 28 April 2014.
7. Byron Tau, 'Obama: America is Back', *Politico*, 24 January 2012.
8. *FT* interview with Chuck Hagel, conducted by Stephanie Kirchgaessner, 29 August 2011.
9. 'Clinton sounds the China alarm as an '08 issue', *NBC News*, 3 February 2007.
10. Quoted in Perry Anderson, *American Foreign Policy and Its Thinkers* (Verso, 2015), 5.
11. Ibid.
12. Stephen Walt, 'The End of the American Era', *National Interest*, November/December 2011.
13. Ibid.
14. Charles Kupchan, *No One's World* (OUP, Oxford, 2012), 89.
15. Robert Kagan, 'The Myth of American Decline', *The New Republic*, 2012
16. Chris Giles, 'China to overtake US as top economic power this year', *Financial Times*, 30 April 2014.
17. Joseph Nye, *Is The American Century Over?* (Polity, Cambridge, 2014), 49.
18. Ibid., 57.
19. Mark Urban, *The Edge* (Little, Brown, 2015), 22.
20. Ibid.
21. Ibid., 11.
22. Quoted in Walt, op. cit.
23. Goldberg, op. cit.
24. Fareed Zakaria, 'Britain resigns as a world power', *Washington Post*, 21 May 2015.
25. Urban, op. cit., 13.
26. Nye, op. cit., 99.
27. Menon, op. cit.
28. Zachary Keck, 'Australia Boosts Defense Spending 6.1%', *The Diplomat,* 16 May 2014.
29. Nye, op. cit., 67.
30. Quoted in Ed Crooks, 'The US Shale Revolution', *Financial Times*, 24 April 2015.
31. Quoted in Morris, *Why the West Rules – For Now*, op. cit., 550.
32. Interview with the author, April 2015.

CHAPTER NINE

1. The best source on this is the Iraq Body Count website, www.iraqbodycount. org.
2. James Mann, *The Obamians: The Struggle Inside the White House to Define American Power* (Viking, New York, 2012), 279.
3. Quoted in David Remnick, 'Watching the Eclipse', *New Yorker*, 11 August 2014.
4. Gideon Rachman, 'Lunch with the *FT*: Mohamed ElBaradei', *Financial Times*, 29 April 2011.
5. Vali Nasr, *The Dispensable Nation: American Foreign Policy in Retreat* (Doubleday, New York, 2013), 252.
6. Bruce Reidel, 'The Saudi Pivot to Asia', *Al-Monitor*, 13 March 2014.
7. Yasheng Huang speaking at the Globes conference in Tel Aviv, December 2014.
8. N. C. Bipindra and Natalie Pearson, 'Modi Revives India–Israel ties as terrorism threat grows', *Bloomberg News*, 20 November 2014.
9. Interview with the author, Delhi, May 2015.
10. Quoted by Michael Maloof on wnd.com, 16 December 2013.
11. Kurt Campbell, 'Obama's whirlwind Asian tour', *Financial Times*, 19 November 2014.
12. Thom Shanker, 'Warning Against Wars Like Iraq and Afghanistan', *New York Times*, 25 February 2011.
13. Vimont speaking at a seminar organised by the Centre for European Reform in Warsaw, September 2014.

CHAPTER TEN

1. He is also a colleague of mine at the *Financial Times*, who later moved to *La Repubblica* in Italy.
2. Interview with the author, Milan, March 2011.
3. Figures supplied by the German embassy in the UK.
4. Quoted in Timothy Garton-Ash, 'The New German Question', *New York Review of Books*, 13 August 2013.
5. Speech by Laurent Fabius on the occasion of the fortieth anniversary of the French Policy Planning Staff, 13 November 2013.
6. Interview with the author, Berlin, April 2015.
7. The phrase was that of a senior British official.
8. Interview with the author, October 2015.

CHAPTER ELEVEN

1. I first visited Moscow in 1986, just after the city's first private restaurant had opened. The National Hotel, where I stayed, was run-down and bleak. By the Putin era, however, it was far too expensive and luxurious for me to stay in.
2. Interview with the author, Moscow, 3 October 2014.
3. Speech by Vladimir Putin, Valdai International Discussion Club, 24 October 2014.

4. Interview with the author, Moscow, 3 October 2014.

5. See Charles Clover, 'In Moscow: A New Eurasianism', *Journal of International Security Affairs*, Fall/Winter 2014.

6. Quoted in Remnick, 'Watching the Eclipse', op. cit.

7. I am thinking, in particular, of Western analysts such as my friends Edward Lucas and Anne Applebaum.

8. Quoted in Mary-Elise Sarotte, 'Putin's Belligerence Today Has Roots in the Fall of the Berlin Wall', *Los Angeles Times*, 8 November 2014.

9. Discussion with the author, 2009.

10. Orlando Figes, *Natasha's Dance: A Cultural History of Russia* (Penguin, 2002), 380.

11. Quoted in ibid., 415.

12. Sergey Karaganov, 'Western delusions triggered conflict and Russians will not yield', *Financial Times*, 14 September 2014.

13. Essay in Kadri Liik (ed.), *Russia's Pivot to Asia* (European Council of Foreign Relations), 18.

14. Ibid., 62.

15. Brian Spegle and Wayne Ma, 'Putin's China Visit Highlights Shifting Power Balance', *Wall Street Journal*, 15 May 2014.

16. Peter Zeihan, 'Russia's Far East Turning Chinese', *ABC News*, July 2014.

17. See Darwin, op. cit., 121.

18. Ibid., 119.

19. Zeihan, 'Russia's Far East Turning Chinese', op. cit.

20. Ibid.

21. Quoted in Liik (ed.), op. cit., 83.

22. See Georgiy Voloshin, 'Hidden Dragon: The Chinese Era in Central Asia', *Global Asia*, Winter 2014.

23. 'China Admires Putin the Great', *American Interest,* July 2014.

24. Interview with the author, Washington DC, March 2014.

25. Interview with the *FT,* Washington DC, March 2014.

CHAPTER TWELVE

1. Quoted in Gideon Rachman, 'Ukraine Still Deserves Our Support', *Financial Times*, 5 May 2014.

2. Interview with the author, Kiev, September 2014.

3. Rachman, 'Lunch with the *FT*: Lee Hsien Loong', op. cit.

4. Quoted in Tyler Durden, 'Why the Chinese Admire Putin the Great', *Zero Hedge*, 10 March 2014.

5. This estimate from Nasr, op. cit., 197.

6. Davutoglu speech in Sarajevo, 16 October 2009.

7. Sinan Ulgen, 'How Political Islamists View the Euro Crisis', *Strategic Europe*, 2 November 2012.

8. Quoted by AFP, 14 November 2014.

9. In fairness, this statistic also reflected the fact that many imprisoned members of the Kurdish separatist movement were journalists.

10. Quoted in Honor Mahony, 'Orban wants to build an illiberal state', *EU Observer*, 28 July 2014.

11. Interview with the author, Berlin, September 2014.

CHAPTER THIRTEEN

1. Barack Obama, speech to the African Union, 28 July 2015.
2. 'African Union Opens China-Funded HQ in Ethiopia', BBC, 28 January 2012.
3. 'The Hopeless Continent', *The Economist*, 11 May 2000.
4. Interview with the author, Beijing, 2008.
5. In terms of fixed investment in Africa, European nations such as the UK and France still led China in 2012 – a reflection of their longer economic relationships, which dated back to the colonial era. However, the pace of Chinese foreign direct investment into Africa meant that this situation was likely to change over the coming decade.
6. Cited in Elizabeth Economy and Michael Levi, *By Any Means Necessary* (OUP, Oxford 2014), 46.
7. 'China Buying Out Africa', *Christian Science Monitor*, 1 March 2012.
8. Economy and Levi, op. cit., 262.
9. Quoted in *China–Africa Relations Factsheet*, South African Institute of International Affairs, 2015.
10. Interview with the author, London, June 2015.
11. Michael Reid, 'Obama and Latin America', *Foreign Affairs*, Spring 2015.
12. 'The Dragon and the Gringo – Bello column', *The Economist*, 17 January 2015.
13. The figure is for 2013.
14. Jennifer Jett, 'Bahamas Mega-Resort Stands Empty', *New York Times*, 2 February 2016.
15. 'The Chinese chequebook – Bello column', *The Economist*, 23 May 2015.
16. 'China's big ambitions stumble at Bahamas resort', Reuters, 30 June 2015.
17. John Authers, 'Diversity Drives The Indian Ocean Region', *Financial Times*, 8 May 2015.
18. 'Japan in Africa: A Rising Sun', Brookings Institution, 14 January 2014.
19. 'Japanese Activism Goes Global', *American Interest*, 20 July 2014.
20. Quoted in 'China in Africa – One Among Many', *The Economist*, 17 January 2015.
21. Abdoulaye Wade, 'Time for the West to Practise What it Preaches', *Financial Times*, 23 January 2008.
22. Quoted in Economy and Levi, op. cit., 78.
23. Katrina Manson, 'The Ethiopia Paradox', *Financial Times magazine,* 24 July 2015.
24. Barney Mthombothi, 'What are we bid for this shining set of principles, barely used', *Sunday Times South Africa*, 5 October 2014.
25. Howard W. French, *China's Second Continent: How a million migrants are building a new empire in Africa* (Knopf, 2014), 68.
26. Quoted in Gideon Rachman, 'The Realities Behind the Cult of Lula', *Financial Times*, 27 September 2010.
27. Peter Baker, '"Nobody Should Be President for Life," Obama tells Africa', *New York Times*, 28 July 2015.

CHAPTER FOURTEEN

1. In conversation with a senior *FT* journalist, June 2014.

2. Robert Wade and Jacob Vestergaard, 'The IMF Needs A Reset', *New York Times*, 2 February 2014.

3. Shawn Donnan, 'Jack Lew Hails End to US foot-dragging on IMF Reform', *Financial Times*, 20 December 2015.

4. Quoted in Susan V. Scott and Markos Zachariadas, *The Society for Worldwide Interbank Financial Transactions* (Routledge, 2013), 135.

5. Ibid., 136.

6. Ibid., 137.

7. Conversation with the author, Washington DC, November 2014.

8. Conversation with the author, Paris, April 2014.

9. Laura DeNardis, *The Global War for Internet Governance* (Yale, New Haven, 2014), 34.

10. Quoted in Monobina Gupta, 'Internet's governance cannot be limited to one server', *Times of India*, 30 July 2012.

11. Quoted in 'Doing the ICANN-can', *The Economist*, 22 March 2014.

12. Cheng Li and Ryan McElween, 'NSA Revelations Have Irreparably Hurt US Corporations in China', *Brookings Brief*, 12 December 2013.

13. Quoted in Steven Levy, 'How the NSA Almost Killed the Internet', *Wired*, 1 July 2014.

14. Quoted in 'US Is Relinquishing Control of Domain Names – Here's Why', *Fortune*, 17 March 2014.

15. Owen Gibson, 'Sir Dave Richards says FIFA and UEFA Stole Football From England', *Guardian*, 14 March 2012.

16. Simon Kuper, 'Why Sepp Blatter Is a Genius', *Financial Times*, 22 May 2015.

17. Gideon Rachman, 'What Fifa Tells Us About Global Power', *Financial Times*, 1 June 2015.

18. 'Exorbitant Privilege', *The Economist*, 10 May 2014.

19. Nick Cohen, 'How Did The English Judiciary Stoop So Low?', *Observer*, 23 September 2012.

20. 'Exorbitant Privilege', op. cit.

21. Ibid.

22. Quoted in Benjamin J. Cohen, *Currency Power: Understanding Monetary Rivalry* (Princeton University Press, Princeton, 2015), 1.

23. Subramanian, op. cit., 106.

24. Ibid., 109.

25. Jonathan Kirshner, *American Power After the Financial Crisis* (Cornell University Press, Ithaca, 2014), 151.

26. *Australia in the Asian Century,* op. cit., 52.

CONCLUSION

1. Fu Ying, 'The US World Order is a Suit That No Longer Fits', *Financial Times*, 6 January 2016.

Index

penguin.co.uk/vintage